The Gentleman Boxer

The Story of a Fighter in the Roaring Twenties

Ion Grumeza

authorHOUSE®

AuthorHouse™
1663 Liberty Drive
Bloomington, IN 47403
www.authorhouse.com
Phone: 1-800-839-8640

Published by AuthorHouse   8/13/12

ISBN: 978-1-4772-5790-6 (sc)
ISBN: 978-1-4772-5791-3 (dj)
ISBN: 978-1-4772-5792-0 (e)

Library of Congress Control Number: 2012914395

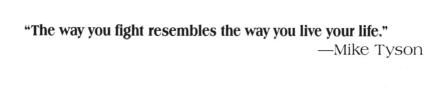

"The way you fight resembles the way you live your life."

—Mike Tyson

Contents

Preface

I learned about Joe "Grimm" Hashim a few years after he died at age ninety-six. Hearing that I had done some boxing in college, his son showed me a scrapbook of clippings, with headline after headline trumpeting the name and achievements of boxer Joe Grimm in the 1920s, an era that has always fascinated me. I was hooked and wanted to know more about the man and his life.

How did a boy who came over on a ship from Lebanon, who lived in the mill town of Fall River, Massachusetts, with his hardworking family, begin his professional boxing career with an uninterrupted string of twenty-four knockouts and become a prizefighter? The odds of scoring so many knockouts in a row are slim. Even "Iron" Mike Tyson scored "only" nineteen KOs in a row. How did Joe evolve from a model Boy Scout who never threw a punch in anger into a fearsome boxer? And what happened to Joe Grimm? Why isn't he included in boxing history? Perhaps most bewildering of all, why did he quit the sport in his prime and become a butcher in his own grocery store?

Before I wrote the first word of this saga, I was surprised to find out that more than ten boxers had taken the name of the original pre–World War I professional fighter Joe Grim, known for his legendary endurance when taking punishment in the ring. My Joe Grimm (spelled with two Ms) was hard to find on the Internet and was often mixed up with other Joe Grims. To make things more complicated, he is also found in boxing records under the name Jimmy Haskins. The only credible trace of his boxing activity was at BoxRec.com, listing his last eight fights—six wins (three KOs) and two losses by marginal points. At that time Joe was twenty-four years old and living in Pittsfield, Massachusetts. He had stopped training and considered himself pretty much retired from the ring. His best fighting years had already taken place in cities renowned for their boxing activities—Fall River, where he grew up, and the neighboring New Bedford, Massachusetts, as well as Bayonne, New Jersey, where he scored his best victories and achieved some greatness in the same ring in which some famous champions made history.

One of my best resources, in addition to the old cut-up newspaper articles, was Joe's personal notebook, where he penciled the date of his ring appearance, place of the arena, name of rivals and referees, number of rounds, results, and brief comments. Joe's immediate family provided additional valuable information about his life. Each bit of information found a place in the reconstruction of his story. I found a man on the cusp of greatness who was learning that winning has different meanings at pivotal times in life.

As I searched for the evolution of Joe's life as a boxer, a larger story emerged. Joe's family, especially his mother, was against his boxing career. Only his older brother Mike believed in Joe's talent and was always present in Joe's ring corner. At first I thought Mike seemed like a controlling and greedy chaperone, but as I got to know him more, he emerged as a valued mentor and an inborn businessman. He invested Joe's ring money well, so their family would own the grocery store, which led to other successful businesses and to the good lives of the future Hashim children.

I made trips to Massachusetts, Rhode Island, and New Jersey, where my hero lived and fought. To my delight, the houses and blue-collar neighborhoods in which Joe lived were intact, along with other relics of the Roaring Twenties. But none of the boxing arenas had survived; they had been reduced to parking lots or were rebuilt as malls and apartment buildings. I was able to locate some family members who recalled their boxing grandfathers who had known Joe, and I listened to their recollections and examined their vintage photo albums. And I found octogenarians, who, with sparkles in their eyes, remembered what it was like "to go to the fights in the old days" and sent me to another person or another place to find out more about those times.

To learn more about the era, I reviewed microfiche archives in the libraries of Fall River, New Bedford, Pittsfield, and Bayonne, reading 1920s newspapers that had articles about Joe's fights. These helped me to precisely document his successful boxing activity and sometimes led me to people and addresses that I would then visit in person.

Indeed, there is no replacement for being there, feeling the energy of the place, and trying to put yourself back in the time when the hero lived. Certainly Joe, whom I never met, was with me in all my visits. I often felt that his spirit was hovering above me, guiding me to people who had known him, and nudging me to detour from my planned highway route, leading me to locations where, sure enough, I found out something unexpected about Joe or his time. Truly, I had a metaphysical experience in connecting with Joe on many levels, and I believe he approves as I write these lines.

Still, retracing Joe's footwork in boxing was arduous. My determined efforts to locate the once–very famous Casino of Fall River, where Joe won many fights, produced no results. It was unbelievable to me that no one remembered the former largest building in the area. Exhausting research at the local library through the local newspapers of the 1920s produced many announcements and promotions for that arena. Sports reporters kept mentioning the name, yet no address was available until I spotted in an obscure note a mention that "any ticket exchange for one of the Casino nights was to be made at its Morgan street entrance."

I drove to the street, and I saw a mammoth red building. With a pounding heart I asked anyone around if that had been the famous Casino. No one, including aging neighbors, recalled that name, but they knew that boxing events took place inside the theater, which now was being renovated, and pointed to the red building. Indeed, inside it was a 1920s theater that could seat one thousand spectators; even the old film projectors were still in place. Yet, days later I was told by an employee in City Hall that the real Casino had been demolished in the 1950s to provide parking space for the theater inside the existing red building, which later became a furniture warehouse; its name, painted on the building, was still visible. To my surprise, there are no pictures of the Casino, despite its having been a massive structure that provided entertainment and a place of gathering for many generations.

I had similar frustrating experiences in trying to locate photographs and reminiscences of the no-less-famous Cycledrome of New Bedford, the New Winter Garden Theater of Pittsfield, and many other landmarks of a glorious bygone era. While many of the theaters of the 1920s remain in cities today, some restored to their previous glory, most of the casinos have been converted into office space or torn down, the land being used for a parking lot or new building. The cycledrome has virtually disappeared from the landscape, and nothing about it could be found on the Internet; little written information and few photographs remain today in library archives and private collections.

Furthermore, I was unable to locate the family of Frank McGrath, the late sports editor for the Fall River *Herald News*, who had written so many articles about Joe. I knew Joe had said, "Frank was a gentleman, great writer, and great friend." Nor could I trace the family of Charles Doessereck, Joe's main manager and promoter from Bayonne, who lived there for almost half of the century; I found his house and his obituary, but neither the current owner of the house nor a neighbor who had lived there since 1960 had any idea who Doessereck was. For half a century his name was recognized by millions and his face was familiar to any boxing fans, but today there is no trace of him, and even his two sons and their relatives have seemingly vanished. My inquiries to various boxing institutions and their officials produced no results. Despite the road blocks, however, in the end I was amazed to realize how things clicked and connected by pure accident or coincidence, as if they were destined to happen, making all the money, time, and effort I had invested in my research well worth it to me.

While I initially intended to write only about Joe and his family, my research convinced me that this book should speak for countless Joes who never entered the history books, but who were responsible for the making of the Golden Age of Boxing. Being able to take or throw a tough punch wasn't enough. You had to have a trainer, a manager, and a promoter, people to "protect your interests" and deal with the politics of the sport. You had to be savvy about contracts, which could take not only the bulk of your winnings, but also your future earnings and those of your entire family. There was little regard for injuries, even those that could be life-threatening. There were countless happenings that were damaging to a boxing career—not that these kept any would-be fighters out of the ring.

Almost a century later, this book about Joe Grimm's life and professional boxing career in the Golden Age of Bantams offers a long-due tribute to the countless little warriors who are not found in the records of the gloved sport. I made a conscious effort to incorporate many of the fighters, trainers, managers, and promoters from Joe's ring years and to narrate his story in the larger context of boxing as part of the cultural era of the glamorous 1920s.

With my modest talent but with a fighter's heart, I have tried to enshrine as many other forgotten but similar Joes as I could in this overdue memory-lane book.

Introduction

Joe Grimm was the fighting name of Joseph David Hashim. His boxing record reads like sports fiction. He scored twenty-four knockouts in a row by the time he was eighteen, and he was never, himself, knocked out. He shared the same ring in the same event with some of the greatest champions of his time, including Eddie "Cannonball" Martin, "Midget" Smith, Abe Attell Goldstein, Harry Greb, Jack Delaney, and James "Jimmy" Braddock, among others.

What distinguished Joe from most other boxers was that he was not a school dropout or a bully, he did not come from a dysfunctional family, and he had not been released from a juvenile correctional institution. Nor was he a street bully or bar brawler. He was an altar boy with disciplined training who was so respectful inside and outside the ring that he was called "The Gentleman Boxer."

This book focuses on seven years in Joe's life during the glory days of the Roaring Twenties, the decade of flappers, jazz, the Charleston, the Model T automobile, heroic aviation, and the beginning of sound movies—the period known as the Golden Age of Boxing, when fistic champions became American and international legends. During that era, most small cities and all large ones had a boxing arena. Bouts were often staged in art deco theaters, "casinos," and huge multipurpose buildings on or near the main street where, for fifty cents, one could enjoy the memorable thrill provided by professional fights. Many cities could boast of a "cycledrome," a large outdoor arena with wood tracks for fast races of bicycles and motorbikes, with a boxing ring in the center. Few of these twentieth-century gladiatorial arenas ever heralded a challenger, and most never saw a champion, but each event showcased gutsy local heroes who were passionately cheered by their neighbors, coworkers, and friends.

Joe Grimm's story illustrates what it was like for some of those valiant fighters who pursued glory—even though, no matter how well they did, there were no guarantees of success. While he weighed almost one hundred pounds less than his contemporary Jack Dempsey, Joe had the ring presence of a heavyweight champion and the mental and physical qualities to conquer the bantamweight world title.

But forces he could not control and demands he could not avoid caused him to quit a promising professional career at the age of twenty-three, when he was at the peak of his fighting ability. This was akin to Cassius Clay (Muhammad Ali) quitting boxing after winning his Olympic gold medal.

There is no doubt that Joe Grimm was not a brainless brawler in the ring, but a superior fighter destined to conquer a world title if he was put in the right circumstances to do so. In Joe's case, his popular bantamweight division generously provided the ring with countless aspiring "little fighters." Typically, a boxing event featured five bouts with fighters in different weight categories. But there were so many bantamweights that often more than one bout featured the 118-pound scrappers who were eager to establish a record in the local hierarchy. In fact, between 1920 and 1928, there were at least ten bantam world champions. Finally, these great openers who went the distance and entertained crowds often dissatisfied with the main event became stars on their own merit. These overly aggressive and hard-punching "roosters" kindled an interest in pugilistic competition for millions of spectators, making boxing the king of all sports.

As one of Joe's managers regularly said to him, "There are no guarantees in life," and there were plenty of times when that saying was meaningful. Yet, none of the hard punches or surprising twists of fate and turns of events ever knocked out Joe—not in the ring, not in life. Yet, whereas a vast majority of fighters made their exits because they were too battered and injured to continue, past their prime, rejected by managers and promoters, and/or broke, Joe retired unscarred and retained the tenacity he had in the ring. Furthermore, he dutifully had turned his winning money over to his needy, tightly knit, Christian, Lebanese family. Joe had made good choices, and the winner in the ring became a winner in life. The young immigrant joined countless other millions who in total anonymity proved America to be the greatest land of opportunity in the world.

Joe would say that his glory days were those seven years of boxing, especially his twenty-four knockouts in a row. And while this book revolves around his boxing career, it also shows how Joe's ring experiences offer a life lesson in rolling with the punches and coming out a winner. A gentleman in the ring, he continued to be a gentleman for the rest of his long life.

CHAPTER 1

ONE MORE TIME!

Walking out of the locker room with his boxing gloves on and a large white towel on his back, Joe Grimm was followed by two men: Bobby Tickle, his trainer and manager, who held a doctor's handbag with a towel folded between the handles, and Mike Hashim, Joe's brother, who carried the spit bucket and two jugs with icy water. Tickle, the blue-eyed older man, was the same height as Joe. He wore a black flat hat, a buttoned green vest with stuffed pockets, a bluish shirt with the sleeves rolled up, and baggy-knee pants. Mike, a little taller and with dark bulging eyes, was dressed in a secondhand navy-blue double-breasted suit, a white shirt with a stiff collar, and a black tie. His black wavy hair reflected its olive oil treatment and matched the color of a pencil mustache above carnal lips.

The small group ceremoniously walked through the crowded aisle of the boxing arena toward the ring, set up on a four-foot-high platform. It was two days before Christmas in 1921, and all seven hundred spectators shouted and applauded when they spotted the teenage fighter as he made his way through the wooden benches. Heavy cigarette smoke swirled in rolling clouds that were pierced by the electric spotlights aimed at the ring, which looked like a pagan altar, spattered with blood, in the middle of glittering Christmas decorations. The hubbub and suffocating smells of sweat and tobacco were familiar to the regulars who attended the indoor events in the Casino of the city of Fall River, Massachusetts.

Hands reached out and touched Joe during his brisk walk toward the ring. "Lookin' good, Joe!" "Go for it, guy!" and "Floor him, Joe!" the excited fans called out. The trim bantam fighter with lively brown eyes, his black hair showing a perfect part on the left, saluted them with his right glove, a flexed bicep, and a big smile. The crowd responded enthusiastically, knowing they were in for a good time with Joe in the ring. It was the second bout of the evening. There would be three more before the main event, and the crowd was throbbing with expectation.

Reaching the brightly lit platform, Joe slipped through the ropes and shadowboxed into the middle of the twenty-foot enclosure, where he then saluted the public by touching his gloves above his head. A little over five feet five inches and only 118 pounds, he radiated power, skill, and, most of all, confidence. The crowd stood and screamed their approval. Then he went to his corner. Referee Degasse, dressed in black slacks and a white shirt with a black bow tie and wearing highly polished leather shoes, checked Joe's face and examined his gloves. Nodding approval, the referee went to the opposite corner to perform the same inspection on the other bantam, Jackie Coogan, who was being massaged on the neck and face by his cornerman. Both fighters were local boys—Grimm residing on Harrison Street next to the factory buildings, while Coogan lived on Morgan, next to the Casino. Neither boxer looked at the other until Mr. Degasse called them into the middle of the ring.

One of the two judges crossed under the ropes and into the ring. The audience quieted as he introduced Coogan, calling him a promising fighter. Polite applause followed. Then the overweight judge—dressed in street clothes, including a bowl hat—turned toward Joe and announced, "In the right corner, scoring eighteen victories in a row by knockout, I present to yoouuu, Joooeeee Griiiimmm!"

The crowd was on its feet, screaming. The shouts of some thirty Boy Scouts emerged from the tumult. "One more time! One more time! One more time!" The boys proudly heralded their assistant Scout master from Camp Noquochoke. Joe acknowledged his faithful troop number 14 by throwing a few fast punches in their direction, triggering another wave of screams from them. After touching gloves, the two fighters went to their corners. Mike leaned over the ropes and whispered into his brother's ear, "You win this!" Joe's trainer had the last word. "Remember to start and end up with a left jab!" Pulling the white towel from Joe's shoulder, he slipped between the ropes to sit below the platform.

Joe nodded as the bell sounded, and pivoted forward, ready to battle in the center of the ring. Coogan was already there, sure of himself. He was taller and opened the fight with a flurry of punches aimed to intimidate the fast-approaching Harrison Street boy, who stepped to the side and promptly sent a quick left-right-left jab combination that landed on Jackie's temple and shook his head. There was nothing more hurtful for an advancing rival than walking into a point-blank stiff jab. The crowd went wild, wanting to see their favorite score another KO. Determined to avoid exactly this, Coogan hugged Joe in a clinch to gain time and recover. Both fighters wrestled until Joe began delivering quick uppercuts to Coogan's midsection, looking for an opening upstairs. The referee stepped in with a "break free" and pushed them apart. Coogan leaped back and began to sail around Joe, delivering long punches, taking full advantage of his longer reach. It was a good tactic that he had used successfully many times, allowing him to score from a safe distance. Joe avoided most of the blows by bobbing and weaving, patiently trying to adjust his range. Fighting defensively, he encouraged Coogan to intensify his scoring jabs.

Each corner screamed instructions that neither of the fighters could hear over the roars of the crowd. Trading punches continued to put Joe at a disadvantage because of his shorter reach. He shifted from side to side, setting his own pace, but Coogan was a moving target. Joe kept strategizing as he calmly eyed his opponent. He knew that in six rounds many things could happen in his favor. Also, he was aware that his rival's punches had begun to lose power and snap. When the first round ended, Joe sat in his corner, listening to Coach Tickle point out that Coogan was ahead in points. Mike stopped fanning the towel for more air and put a firm hand on his brother's shoulder, squeezing hard as he urged Joe to finish him—the faster, the better. Joe rinsed his mouth with icy water and spit it out in the bucket.

When the bell rang, Joe rushed across the ring and assailed the opponent in his corner with all the punching combinations he knew and all the strength he had. The public went ballistic! Coogan tried to duck and pull back from the unexpected relentless punishment. Skillfully he managed to slip out of the troubling position he'd been in and retaliated by sending long blows into Joe's face. But he telegraphed his punches, and most of them missed their target. Even so, the barrage kept now-attacker Grimm in check. Joe realized he was doing Coogan's fight. Unlike in previous bouts, when he succeeded by engaging in a close fight and using his merciless right cross and left hook to wrap up the match, this time Joe was being outpunched for too long. Coogan knew he had the edge, so he kept dancing around. His safe tactics suddenly ended when he found himself rushed into the ropes.

What happened next was succinctly described in the local paper: "Jackie Coogan was in the lead at the time Young Joe Grimm crossed a quick right to his chin that floored the Morgan street fighter for the full account." Referee Degasse signaled with his spread arms the end of the ten count and lifted Joe's right arm as a mark of victory. The Boy Scout troop went wild and rushed to the stage to carry Joe on their shoulders, but two policemen pointed them back to their seats. In his corner, Joe took a long sip of icy water and, wrapped in the white towel, stepped into the middle of the ring, where the referee once again raised his victorious arm high as the announcer shouted, "Nineteen KOs now in a row!"

With Tickle and Mike on each side, Joe stepped out of the ring and headed for the dressing room, waving at the spectators, giving them his big grin and a few loose jabs that had the crowd screaming even louder, "Joe! Joe! Joe!" He was almost seventeen years old and a very happy winner.

In the calm of the dressing room, Tickle pulled Joe's gloves off. "It was a good fight!" he said as Joe nodded. As usual, the small leather bag stuffed with bandages and ointments that Tickle carried to the ring remained unopened. So far, Joe hadn't needed it; his face was unscratched. While Joe dressed, Tickle walked out of the room. Mike stayed, lit a cigarette, and calculated in his mind how much money he had made betting on his brother's win. The coach returned with an envelope and went to hand it to Joe, but Mike intercepted it. "I'll take care of that." He opened the envelope and counted five $5 bills. Inhaling deeply from the cigarette, Mike raised his bushy eyebrows. "That's all?"

"For now, yes! Joe, I'll see you at the gym after the holiday. Merry Christmas, everyone!" Tickle shook hands with both brothers and left.

"I wonder how much he got in his envelope," Mike mumbled as he inhaled deeply and then blew out a stream of smoke.

"Hey, it's okay. Remember, I used to make just $5 a fight!" Joe smiled. "Twenty-five bucks is five weeks' pay at the mill. I made that in four minutes!"

"Others make four thousand in the same time." Mike frowned.

"Yeah, but I'm not there yet."

"We will be, don't worry!" Mike ground the cigarette butt beneath the heel of his well-polished shoe, and the brothers went back to the arena. Joe always wanted to see how others conducted themselves in the ring so he could learn from their mistakes. Mike collected his winning bets and looked around for other managers and trainers, hoping to overhear their conversations.

The winter cold chilled the Hashim brothers as they walked home. After they washed their hands, they joined their younger siblings, Evelyn, Catherine, and George, at the collapsible aluminum table in the small kitchen, where the family not only ate meals, but also shared news and relaxed. The aroma of cinnamon and allspice signaled the Lebanese food their mother, Rafka, had been preparing. Saying nothing, she took a plate filled with pita bread still puffed and steaming from the wood burning stove and placed it on the table, next to a bowl of hummus. Mike and Joe split the pita open and tore off pieces they then used to scoop up the food. Their mother quietly searched Joe's face for cuts, scrapes, or bruises. Before long, the boys' mustached father, David, came from another room and said in Arabic, "How was it?"

"We won again by another KO!" reported Mike as he handed the envelope to his father, who sat down and carefully pulled out each bill. No one looked at Rafka, who went to the stove to check on the rest of the food. She wiped away the quiet tears that slipped down her cheeks. She had made it clear she did not want Joe to fight for any reason. But despite her pleas, Joe kept sneaking out of his second-floor bedroom window to go to the gym or to the fights. Her husband was more tolerant—the winning money was a big help to the impoverished immigrant family with nine children.

"A few more wins and we can buy a Model T Ford!" David smiled as he took the money into another room. Rafka glanced at the large crucifix that was on the wall above the ice box. Quickly crossing herself, she turned back to the stove top and, with heavy oven mitts, lifted the large casserole filled with *kusa mihshi*, squash that had been hollowed out and stuffed with chopped lamb and rice, all in a tomato sauce, and placed it on the table.

Glancing out the window over the sink as she did the dishes, Rafka saw that it had begun to snow; large, whirling flakes ensured a white Christmas. Mike started to describe the fight, but no one seemed to be interested. Before long, the entire family was sound asleep.

The family's life had begun to change when one day a stranger, seeing Joe fighting in the street to defend his sisters, asked him to come to the YMCA. The teenager ended up in a huge room with the running track suspended around the brick wall above the floor, exactly at the height of the basketball hoops attached to it. A ring was anchored to the walls in a corner, and a large punching bag was hanging next to it from the suspended track. A bunch of other teenagers were watching a boxing exhibition among amateur fighters who kept pelting each other with large brown gloves.

Joe observed all this with a racing heart. He noted that the faster a guy threw punches, the better luck he had of reaching the target, while the one who kept his arms up all the time received fewer hits, especially in the face. However, regardless of giving or receiving the punches, the guy who was out of balance was easy to hit. Worse yet was to close the eyes and throw an aimless punch. Clearly, winning meant to hit more and be hit less. Watching, Joe's muscles tightened with excitement. When the match was over, he picked up a glove and found he could hardly push his large hand inside it.

"You do have quite a fist," said the referee, struggling to pull the glove off. Joe didn't know if that was a good or a bad thing, but before leaving the gym, he threw a punch against the big punching bag that seemed to be filled with sand. The muffled sound of impact came with a pain in his arm. No doubt, that was not the way to hit the bag, but Joe loved it anyway.

The next day he came back to the Y and saw guys doing calisthenics, jumping rope, throwing a heavy ball to each other, and punching the large bag with smaller gloves than those he had seen in the previous day's fight. Perspiration covered their faces and soaked their workout clothes. They were breathing loudly, as if letting brief whistling steam mark each movement: *hegh hegh hegh*. They knew how to blow their noses without touching the nostrils with their fingers, a skill that highly impressed Joe. But what captivated him the most was the small speed punching bag dangling under a round platform attached to the brick wall. The rattling *ta-ta-ta-ta-ta-ta* went faster and faster, the rhythm changing as the guy used different parts of his fists or changed the hitting direction.

Joe returned to the Y every chance he had, and little by little he was accepted by the regular group of beginners, many of whom were wrestlers who liked to put on gloves. In time a few professional boxers showed up. Joe learned something from everybody. Before long, he stepped into the ring with another rookie. The sparring was uneventful until Joe snapped a punch, and the other guy dropped to the floor. He pulled himself up, with a confused look on his face, and went down again with the next punch. The referee pulled him out and put a heavier guy in the ring. Joe put him down in no time. Then one of the older pros stepped in the ring; making his moves and faking blows, he struck and gave Joe a black eye and a swollen lip. But then the pro found himself on the floor—and then again he took a dive! Visibly hurt, he called it quits. As Joe left the ring, Referee Tickle patted his shoulder and said, "Kid, you got a million-dollar punch!"

Joe went home and announced to his parents in Arabic that he had a "$1 million punch" and he was going to be a boxer. His mother looked at his bruises, walked out of the kitchen, and went into her bedroom, followed by Joe's father. A few minutes later, his father came back into the kitchen alone. "Your mother is crying. No more fighting!" Mike overheard the conversation, and after their father left, he asked his younger brother, "What was that about a million bucks?"

The next day Mike went to the Y and found Joe in the ring. Mike watched and could scarcely believe how well his kid brother was doing. As they walked home later, Mike was thinking about how Joe could get out of the house without upsetting their mother. Then it came to him: Joe could get a job with the Boy Scouts. After all, he had been a devoted member for years.

Within a week, the plan was in motion and Joe was the new physical instructor for Troop 14 at summer camp, which had just started. Drawing on his few weeks of training at the Y, Joe demonstrated exercise routines for the troop members, challenging them to copy his push-ups with three claps between jumps and one-arm chin-ups. Before long a ring was installed in the summer camp between four trees. He still slipped away from camp and his family house to get into the ring at the Y, often with Mike covering for him and then watching him from ringside.

At the gym Joe worked harder than anyone. His warm-up consisted of running from his home on Harrison Street and then uphill on Quarry Street, both lined with factory buildings. Many of the mill workers knew him, and upon seeing him running, they would cheer him: "Go, Joe, go!" Encouraged, he would accelerate his steps as he turned onto Bedford Street, with its beautiful mansions overlooking the water, and continued onto North Main Street until he reached the YMCA building. He was the first to show up for training and the last to leave.

Before long, Joe's uninterrupted wins-by-knockout record led Referee Tickle to introduce Joe to his brother Bobby Tickle, a veteran boxer-turned-manager. There was something appealing about his reddish face, with its radiant blue eyes, strong chin, and inviting smile. His pug nose advertised a rough past in the ring, and his still-athletic body imposed authority. Joe accepted him as his manager on the spot. A handshake sealed the deal that also split in half any money resulting from Joe's boxing earnings, minus expenses. When Mike learned the news, he rubbed his face nervously, smoothed his pencil mustache with his thumb and index finger, and shook his head. "Do you realize you just handed half of our money to a stranger!"

But Bobby Tickle was a needed stranger, and Joe not only liked and trusted him, but he felt privileged to be associated with him. Tickle was an ex-professional fighter who, in 1910, lost to the future featherweight champion, Johnny Kilbane, in six rounds by a narrow decision in Boston. Kilbane continued to hold the world featherweight champion title that he'd won in 1912—the longest reign of any title holder in the history of boxing.

Tickle wanted Joe to have a new last name—a boxing name, not as ethnic as "Hashim." Something memorable and catchy. "How about Joe Grim? Sure, he never won, but the public loved his guts." And Tickle began to talk about the original Joe Grim, whom he had met and seen fight. Shaking his head and chuckling, he described how the fighter shouted to the spectators before every fight, "I am Joe Grim! Nobody can knock me out!" Born in Italy in 1881, Saverio Giannone was living in Philadelphia by 1900. His first known fight was in 1899, when he was eighteen years old; he was knocked to the floor in every round but kept getting up. Called "the human punching bag" and nicknamed "Iron Man," he was famous for never surrendering in the ring in his 134 bouts (according to rumor, the number is as high as 300). He was the type of boxer spectators loved the most—a fighter with a tiger's heart.

Joe loved the story. How good to share a name with a boxer who ended each fight on his feet, screaming to the public, "I, Joe Grim, I not quit for no man in the world!" It sounded so heroic. But, he vowed, the new Grim would do right where the old Grim did wrong. "Let's spell it with two Ms to make it a little different," said Tickle. He added with a smile, "With this name, your mother will never know you're fighting." And so another boxer took on the name of the legendary iron man; more than ten other young boxers would subsequently also use the name that had come to embody the spirit of a fighter who just wouldn't quit in the ring.

After his nineteenth victory, Joe was wrapped in the good feeling that he was doing exactly what he should do to help his parents and siblings by making more money in one night than the entire family made in two weeks. He sighed with pleasure as he reviewed in his mind the assurances so many were making that he had a bright future as a successful prizefighter. What he did not realize at this point, however, was that his weight category had numerous teenage competitors, all under 120 pounds, cocky, and eager to jump into a ring.

Each American state, each county, and countless small cities and towns had excellent bantams ready to achieve national recognition. Within Joe's hometown there were at least four good fighters in his category, namely Tony Carney, Joe Dias, Joe Pete, and veteran George Vanderbilt, all fighting some other ten rivals who lived in neighboring areas. Well-ranked boxers like Charley Manty and Chick Suggs, who was already a household name and on his way to stardom, lived in nearby New Bedford. Others, like Young Montreal, lived in the vicinity of Providence, whose fighters faced tough competition from nearby Boston and its surrounding cities, like Worcester, where Tony Mandela lived. On top of this, there was the rest of the Commonwealth of Massachusetts, whose boxers battled each year to conquer the New England title. To achieve that honor, boxers from Connecticut, Maine, New Hampshire, Rhode Island, and Vermont eliminated each other through tough contests. However, the New England title meant little when it came to national boxing recognition. Its champions too often paled in comparison to the exceptional crop of boxers who lived in New York City or its boroughs of Queens and Brooklyn, and in the cluster cities of Bayonne and Jersey City across the Hudson River.

Meanwhile, Chicago and Los Angeles, as well as major cities in Florida, Texas, Georgia, Ohio, Missouri, and Utah, among others, kept producing fighters who in Europe would floor any contender in any category but here had to slowly fight their way through the ranks just to receive some recognition. They all hoped that they would be spotted by a good manager or promoter who would advance their careers. It was a close-to-impossible wish, since the best of the best fighters were already signed up and waiting for their turn to fight challengers who, in their turn, hoped to become contenders and fight a champion for a title.

Joe knew about boxing activities only in the area in which he was living. His job was to be a winner, while Mike, three years older, acted as his mentor and protector. Joe had won all his fights by knockouts, and Mike's bets had paid off handsomely. It was a win-win situation for both young men. So far, so good for the two brothers and the rest of the Hashim family.

Chapter 2

More Knockouts

Joe Grimm was undefeated at this point in his career. An immigrant, he was born in 1905 in Lebanon (part of Syria at that time), where he was Christianized as Nageeb David Hashim. His first name was written "Hagil" in the "List of Alien Passengers" when he arrived at age eight in America and settled with his family in Fall River. Wanting a more American name like his schoolmates, he became "Joseph" and was called "Joe." He liked to play stickball with the other kids on the street and inevitably got into fights, one of which would lead him to the ring. And so Joe took on a new identity and became a serious boxer.

Coach Tickle had quickly identified Joe's raw talent. The boy had excellent reflexes and arm speed. He was blessed with heavy hands, a strong neck, a granite chin, and tremendous determination to succeed. With these qualities, Joe needed only to know how to use them. This would be Tickle's job. Countless hours and repetitions taught Joe how to initiate a punch from the feet, hips, and shoulders, and how to deliver a precise snap without pushing it into the target. He learned that not all punches were equally efficient when it came to score a KO, and that each fighter had his favorite punches. Joe decided to stay with his right cross and left hook, and he perfected this move over and over, practicing against the heavy sandbag and speed bag. As for style, he discovered that having flat feet meant that running around the ring was not advantageous for him. Therefore he practiced the old routine of bobbing and weaving that also felt more natural to him. As Tickle told him, he was an infighter and a counterpuncher, waiting for the opponent to make mistakes in defense. All in all, he was better suited to carry out a close fight, which he instinctively did from the very beginning. He had natural power and stamina and did not easily run out of gas.

Because he was the same height as Joe, Tickle was comfortable sparring with him, and at the same time he shared valuable tips with the eager student. He showed Joe how to use punch combinations at different angles and speeds, how to pace himself during a round and the entire fight, and how to avoid wild punches. He pointed out that many fighters had a "glass chin" and demonstrated how to hit it most efficiently to give opponents "spaghetti legs." He taught Joe new vocabulary, like "solar plexus," related to how "to plant a blow in the pit of the stomach." And he taught him that "perfection comes from practice" and "there is no substitute for practice."

Joe learned that mental attitudes were as valuable as fight tactics in the ring. It was important not to resent or be furious with an opponent. These strong emotions didn't help in a fight; to the contrary, they led to less control of muscles and nerves. Fighting smart was the way to win. The more Joe trained and sparred, the more he learned that keeping a cool head was a must. This was not always easy for a teenager overcharged with adrenalin and hormones. But Joe was one of those fighters who showed no pain or panic, and therefore it was difficult to intimidate him in the ring. His determination to win was endless. He learned that, to end a fight by flooring his rival, he needed to deliver one punch, not necessarily swiped from the floor—his half hook and half cross had given him nineteen knockouts in a row. His heavy fists seemed created for that purpose.

Tickle (the referee) and Tickle (the coach) both recognized Joe's strong, innate learning ability and determination. They knew his gameness was genuine and saw that the public loved him. Yes, Joe Grimm was young and lacked experience, but he wasn't afraid to enter the ring, and he dreamed big. The teenager projected a glowing confidence that no training could provide. He had the potential to be a challenger. He might even have what it took to be a champion. Lying about his age, Joe became a professional prizefighter at age sixteen.

Because his many boxing victories were covered in the popular sports section of the local newspapers, it was inevitable that the news reached the Lebanese community and ultimately his mother, who spoke only Arabic. Mike and Joe tried to explain to her that boxing was part of the Boy Scout program, but she would have none of it. She looked at her two sons, shook her head, and turned to the stove. There would be no more discussion about fighting. Still, Joe used any excuse and trick to get out of the house, mostly lowering himself with a rope from the second-floor bedroom window to go training or fighting, and then returning the same way.

But the obvious bruises, sweat-soaked outfits, and dirty hand wraps were a giveaway, and Joe finally decided to make everything "legal" by announcing that he was turning professional and would fight for money. His mother openly cried; his father shrugged his shoulders, reluctantly proud that everyone else was talking about how his youngster was winning by knockouts. "What will be, will be," he told his wife as he thoughtfully twisted both ends of his long mustache.

The second day of the new year of 1922 found Joe in the Fall River Casino, getting ready to fight Young Murphy from neighboring New Bedford, a city with a long and strong boxing reputation. Whenever boxers from the two cities met in the ring, they fought not only to score a victory for themselves but also to defend the reputation of their city. The two communities had a perpetual argument over which produced the better textiles and had more skilled seamstresses and tailors, and this rivalry spilled over to every competition. Basically, Fall River residents believed that those who weren't skilled enough to work in their city found employment in New Bedford. In fact, New Bedford people were called "whalers" since that was the trade that put them on the map, not the new industry of textile and thread production. On the flip side, the workers of New Bedford believed only they could sew straight and perfect lines on any garment, since their textiles were only white and any imperfection would be noticed. The more numerous workers from Fall River, the New Bedford workers would say, handled only floral designs that camouflaged their defective work. Now, in the ring, it was Joe's duty to prove who was the best.

While Joe put on his gloves, the event promoter came into the dressing room and announced that Murphy could not fight, but another fine fellow by the name Jimmy Enos, also from New Bedford, would be the last minute replacement. Immediately Mike suspected a set-up. Fearing for his bet on Joe, he quickly lit a cigarette to calm himself down. The walk to the ring was the same as usual, with spectators trying to shake Joe's hand and patting the white towel on his shoulders, while the choir of Boy Scouts and their relatives chanted, "Joe! Joe! Joe!" Cigarette smoke enveloped the Christmas decorations and the ring itself in bluish clouds. The arena was filled with spectators from both cities, separated in two groups by other out-of-towners, many of them women, and by the noisy members of Troop 14, who had paid an entrance fee of only twenty-five cents instead of the regular half a dollar, or one dollar for ringside seats. Just like the last time, people were dressed up, indicating they came or would go to some party after watching the fights. Boxing events were often the prelude to an evening of dinner and dancing.

Once in the ring, Joe saluted the viewers by tapping his gloves above his head, attracting stomping ovations from one side of the arena and booing from the other side, clearly where those from New Bedford were seated. When Jimmy Enos entered the ring, he punched the air a few times and was likewise greeted with screams of support from one side of the arena and booing from the other. The announcer introduced the opponents. When he mentioned that Joe had already set a record of nineteen wins by knockout, the noisy spectators reacted as expected, pro with cheers and con with boos. The sound of the bell changed the nature of the noise, now a hubbub of mixed encouragements.

Joe walked into the middle of the ring and waited for Enos to step forward, which he did in an aggressive way by hitting his face with his own gloves. Obviously, the guy was tough. They exchanged a few heavy blows because Enos asked for it, and Joe realized he was a typical brawler, much feared in any back alley or saloon. The boy simply began to swing his gloves from the floor in Joe's direction, missing each time by a mile. Joe refused to brawl and kept moving back and away from the dangerous swirls of punches that forced their sender to pivot to the right and to the left, exposing his back. But Joe knew better and waited for the jaw. So far, there was no way to predict which way the fight would go.

With each of Enos's wild punches, his supporters screamed their support. Joe's fans were frozen in their seats, believing him to be badly bullied or even scared. It was so rare to see Joe on the defensive that even the Boy Scouts were silent. A little more than one minute into the first round, the slugger was relentless; he showed no indication of slowing down or getting tired, and continued chasing Joe around the ring. There was no style, just furious hitting power. However, his movements were predictable, and Joe carefully began to do his bobbing and weaving. Joe threw a few fake punches to lure his adversary into an even more chaotic reaction. Then, in a split second, it happened: Enos leaned in for a big swing and missed as Joe had stepped back. This left Enos wide open. Joe leaped forward and landed a punch to the face that put Enos down for good. Referee Jackson, who so far had very little to do, dramatically counted a full ten seconds and then raised Joe's hand, declaring the winner. While Enos's corner aides tried to revive their boxer, the Boy Scouts were joined by the rest of the Fall River fans as they rejoiced with ear-piercing "We won again! We won again!" The victory against Enos was "the result of a terrific rain of punches to his midriff," wrote the local newspaper the next day. "Grimm won the fight without any trouble scoring his twentieth KO after less than two minutes of fighting."

As he did after each fight, Joe got dressed and went to join the Boy Scout troop, shaking numerous hands along the way and being proudly slapped on his back by countless fans. He always stayed in the audience until the last fight was over, because watching others fight helped him analyze different styles and learn from others' mistakes. But this time was a little different, because Jack Delaney was to appear in the last bout of the evening card.

Delaney was a boxer from Quebec, now residing in Connecticut, famous for his spectacular fights and equally good looks, including dimples. He became an instant attraction for young women who were huge fans of his, and many of them, well perfumed and colorfully dressed, had come to the Casino to see him. His record consisted of some twenty-five wins, half of them by KO, one draw, and only one loss by points. He was opposed by the gutsy, light heavyweight Jackie Clark, a local boxer with eight wins, two draws, and two losses. Not at all intimidated by his superior adversary, Clark appeared in the ring ready to do his best.

That night, Joe saw a close encounter of two good fighters who went toe-to-toe for ten rounds. Delaney was a smooth combatant with clear judgment. He won by decision. Simply put, he was a smart fighter who could punch hard, to the delight of his female cohort. His performance deeply impressed Joe, who afterward was introduced to the smiling Delaney and shook his hand. Unwittingly, Joe had touched and talked to the future world light heavyweight champion of the world (1926–1927).

Back home, Father Hashim counted another $25 and twisted his long mustache with a hidden smile. Mike, with a full grin, was rubbing his hands. Mother Rafka looked at the crucifix and crossed her heart.

Conforming to his belief that there was no substitute for practice and hard work, Coach Tickle intensified the training sessions as Joe approached the age of seventeen. His many winnings by KO had already made him a local household name. Suddenly Tickle told him that a manager from New York had called about bringing a boxer, Eddie Lester, to Fall River on January 27 for an evenly matched bout. It just happened that Tickle was the event promoter, and the managers agreed that Ralph, Tickle's brother, would be the referee. The news quickly spread and the arena was overpacked with supporters, including many from New Bedford. The two cities might fight against each other all the time, but when someone came from another town, it was all for one.

The night of the fight came quickly, with Grimm–Lester opening for the main event, again for another Delaney card. As usual when Delaney fought, the arena air was scented with the clashing odors of cigarette smoke and the fine perfume worn by the female fans of the charming fighter. Their colorful hats looked like flowers in the muddy-looking arena. It happened that Joe shared a dressing room with Delaney, so he watched how Delaney did a little warm-up and talked to his corner people, always smiling and looking more like a handsome actor than a boxer. He was cheerful and so relaxed that he seemed like he was going out with some buddies, not facing a brutal opponent in the ring.

There was a thing about the New York boxers—they had an often-inflated reputation, so it was no surprise that most of the bets were placed on Lester even though the fans were screaming support for Joe. Hoping the hometown boy would win didn't necessarily correlate to where hard-earned dollars were placed for a bet. Soon enough, Lester entered the ring. Shrugging off his black robe and moving about, he revealed an athletic body, a sharp attitude, and a readiness to fight hard. When the bell rang, the fighters raced to each other, both eager to throw the first punch, only to lock in a tight clinch. Referee Ralph pushed the wrestlers apart while the entire audience hissed at him for sabotaging the fight.

That first contact showed that Lester had not only strength, but a huge desire to win. He was certainly not intimidated by Joe's record of twenty knockouts in a row, and he was determined to stop it with this match. Methodically, the taller Lester began to score by jabbing with his left hand from a distance. Joe tried to close in for his best shots. It didn't happen in the first round, nor in the second. Taking advantage of his longer reach, Lester was standing his ground with fast-repeating jabs that prevented Joe from doing his fight.

Before the third round, Tickle coached Joe to move a lot more, aiming to make Lester tired as he continued to come at him. Joe did just that, but the round went again in favor of the New Yorker, who easily kept up with Joe's leg work. Whatever Joe tried, the other would return in double with great ease and good form. At the third break, Joe was losing. "What are you doing to me, brother?" cried Mike while fanning the towel in Joe's face to bring more air into his lungs. Tickle was still confident that Lester would collapse if forced to move a lot, and simply ordered, "Harass him a lot!" But in the fourth it was Lester who did the chasing all over the ring, looking for an ultimate punch delivery. Joe's fans were on their feet screaming their lungs out, and the Boy Scouts blew sharp whistles to energize their troop leader. It was a round during which the two fighters tried to see who was faster and smarter. Suddenly Joe slipped inside and pelted Lester's face and body nonstop at close quarters until the bell rang. He saw Lester wobbling toward his corner chair, showing that the knees go first.

With his eyes closed, Joe breathed deeply as he planned his next round, ignoring his brother's voice in his ear, pushing him to win. Within seconds of the bell ringing, Joe was all over Lester, who so far had put up a hell of a fight, but the action was now beginning to turn against him. The newspaper reporter who covered the event would write in his column the next day that "Grimm was determined to take everything that Lester shot out and he waded right into Lester in the fifth round and gave him such a beating that Lester dropped from exhaustion." But Lester was too strong and too proud to stay down for the complete count and, hooking on ropes, he stood up.

Disoriented and with his knees bent, he walked to Tickle's corner, believing the round was over, only to be redirected by the referee to the center of the ring. There he tried again with his distance jabbing until Joe's short but merciless left hook flattened the New Yorker for the full count. The fight was over and the crowd went crazy with cheers: "Our Joe wins again!" Those who had bet against the local hero ruefully shook their heads as they cheered for him; the handful who had won their bets raced to collect them, waving the money in the faces of all the losers. Joe was the man of the hour. Delaney came over to him and shook his hand again. "Those fists will drop anyone!" he commented. Joe gave Delaney his big smile. Over Delaney's shoulder, Joe saw Mike. Their eyes met, and Mike nodded in admiration. Another win for Joe, and a big money day for his brother.

The night was not over. The main attraction was Delaney, now opposing Jack McCarron, once famous for fighting a few times within a week, now a ring veteran who kept on boxing after some ten years of ups and downs in his professional career. Round after round, Delaney kept on jabbing to set himself up for his famous deadly right cross, but his intentions were diffused over and over by the clever and alert Pennsylvanian. It was obvious that Delaney was the superior fighter, with his feline moves, good technique, and well-planned attacks. Yet this exceptional KO boxer was outsmarted and often outpointed by the older McCarron.

While factions of spectators switched cheers back and forth according to what happened in the ring, Joe was quiet and focused on learning what he needed to know better. Sometimes he saw himself as a stiff puncher like Delaney, and other times as a smart counterpuncher like McCarron; he liked both of them. Delaney was more aggressive and won at the end of the ten rounds, but to Joe, both were winners; he could have watched them fighting all night long. The public reacted in the same way, and Delaney's women were jubilant with happy screams and laughter. Joe left the Casino with the cheers of the Delaney follies in his ears and a strong feeling that indeed boxing was his calling.

That night he brought home a record $40, and his career began to make sense for the entire family.

Despite Joe's win, Lester and his manager believed that Joe could be defeated and asked for a rematch. To Tickle, who would again be the fight promoter, this sounded like striking gold. On February 3, 1922, Fall River witnessed a boxing event heralded as the fight of the year; it attracted a record audience. Lester came with an entourage. He was determined to demolish Joe's growing reputation. Joe was more than ready and appeared in the ring with new trunks made of white satin, with "JG" monogrammed in red and encircled with a red border; they were a present from his mother and sisters for his seventeenth birthday, which would be in three days.

As Joe entered the ring, the home audience stood up and cheered for their undefeated boy. It was an emotional moment in the middle of a brutal arena. Lester in his corner ignored the cheers for his opponent and kept shadowboxing, so as not to lose his warm-up.

The bell announced the first round. Lester knew this time exactly whom he was facing. He'd been coached specifically on how to handle Joe. He initiated the fight with terrific left jabs, doubled up with stiff rights that landed a few times on Joe's face. As neither fighter was willing to step back, a toe-to-toe engagement took place in order to establish who was the stronger and better boxer. Lester stood tall on his feet to dominate, but his arm speed was no match for Joe's. And Joe, who ignored any blows he absorbed, kept throwing one combination after another, just like punching the heavy bag in the gym. His brief respiratory sounds, *whoosh whoosh whoosh*, were in perfect harmony with his blows, forcing Lester to shield his body and face. As the minutes went by, Joe revealed his tip-top shape, compared with his opponent, who was equal in skill but showed signs of fatigue. When Lester's arms dropped for a second, Joe threw a lightning-fast half cross to the boy's chin and then waited. Lester's knees gave up in slow motion, and he simply melted like a candle toward the canvas, where he lay sprawled on his back.

"We did it again, brother!" Mike happily exclaimed, forgetting to give Joe water or to fan the towel. He was right. After the break, Lester could not answer the bell. Still on his round chair, he could not get up to continue the fight. It was over. The audience went berserk. In the middle of the ring, Joe saluted by pumping his arms up and down in a sign of victory. He looked down at his new white trunks and was relieved to see them unstained. As he left for the dressing room, he heard the chants: "Our Joe won again!" and "Twenty-two in a row!" The pay was another record of $50.

Little by little, the Hashim family was getting used to Joe's boxing. They all went to Bobby Tickle's home to celebrate Joe's birthday. Joe was slowly being integrated into the American way of life. His parents were proud of him—not sure where this was all going but relieved that Joe was unhurt and grateful for the ring money.

Chapter 3

The Family and the City

Hashim was a popular family name in the former Levant nations, which at the beginning of the twentieth century were under the rule of the moribund Ottoman Empire. One Hashim clan happened to live in the mountain city of Aley, around ten miles from Beirut, capital of Lebanon, at that time part of Syria. Aley's population of some five thousand was the result of many racial mixtures dating from the Phoenician, Greek, and Roman times, to which the crusaders and the Turks added their genetic toll. Maronite Christians and non-Christian Druze found a good refuge in Lebanon, where they settled in solid communities, never to intermingle religion boundaries or their traditions that were written in stone. Some of them lived in Aley, where one Christian, David Abu Hashim (David son of Hashim), entered into a bitter dispute with a Druze neighbor whose children bullied the Hashim children. The exchange of bitter words and insults escalated to a fistfight between the fathers, who both carried daggers. David killed his neighbor, and that settled the argument.

An Ottoman investigation of the common dispute dragged on for so long that David, fearing capital punishment, borrowed money from his wife's family, the Haddads, and left the city with his oldest son, Elias, and second-oldest daughter, Edma. The father was a trader, while the son was a barber, both easy professions to practice while on the run. Edma, who sometimes had to dress as a boy to escape unpleasant situations, was to cook and take care of the two men. They traveled until they reached Patras, where they boarded a transatlantic ship whose destination was America.

This was a few months before the *Titanic* sank during its maiden voyage to New York. What the three Hashims knew about the new land was two words in English: *Fall River*, where a relative of Rafka, David's wife, lived and worked.

Upon arrival in Fall River, they were welcomed into the existing Lebanese community, which dutifully helped with job and living arrangements. The fifty-one-year-old father worked as a janitor in one of the mills, while seventeen-year-old Elias, who quickly learned a few hundred English words, was hired by a barbershop. Edma made a home out of two rented rooms and kept the expenses to a strict minimum. Within a year, they had enough money to bring the rest of the family to Fall River. Records show that Rafka Hashim and four children disembarked at Ellis Island on July 10, 1912, having crossed the ocean on the *S.S. Argentina* in its last voyage to America. Frieda, the oldest daughter, had stayed behind in Aley; she was married and pregnant (and would shortly thereafter die in childbirth). The family reunited in Fall River: David, the father; Rafka, mother; sons Elias, Mishael, and Nageeb; and daughters Edma, Emma, and baby Evelyn. They settled in the Lebanese section of the city, residing for a while on Flint Street in a three-room apartment. That summer everyone worked hard to put together enough money to rent part of a multifamily house nearby on Harrison Street. The three-story house was across the street from the Aldrich Elementary School, where the younger three Hashim children attended classes in September. Elias continued to work in the barbershop; Edma was now employed in the mill (she never went to school or learned how to read and write, and she would, for the rest of her life, speak minimal English). Each Sunday the entire family went to the church.

Fall River was a city of ethnic neighborhoods, each with grocery stores that catered to the local population. It wasn't difficult for the Hashim family to find the ingredients for foods they'd had back in Aley. Rafka, with the younger girls helping, prepared meals of lentil dishes, yogurt, squash stuffed with lamb and rice, fish topped with tahini and pine nuts, rice mixed with lamb and cinnamon, and, when they could afford it, kibbi (a finely ground lamb and bulgur wheat dish). On special occasions David and Rafka sipped *arak*, a strong wine that was 65 percent alcohol. It went well with the family's favorite dish, head of a lamb, pork, or deer cooked in a pan with a lot of Middle Eastern herbs.

The only language spoken in the household was Arabic. Similarly, other neighborhoods revolved around the languages and foods of the recent immigrants from Portugal, Italy, Ireland, and Germany, among others. While the immigrant parents struggled to learn enough English to get by, the children quickly became bilingual. As they intermingled in school and later in the mills, they became more Americanized, experimenting with different foods, having friends who came from different countries and cultures. To fit in the new society, it was easier to have an American name. In the Hashim family this meant changes for the boys, who had ethnic-sounding names: Elias was called Louis, Mishael became Mike (Michael,) and Nageeb, whose name was often misspelled Nageb, Nagib, and Nagil, was now known as Joe (Joseph). Thanks to Louis the barber, the Hashim children had hair that was always well groomed; their mother and older sisters made sure everyone's clothes were immaculately clean and ironed. The boys wore black ties with their white shirts, which, like their sisters' skirts and blouses, were stitched by their mother.

David Hashim was just over five feet tall; walking on the street or working in the mill he was unprepossessing, unless one noticed his proud long mustache and steely eyes. His wife, Rafka, was shorter than her husband and fourteen years younger. Always dressed in black, she was modest, hardworking, and soft-spoken. Looking fragile, she was strong both physically and emotionally. Deeply saddened to have had to leave her eldest daughter in Aley and not to be by her side when she died, she was religious and proud of her brother, who was a Greek Orthodox priest. She bore nine children, the last two after she was over forty years old. Both David and Rafka were well liked and respected in the Lebanese community of Fall River. Their children were well behaved, and all went to church. Their circle of friends was limited to the Lebanese families who often visited each other, bringing presents, mostly cooked food or pastry, according to the old saying, "An empty hand is a dirty hand."

It was the Roaring Twenties, when jazz music blossomed and flappers took over the towns, the Model T pushed aside the horse and carriage, and Hollywood movies and radio showcased a new modern age. But within the walls of their household, the lives of the Hashims did not differ much from the way they had lived in the old country. There were two more children now in the family—daughter Catherine and son George had been born in Fall River. David, with eight children living in the house, was the supreme tribal ruler. Children spoke respectfully to adults—talking back was unthinkable. Everyone crossed their heart and murmured a prayer before and after eating a meal around the table, and good manners were expected and enforced. Hand-knit afghans covered the sofa and beds; some artifacts from the old country could be seen on the walls and counters, including a Greek Orthodox cross in the parents' bedroom. A few Americanisms did make it into the household; for example, the children began to introduce some English words into their conversations. Still, the one time one of the girls called her father "Daddy," she received a silent look from him; Papa remained "Baba" from that moment on.

As was the case with most of the immigrant families in Fall River, when they were not in school the Hashim children worked and made money to help support the family. Altogether they might make no more than $10 a week, but that would pay the rent for a month. The main provider was the oldest son, Louis the barber, along with Edma, working in the mill. Mike also worked for a while in the mill, but when he was thirteen years old, he thought he could get more money from tips and left to work as a delivery boy for a grocery store. Having quickly learned how to stuff the shelves, he was soon allowed to fill in for the cashier and even to order goods on behalf of the Lebanese store owner, who spoke very little English. Two years later, Mike left the grocery business and joined Louis, who was now part owner of the barbershop. This, he said, was "where the big money was." As an apprentice, Mike mastered how to please the clients, including opening the door for them and brushing their coats. He made good money in tips. How much, only he knew, since he always put his share of $5 on the kitchen table each week and pocketed the rest.

Three years younger than Mike, Joe had specialized since the second grade in delivering hot meals with a pull wagon; he picked up the food prepared each day by Lebanese and Portuguese women and delivered it to their relatives working in the mills. He made a few dimes a day. On his way back home, Joe would drag the now-empty wagon alongside the rail tracks and pick up the chunks of coal that had fallen from the freight trains. There was a lot on the ground. He would unload the wagon and pile the coal in the basement, bringing some upstairs to the wood-burning stone in the kitchen and thus saving money for the family to use in other ways. After Mike left the grocery store, Joe took his place there, but only as a part-timer, since his job with the Boy Scouts and boxing training were almost a full occupation.

Shy and obedient Joe surprisingly turned out to be the most willing to step out of the immigrant way of life. Choosing the violent sport of boxing, he became the first "black sheep" of the family. He was also the first to be

Americanized, when he joined the Boy Scouts at their summer camp on Fall River's Stafford Pond. He slept over in the camp, marched with Troop 14 in parades, and was involved in any activity in which the troop participated. In 1918 he took the job of physical instructor for the troop (giving him a cover for going to the gym to box). He also trained the baseball Junior City League, and his Cubs kept winning at Crane Field. His good deeds and devotion to his troop resulted in his becoming second-in-command at Camp Noquochoke on the west shore of the Westport River. The camp's Spartan discipline was intended to make patriotic citizens and good soldiers out of Scouts, teaching them duty and responsibility. They learned what the American flag stood for, pledged allegiance to it each morning as it was raised on a pole, and played "Taps" at dusk when the flag was lowered and carefully folded. Rejected from military conscription because of flat feet, Joe loved the military aspects of being with the Boy Scouts. He proudly wore the Scout uniform, insignias, and merit badges and readily participated in the military-style drills and ceremonies that were a common part of camp life. Most of all, Joe was proud to be the flag bearer and to march in the front of his troop's formation.

At home, however, Joe was in the shadow of his brother Mike, who deserved respect by virtue of his being older. Still, when three teenage boys picked on a Hashim sister, it was Joe who stepped in and confronted the bullies. The bigger boys tried to grab Joe by the neck and hair. He punched them, and one after another, all three dropped on the pavement. A pedestrian asked Joe if he did any boxing, and he shook his head, saying the boys had it coming. The stranger invited him to come to the YMCA the next Monday night to see how boxing was done. "You'd be very good at it!" The stranger was boxing referee Ralph Tickle. At that time, Joe was almost fifteen. He went to the Y and that night ended up not bowling in the basement, as he had done in the past, but walking through the main lobby to the large basketball court with a boxing ring in the corner. There he soon discovered he could throw and take a punch. Since then, the ring had become his main destination and training his most loved activity. He was now committed to becoming a prizefighter.

The ring became Mike's destination as well, once he realized that Joe's talent and tenacity in boxing could bring "serious money" to the impoverished family. Mike instantly became the decision maker for his kid brother and learned to be a cornerman. He never asked for any payment, but he bet heavily on Joe, who kept winning all the time. In a few instances

Mike was able to count "big bucks;" later admitting that he kept "the loot" stashed "in case of family emergency."

As the older children reached the age when they might marry, David and Rafka carefully considered their prospects in the Lebanese community; they were also in touch with others who had emigrated from Aley, who might make a good husband or wife for one of their children. Louis married a Lebanese girl living in Fall River, and Edma married a Lebanese man. Emma was sought after by Louis Massery, who had known her family in Aley; he now lived in Pittsfield, Massachusetts, where he had a confectionary and tobacco wholesale business named the White Star, after the transatlantic liner that brought him to America. He would have a strong influence on the Hashim family.

An imposing man of six feet two inches, Massery spoke French in addition to Arabic and English, all with no accent. Handsome, always impeccably dressed and wearing rimless glasses, he had inborn charm and was one of the young immigrants who quickly and easily adapted to American society. He already had a successful business, supplying most of the grocery and convenience stores in western Massachusetts; he handed the Hashim children their first Hershey's milk chocolate bars, as he was the first to deliver this candy to the stores he serviced. The White Star was located in center of Pittsfield on Summer Street, close to the house where he moved with Emma after their marriage in Fall River. With three of their children well married in the United States, there were now seven living in the Hashim house on Harrison Street in Fall River: David and Rafka, with Mike, Joe, Evelyn, Catherine, and George.

Thus far, life was getting better for the Hashim family in America in 1922.

❧❧

Despite the Hashims' bastion of ethnic fortitude, the American way of life and the industrial surroundings of Fall River forced changes. Weeks after their arrival, they began attending services at the Congregational Church, where their neighbors on and around Lebanon Street went. There was no Orthodox parish in the city. The house in which they lived was between Alden Street, where one of the mills in which they worked was located, and Pleasant Street, a commercial avenue with all the goods the family would need to buy. It wasn't a far walk, even though they would end up on Main Street and make their way through the stream of shoppers rushing from one department store to another. The thrill was to avoid the noisy and smoky automobiles and tramcars pulled by electric power that crowded the streets.

Too poor to buy much, the Hashims enjoyed browsing and commenting about window displays, where gramophones and music boxes competed for attention with wristwatches and alarm clocks, statuesque lamp stands, and beautifully ornamented chandeliers, not to mention electric toasters, pressing irons, mixers, and hot plates. The modern gadgets made the new immigrants rethink the old way of cooking and living. Other windows tried to lure them with perfumes; deodorants; cosmetics; hair products; hand mirrors; purses of multiple colors, materials, and sizes; elegant shoes and dresses; and endless styles of hats, furs, and expensive pieces of jewelry. Gold, diamonds, and other precious stones, exposed so abundantly, validated how rich America was. One of the Model Ts that was honking its horn on Main Street sold for $440 in 1915, which was two years of the entire Hashims' earnings.

The boys hung out at the beautiful train station that resembled a clubhouse and connected the city of more than 120,000 inhabitants, mostly of Portuguese extraction, with the rest of the world. The railroad crossed a huge steel bridge elevated over the water, a marvel of technology. But the unmatched pride of Fall River was the country's first electric elevator in one of the massive mills that provided most of the employment for the city's residents.

At a personal level, the Hashims' lives were positively affected by the use of the electric lightbulb and indoor plumbing, including a bathtub. Soon, taking a shower and brushing teeth became a daily routine for everyone. Writing with a fountain pen, listening to the radio, and cooling the room in the summer with an electric fan were other adaptations to the new life. Nonetheless, laundry was washed by hand and hung in the backyard on a suspended line to dry. Lebanese cooking was done on the round burners of the wood-burning stove that had an inbuilt oven. The hot dog, hamburger, or the ever-popular peanut butter sandwich had no place on the kitchen table. The children walked anywhere they needed to go and carried whatever was needed from the grocery shop—there were plenty of Hashim children to run errands, without even thinking about paying someone to help with deliveries. Nothing the Hashims bought involved a payment plan or credit, because all was paid for in cash. The handkerchiefs, sewed, embroidered and ironed by the girls, were never replaced by disposable paper tissues. All in all, the family was grateful to be living in prosperous Fall River.

⍍⍔

Fall River was well situated at the end of the mouth of the Taunton River, connecting with the bay of Mount Hope and Narragansett. The city's name came from the Native American word *quequechan*, describing "the falling water" of a short but cascading river that connected two large ponds in the area. The city was located only twelve miles west of New Bedford, previously known as Bedford Village in the Plymouth colony, and present dwellers were immensely proud of its Mayflower and Protestant heritage. Both sister cities were densely populated, because the many industrial developments guaranteed employment and good services. Both were the result of the population explosion after the middle of the nineteenth century. Millions of immigrants arrived by steamships, mainly from Europe, to colonize huge territories and establish settlements that soon became large cities and metropolises.

Among them was one-fourth of the population of Lebanon, escaping the Ottoman yoke and poverty. After Dearborn, Michigan, the largest Lebanese community in the United States was Fall River, which provided the newcomers immediate employment in the textile industry. With its convenient water transportation, the city prospered, producing yarn by spinning raw fibers of cotton, wool, linen, and hemp, all woven, knitted, crocheted, or pressed into felt. The strong manufacturing industry and the fact that it had more looms than any other place in the world led to the city's nickname, "Spindle City."

Fall River was thriving in 1918, when up to ten thousand workers were employed by the American Printing Company (the largest cloth printer in the world), now a landmark of the city. The World War I years had generated even more business for Fall River—new and bigger mills opened, ensuring ready employment to thousands of immigrants who poured into the industrial area, unable to speak English and having few skills of use in their new country. The low wages were sufficient income to get them started, and the factory work provided abundant employment opportunities for women who specialized as spoolers, winders, reelers, and seamstresses. When the Hashims arrived, any job in America paid three times better than the same job in Europe, and at least ten times better than in Aley. Fall River's payroll was the fourth largest in the nation, with $1 million paid in salaries each week. The work came with child exploitation and sweatshops, but the Hashim family was thankful that the children could make forty cents a day.

While little aware of it, the new settlers also benefitted from the Anglo-Saxon laws and capitalistic know-how that made penniless immigrants and school dropouts rich and famous. One of them was Cornelius Vanderbilt, who in 1892 gifted his wife with a summer cottage costing $11 million to build in Newport, close to Fall River. It was, in fact, a palace built in the middle of the city's wooden houses that faced the ocean. More than half of the astronomic sum was spent on marble. It was a supreme example of how American entrepreneurs succeeded in running megabusinesses—in Vanderbilt's case, from shipping by water or by railroad. While not at the level of Vanderbilt, everyone seemed to do well in Fall River, where its mill industry reached its heyday, trickling its prosperity to each of its workers and residents, including the Hashims.

Now it was era of endless opportunities of the 1920s, and prosperity was within reach to anyone. Money could be made by doing something well that many others wanted to pay for. In the mind of teenage Joe, it was clear that professional boxing was his ticket to a better life. Proudly he read and reread what the *New Bedford Standard Times* wrote on January 19, 1923, about him: "With intelligence far above the average, and a willingness to learn from others, it looks like a brilliant future for him in the ring." His name was even in the big-type headline: "Scout Joe Grim, Coming Champion." Making a headline in the newspaper was reason enough for Joe to feel confident that his future lay in the ring, prizefighting.

CHAPTER 4

A BUSY SPRING

Now that Joe was seventeen years old, everything seemed to go his way. He kept on winning via knockouts and had a trainer and a manager, and his parents seemed to accept his boxing career. He began to make significant money in the ring, plus tips from his brother's barbershop, where he was an apprentice. While only a month ago the business had struggled to stay afloat, now because of Joe's presence, clients waited in line to be served. Responding to the demand, Louis hired another Lebanese boy who did the shoe shining. Listening to patrons talking about numerous problems, Joe realized why his brother Mike had become clothes conscious and knew so many new things: he simply learned a lot from the farmers, workers, teachers, salesmen, bank employees, city officials, and well-to-do businessmen, all of whom mingled in the barbershop. Joe, too, was keen to listen to any discussions that shed light on what it took to be a success or why someone was reduced to failure. He learned that it took money to make money and nobody could make money alone. There was lots of talk in the shop predicting that Joe would become famous. "Make sure you remember us!" he was good-naturedly chided. He was already called "champ," and Joe was very determined not to disappoint his supporters. His focus was on training harder.

Coach Tickle believed that Joe had what it took to be a good fighter—gutsy attitude, unshakable confidence, and an inborn desire for fighting. Furthermore, Joe's strong neck and chin could absorb blows that would easily put down another fighter. His endurance was excellent and his hitting power already proven. Somehow, ironically, due to his flat feet, he had great balance, helping him counterpunch or send speedy combinations that ended with crushing left semihooks to the liver, or right half-cross hits to the chin. He was always ready to enter the ring at a moment's notice. It was with all this in mind that Tickle arranged for Joe to meet Young Francis of New Bedford on March 1, 1922.

The fight took place in the 4,000-seat Bristol Arena in New Bedford, where Joe's fans were considerably outnumbered by the local audience, enthusiastically supporting their "whale" boxers. The mood in the arena was positively charged until the promoter announced that two fighters, one from New Bedford and one from Newport, were eliminated because they tampered with the scale, and the event was reduced to five bouts. The public was not happy, and their disappointment increased when their homeboy, Barney Rivers, was flattened in the third round by Young Lewis of Newport. It took the confident smile of Young Francis and his fancy shadowboxing to reenergize the crowd. Joe's presence in the ring was almost unnoticed, and no one seemed to pay attention when the announcer mentioned that he had so far scored a perfect string of twenty-two knockouts. Also unaffected by this news was Francis, who carried on a conversation with his fans on the ringside. Joe sat in his corner, waiting for Referee Bouchard to start the fight. Mike quietly stood behind his brother, eyes scanning the crowd and the ring, his body tense. He had a large bet on Joe's winning.

When the bell rang, Joe immediately went to the center of the ring, anticipating a tough round. Instead, he saw the "whaler" doing an elegant ballet in a large circle, sending long lefts and rights. Clearly he had been told exactly how to fight close-range Joe, who now was doing speedy bobbing and weaving, looking for an opening. The "I am in charge" tactics worked for Francis, who scored with many well-aimed jabs. He kept punching and smiling, as if the entire scene were a joke. His fans loved it, expecting an easy win. This nonchalant attitude was disconcerting to Joe, a serious fighter. After two minutes of "dancing," he launched a punch combination that threw Francis into the ropes, and there he stayed, under a shower of hits coming from all directions and angles. The taller and skinnier Bedfordite covered and defended himself as much as he could, but it was futile. Joe kept pressing with rapid punches, as if he were doing his routine against the heavy bag, until his opponent was nearly pushed behind the ropes, outside the ring. Unlike other boxers who would now go for the kill, Joe stopped and stepped back to the center of the ring. The gallant move was acknowledged with silence. Seconds later the entire audience erupted in applause. At this point Francis realized with whom he was fighting, but Joe was still on guard, eyes glued to the other fighter, unsure of what to expect. The round ended with sparring, and the crowd loved it, believing this was the real action.

At the break Mike whispered in Joe's ear, "Are you going to babysit him? Take him down!" The bell rang, and Joe leaped to his feet. He charged forward and battered his opponent with an arsenal of stiff punches. The fight was so one-sided and badly against Francis that his fans were silent. After one minute in the round with Joe swarming all over his opponent, everyone expected to see him dropping on canvas. There was no need for this, though, as the Bedfordite's second tossed a towel into the ring, ending the fight before Francis was hurt even more. It was a surprising mismatch, and Joe won by a technical KO. Francis was one of those boxers who excelled in gym practice, but he could not face the brutality of the ring. Briefly put, he was not born to fight. The referee lifted Joe's arm, and the announcer shouted that Joe had won his twenty-third knockout victory in a row. The Fall River Boy Scout troop, which had followed Joe to the New Bedford fight, cheered, "Twenty-three in a row! Way to go, Joe, way to go!" Joe felt like he was on top of the world. So, too, were Coach Tickle and Mike (who also had "scored heavily" with his bet).

That same evening at the Carlyle Arena in Boston, another pair of bantamweights crossed their gloves in front of a delirious public who expected local guy Abe Friedman, the best contender for the New England title, to defeat George Dixon of California. From the start, the Jewish boxer was a favorite because of his previous winning and also because he outweighed (and surely could outsmart) the black visitor. But reality proved the contrary: Dixon kept charging and collected points for eight rounds against hesitating Friedman, whose anxious supporters waited for their man to score a KO in the last round. It didn't happen. Friedman lost by unanimous decision. Scenarios like this were happening throughout America, especially in the larger cities. Countless Dixons and Friedmans were fighting, aiming to be winners in arenas packed with screaming fans. Joe, with virtually no knowledge of the world beyond Fall River and New Bedford, could not conceive of now belonging to a legion of the most eager and toughest fighters in his weight division.

The unquestioned champion of the bantamweight category was the veteran Joe Lynch of Brooklyn, who in 1920 took the world title from another veteran, Pete "Kid" Herman from New Orleans, who regained the title the next year only to lose it to Johnny Buff of New Jersey, who lost it again to Lynch, who closed the contest circle in his favor. In order to fight these title holders, one had to defeat those closer in rank to themselves and advance to the top of the list; only then could they be considered for a shot at the crown. The famous veteran Jack "Kid" Wolfe of Cleveland found the bantam category so highly and bitterly competitive that he moved up a category and won the junior featherweight world title in 1922. Many other states could put serious challengers in the ring, such as "Bud" Taylor of Indiana, Young Montreal of Rhode Island, Chick Suggs of Massachusetts, and Johnny Curtin of New Jersey. Another perfect contender could be the already-legendary Jimmy Wilde from distant England, the punching champion of all time, nicknamed the "Mighty Atom."

For Joe at this time, it was most important to win over the bantams who lived within a radius of fifty miles; they were his immediate competition. In fact, only four days after he defeated Francis, he was scheduled at the last minute to fight Young Dawson of New Bedford. The entire uneventful encounter ended early in the first round, when Joe's crashing combination of left hook and right cross found an inviting opening that put his rival down for more than ten seconds. The Scout troop jumped and hugged each other, happily screaming, "Twenty-four in a row! Way to go, Joe! Way to go!"

Four days later was a match with Red Young Larabee, an experienced fighter who had been around for some time and had scored many tough winnings. The bout took place March 10 in the Fall River Casino, filled to capacity with a heavily smoking audience.

From the opening bell, Joe faced a rival who looked much bigger than his category and displayed an unusual style, tricking his opponent into punching to the point of exhaustion. This meant that he didn't care if he was hit or not. And that was exactly what happened when "Grimm started off by ripping some clean punches to the body, and carried the point advantage for a number of rounds," as the local paper described the action the next day. Joe was scoring big, and he battered Larabee at will, but to his surprise, the guy refused to fall. If that was not bad enough, once in a while his rival, quick with his hands, would charge in rage and throw some mighty punches that forced Joe to step back. Each time that happened, the spectators went wild, in spite of their loyalty to Joe. This was the kind of action that the public loved, and Larabee was too gutsy not to be rewarded for it. After each round Joe asked Bobby Tickle what was wrong and what to do. "As long as you score and don't hit the deck, you are winning!" was the calm answer. In reality, Tickle saw that Joe was outpunching himself, he had lost his KO power, and he was getting tired.

Unintimidated by Larabee's cat-and-mouse tactics, Joe kept on punching, just as Tickle had told him, scoring big while waiting to place his lethal half hook or his right cross. He was clearly in the lead, but his usual KO refused to materialize. The Scouts kept chanting, "One more time!" and "Do it again!" each time Joe stormed with fast combinations, chopping hooks at the liver and head, but Larabee was still standing. Both fighters were amazed: one could not believe how many punches the other could absorb, and the other how much stamina Joe still had left. It looked like Larabee was almost glad to be battered, perhaps holding onto an idea that Joe would collapse from exhaustion. In fact, he was almost right: even though Joe kept scoring from bell to bell, his strength was gradually diminishing. Somehow, in the eighth round, Larabee suddenly came alive with a second wind and began counterpunching so successfully that he made Joe retreat.

When the bell ended the fight, the audience's cheering for Joe was subdued. For the first time since they'd seen their local hero fight, he did not win by a knockdown. Some feared that Joe might even have lost the fight because of his poor showing in the last round. But Joe had won by points. The referee raised his arm. Joe's record of twenty-four consecutive wins by KO would stand—but there wouldn't be twenty-five KOs in a row. Joe would blame this on being too tired because it had been only four days since a previous KO fight. He also factored in Larabee's iron chin.

Nevertheless, without knowing it, Joe Grimm had established a mighty and lasting record with his twenty-four consecutive knockouts. Only one fighter came close to this outstanding record: the middleweight Tommy Gibbons from Minnesota had won nineteen fights by successive knockouts—and nine of those occurred in the first round! Out of 106 fights, he lost only 4, but he never conquered any title. Gibbons had the distinction of being knocked out only once, by the legendary Gene Tunney in 1925.

When Joe came home that day, Mike handed only $35 to his father and complained he had lost heavily on his brother. Joe's boxing fee went down even though he had won the match. Piling up points was good, but scoring a knockout was a definitive way to win, because at the end of the fight, only one boxer was standing up in the ring, the uncontested winner. He knew he would continue to fight, and win, but never again would he hear the announcer shout, "And now, ladies and gents, winning every fight by knockout and still undefeated, I present youuu … Joeee Grimmm!"

From his facial expression and body language, "Red" Larabee looked to be a proud fighter. He was determined to score against Joe Grimm and had asked for this return engagement. It took place at the end of March in front of another packed Casino, where the spectators led by the Scout troop shouted, "Joe KO!" and "Lick him, Joe!" as soon as their hero walked into the arena. For the first time, Joe felt the pressure of winning, but smiling, he pumped his arms up and down in rhythm with the chanting. Larabee entered the ring, determined to win, and his red hair was definitely an apropos addition to his overall aggressive posturing. To Mike, he looked even bigger and heavier than the last time. From his corner, Joe watched how furiously his rival was shadowboxing. As usual, the announcer's thundering voice was overwhelmed by the wild screams of the fans, which increased the dramatic atmosphere as the bell announced the opening of the first round.

As expected, at the bell the two rivals began with relentless furious exchanges and little regard for defense, both determined to deliver a fast KO. It was the kind of fight worth any money to watch, as the two roosters entangled in a contest of who could take and give more punches. "At the opening of the second round Larabee went after Grim[m] like a bull at a gate, but Bobby Tickle's youngster fought back like a demon, although he was unsuccessful in evening up the round," wrote one reporter. Larabee won the second round, gaining confidence that he would win the fight. That would make him the guy who defeated the undefeatable Grimm. However, "the tables were reversed in the third when Grimm flew into Larabee at the bell and belabored him with rights and lefts," continued the reporter. For the next three rounds Joe dominated the fight while patiently seeking an opening for his left hook or right cross, which did not happen. "Are you going to win?" demanded Mike, whispering in Joe's ear during the break. Joe frowned and nodded his head. Tickle leaned in, speaking softly but firmly. "Don't do his fight. Corner him and knock him off his feet."

This was easier said than done with Larabee, a resourceful fighter who had figured out how to tackle Joe. Sensing the danger, Joe did what he did best—hit hard and from all angles and directions. Little by little, and round after round, Larabee kept taking more and more punches, while Joe kept scoring, with the hope that one blow would end the fight. Once again it did not happen, because his opponent showed an amazing capacity to absorb punches, his chin refused to go numb, and his legs did not wobble. The public went wild with screams, applause, and whistles while watching the two brave, small gladiators fighting for their lives as wallops that could have put either of them down missed their target.

The last round was so intense with pummeling from both sides that one could easily mistake it for the first round. Toe-to-toe, the ambitious bantams refused to step back, each still hoping to win by a lucky knockout. "Grimm appeared the strongest of the two and there was a terrific fighting all the distance," wrote the reporter on the second day, concluding that during "whole six rounds they did nothing but slam each other from rope to rope." In the end, he wrote, "Larabee put up a good fight for his second time in, and will be heard from later. Joe Grimm is one of the toughest six round boys in his section, and he is worth watching." That "worth watching" brought Joe the decision by points, and he received $40 for the second fight for which he again failed to score a KO.

Coach Tickle surprised all his boys by moving his training sessions from the YMCA, with its improvised ring, to the Tower Athletic Club on Haffards Street, which had a professional boxing ring in the middle of the room with other installations properly secured. It definitely had a lot more to offer training boxers, even though it was located below Bedford Street, and therefore closer to Joe's home, and his warm-up runs were shorter and along busier streets. Still, this was a minor problem that could be easily dealt with, and in the meantime, there were many other benefits, not the least of which was training with his stablemates. Joe met and became friends with "Jabber" Smith and "Slip" Higgins, who were also trained by Tickle. The taller, heavier Smith, who was highly specialized in throwing long jabs, was a welterweight and proved to be extremely useful to Joe when sparring together. He was exactly the type of opponent Joe had trouble dominating in the ring, so Joe was able to learn how to overcome that handicap. The highly mobile Higgins was a true artist in faint moves and slipping punches through any defense, and Joe learned a lot from him as well. These experiences would be highly beneficial to Joe in his upcoming fights. Stepping up to the top of the charts, he was going to be facing stiffer opposition in the ring, with fights that would be more challenging and increasingly difficult.

Chapter 5

An Industry In The Making

Boxing was practiced in the ancient world; the Greeks, for example, included it as an event in their Olympic Games three thousand years ago. During the industrial revolution in England and other European countries, the bare-knuckle fighting was a popular entertaining contest while also playing a role in instant social justice, much as dueling did. The bloody sport was rooted in street and saloon violence that produced fisted prizefighters. The contest included wrestling, kneeing, head butting, hitting below the belt and in the kidneys, and hitting the fallen adversary, all wrapped in verbal insults and punctuated by spitting. No title was awarded to the winners of these bitter and brutal contests until 1888, marking the beginning of organized official competition.

In America, boxing was a watch-from-the-sidelines version of cowboy fights, when the weak challenger (usually the bad guy) went down. Gunslingers were replaced by ungloved boxers who subsequently became professional fighters, meaning that one paid boxer fought against another paid boxer. It was a savage contest. In 1889 a marathon seventy-five–round match took place between John L. Sullivan and world champion Jake Kilrain, both from Massachusetts. Sullivan was the winner. He would win some 450 fights (most of them outside the ring), and he was the first American athlete to earn $1 million. His legacy was enormous, reflected by the proverbial "shake the hand that shook the hand of John L. Sullivan." Kilrain went down on his luck and ended up as a night watchman in a shipyard, but survived Sullivan by eighteen years and served as an usher at his burial.

After that famous marathon fight, boxing entered a new era under the Marquess of Queensberry rules that regulated the young sports industry. These spelled out the size and the way to fight in the ring with gloves, including the role of the referee, the ten-second count, and the prohibition of shoes with spikes. By the end of the nineteenth century, many athletic clubs in major American cities agreed to strictly enforce additional regulations, such as weight categories, the weight and cushioning of gloves, three-minute rounds, twenty seconds to get back in the ring with no assistance or it's a knockout, and other rules. Yet, there was no three-knockdown rule to end a fight if a boxer dropped on the canvas more than three times. As long as he got up before the count of ten, he was allowed to continue fighting regardless of how many times he hit the ring floor. This rule was absent during the entire era of the 1920s, in spite of official efforts to prevent unsportsmanlike behavior in the ring. During this period, the signal for the beginning and end of each round went from a whistle, to a gong, to a bell struck by a hammer.

While there were many noble efforts to beautify and legitimize boxing, which was sometimes called "fencing with gloves," especially in England where the referee was sitting outside the ring until 1917, it remained a sport of dubious morals. This was mainly because of fixed fights and betting, a vice highly condemned by religious and political leaders of those days. Yet the public could not get enough of it, and some of the longest films made before 1900 showed boxing contests. For some twenty years after that, "No Decision" bouts were enforced, especially in Florida, Michigan, New Jersey, Pennsylvania, and Texas (but not states, such as California, Connecticut, Massachusetts, New York, and Rhode Island), to discourage betting and the involvement of the syndicates in the industry of boxing.

Prizefighters were also known as "gamesters." Unless a disqualification took place, or an undeniable KO was scored in the ring, the winner was decided the next day by a "Newspaper Decision," rendered by the ringside reporters who witnessed the fight. This was still common in 1927 in Indiana, in 1928 in Ohio, and in 1931 in Minnesota. That "No Decision" ruling plagued the records of many outstanding boxers who won by points yet could not prove their wins. However, there was (still) no three-knockdown rule to end a fight, nor a rule for the stronger puncher to go to a neutral corner.

In the United States there was no national regulation of boxing competitions. In fact, boxing was outlawed in many states in the early 1900s; in New York, for example, it was illegal off and on from 1900 to 1920, when the New York Athletic Commission was established and legalized prizefighting. One year later, the National Boxing Association was formed in Rhode Island. It was intended to undermine the power of the NYAC, and because it was adopted by seventeen states, but not Massachusetts and New York, it became the legitimate body for recognizing national and international champions. New Jersey—especial Jersey City, with its boxing-enthusiast mayor—was one of the most important centers to hold fights and crown champions. The boxing-friendly state had the honor in 1921 of holding the first legal international fistic contest between Jack Dempsey and Georges Carpentier, promoted in ballyhoo fashion as the Man Killer versus the Orchid Man. The admission fee was between $5.50 and $50 for ringside, and all 91,000 seats were sold out, establishing a new gate record of $1,789,238. From then on, whoever aspired to fame and money was most likely to fight in New Jersey in order to establish himself. What made fights there even more appealing to boxers was the state's "non-decision" policy, meaning a fighter could take a severe beating, but there would be no record showing the defeat, unless he was knocked out.

One year later, *The Ring* magazine was published and began to cover boxing (and wrestling) events, providing hungry readers with pictures and commentary about top contenders. It exposed many scandals in boxing, followed successful careers, and brought otherwise unknown fighters into the limelight, making them known to the public and building their reputations. It became the ultimate authority on who's who in the boxing industry, and a tremendous archive for future generations. The popular magazine legitimized a sport of murderous intent between two nearly naked men paid to cripple each other in the ring. Boxing could be viewed as a kind of dream for modern outlaws—a way to get away with a crime and be admired for it. Those who did the most damage received the larger payment. In any other circumstance, the fighters would be jailed as lethally dangerous people and scorned by the public. Instead, the paid-for display of male ferocity appealed to law-obedient citizens whose animal instincts were dormant until they witnessed the sanctioned bloody confrontation from a safe ringside position.

Racial conflicts and personal dramas in and outside the ring increased the mass appeal of boxing. As a rule, the Anglo-Saxon audience disliked the ethnic-looking boxers who, because of massive waves of nonwhite immigrants, soon outnumbered the white contenders. With all sports highly segregated, racial cards in the ring could be extremely dangerous. Riots and lynching took place after Johnson retained his title in 1910 against white challenger James J. Jefferies. In some cases, black versus black was also a problem, like Johnson refusing to dispute his world title with the black challenger Joe Jeanette, the most famous underdog ever. In other cases, the boxer's manager made the decision. Jack Dempsey's manager, for example, turned down a match with powerful black contenders Harry Willis, Sam Langford, and Sam McVey, who might snatch the world title from the white champion and humiliate him. Nevertheless, "mixed" fights attracted an ethnic paying crowd that increased the revenue. Regardless, only whites were found in the ring seats, which were very expensive and officially segregated.

Drama and tragedies in and outside the ring always made news and offered exciting stories that showed what the champions were made of. Those manly qualities were worshipped by the public, as many boxing spectacles produced "awe" moments that evolved into legends that continued into the next century. In no time, boxing matches were being held all over the United States, with all social strata in the stands, just like in horse racing.

American soldiers returning from World War I to civilian life greatly expanded the interest in boxing, since it was part of compulsory training for some three million of them. Already hooked on it, they loved to go with their families to the arenas and see prizefights, now a booming entertainment business in prosperous America. Boxing competitions typically featured four to six rounds. Each bout and round had three distinctive parts that everyone anticipated: the unclear beginning; the climax, when one opponent dominated the other; and the end, which could be predictable or a total surprise. It all depended on who was fighting and how well the public knew the boxers. Betting on a winner was part of the boxing event and could bring a lot of money when the odds were upset.

Unlike in other professions or walks of life where individuals' values and merits were cultivated over time and rewarded arbitrarily, in boxing there were no requirements to walk in the ring, other than to be young and healthy. In fact, Charles Green was among the spectators when one of the scheduled boxers did not show up. He volunteered to fight in his place. He did so well that he took the name of the absentee Phil Rosenberg and years later became the bantam world champion.

Boxing training took place in the armed forces, summer camps of the Boys Scouts of America, and other paramilitary organizations that required fighting skills. Boxing gyms also were associated with various institutions, including private clubs, even churches, and the YMCA, the latter being the American version of the Roman gymnasium. It was the most reliable patron of boxing, since it had all the facilities needed for training and hygiene.

A boxer required a little space to train and a limited amount of personal equipment, which each athlete could either afford to purchase or share with someone else. Managers, trainers, and promoters signed up boxers for their "stables," associating their men with racehorses, both training and competing under the care of one owner. Around the 1920s there were more than four hundred boxing fight clubs in the United States, producing nine thousand good boxers from which remarkable elite emerged to dominate the rings of the world. Rarely was anyone better recognized, respected, or heralded than a boxing champion who was regarded as a superhuman. Chewing gum companies claimed that their product built the boxers' iron jaws.

Often boxing events were held during public festivities or on holidays. County fairs brought together thousands of people who watched shows from juggling acts and rodeos to incredible, dangerous flying stunts by ex-military pilots who were now true daredevils. A noisy biplane might feature acrobats on the wings or chase a racing car only feet above the thrilled spectators, who afterward ended up watching lengthy boxing matches held inside a fenced enclosure. A crowd of more than five hundred would pay enough for the promoter to break even. Boxing events also took place in specially enclosed ring areas at beaches. Baseball and football stadiums were easily converted into boxing arenas, but they were too large for local fights, and their prohibitive rental fees meant most promoters avoided them.

Popular sites for entertaining under the open sky were oval cycledromes, with their raised elliptic tracks, like the one in New Bedford, Massachusetts, on Kempton Street, with a capacity for six thousand spectators who paid as much as fifty cents for the entrance fee. There they would watch running competitions and bicycle or motorcycle races, cheering as local records were established, only to be broken the next time. The cycledrome offered an ideal arena in the center of which could be placed a ring for boxing or wrestling matches; furthermore, another one thousand seats could be added around it. Polo grounds also offered good open arenas for boxing.

In case of rain or other bad weather, an outside event would be rescheduled inside skating rinks, like the Bristol Arena in New Bedford. There, roller skaters did laps around the flat infield section, which was suitable as well for figure skating and also presented a perfect place to install a ring for boxing matches. Casinos, like the one in Fall River, Massachusetts, on Morgan Street, were usually massive cubical buildings that served as places to hold large meetings, conventions, or sports events, boxing proving most popular for drawing spectators and heavy bettors. Almost every reputable boxer from New England and from the rest of the East Coast fought in the Fall River Casino, nicknamed the "Place of Action," including Joe Grimm. Armory buildings and movie theaters that offered a stage large enough for a ring often hosted boxing matches for an audience of up to 1,500. There were also specially built arenas, Madison Square Garden being the most famous and the mecca of boxing. Almost anyone who fought there, in front of more than ten thousand spectators, entered the history book of boxing.

Unlike other professions, in boxing there was an instant separation of winners from losers. When the referee raised one boxer's hand, the fight was over and there was a winner. The beauty was that a preset payment came automatically for the winner and for the loser, as well as for everyone who was involved in that boxing event. Until the next defeat, the victorious boxer enjoyed full recognition, and it was up to him to keep it or lose it. On the other hand, there was nothing more ephemeral than a prizefighter's career; a countless number of accidents and unforeseen factors could demolish or end it.

The lure of boxing for fighters and spectators alike revolved in great part around one question: in what other profession could an illiterate young man make more money in a few minutes than the president of the United States made in one year? Of course, to do so meant one had to become a champion who could attract huge crowds to see a fight. This is what was happening in 1920s, the age of heroes.

The great Jack Dempsey fought for years just for lunch money, but that changed when he became champion. Between 1921 and 1927, Dempsey, his manager Jack Kearns, and his promoter Tex Rickard grossed $8.4 million after only five fights. The man was an industry in himself, and his heyday coincided with the Golden Age of Boxing in America. His fame kindled a dream of riches in each youngster who decided to walk into the ring. It was also all it took to attract the underground world of illicit "businessmen," who, regardless of official regulations to keep boxing away from the criminal element, were always present around and even in the ring. Like prohibition, which turned into a profitable industry for the underworld, sports competitions. particularly boxing, became a sure source of legal and illicit income for many mobsters, when cash was king.

One such person was Abraham Washington "Abe" Attell, known as "the Little Hebrew" Attell, a former world featherweight champion who for one decade defended his title eighteen times but turned into a henchman for the renowned gangster Arnold "The Fixer" Rothstein, the actual model for the hero of *The Great Gatsby*. His most famous swindle was fixing the 1919 baseball World Series, and later he was involved in other similar money-making schemes. On July 4, 1921, he bet $150,000 on his own horse and made $500,000 plus the purse. One month later he won $500,000 in the same manner but paid an income tax of $35.25 for the entire year. Before the Dempsey–Firpo heavyweight championship title fight, Rothstein personally helped Lucky Luciano with his new wardrobe to attend the fight. When Gene Tunney lost the only fight in his career to a much smaller Harry Greb, Abe Attell was in Tunney's corner. In another instance, Rothstein bet on Mickey Walker, who won against Dave Shade and made $80,000. He made $500,000 after the first Dempsey–Tunney fight, betting $125,000 on the underdog, Tunney.

As no bet was a sure winner, being a bookie was a risky profession, as most money was made if one could predict a draw or the end of the fight in a certain round, almost an impossibility. It was a nerve-racking way to make money, nearly as dangerous as the fight itself. When the losing bettors suspected a "fix," they rioted. During one of the six dramatic fights when Harry Greb (who often bet on himself) fought Tommy Loughran so maliciously, including hitting him during the break and using his head in clinches, the losing bettors charged the ring, asking for their money back. Loughran's fans wanted no more and no less than to lynch the dirty winner. This kind of gruesome do-or-die fight stirred even greater interest in boxing, and the public packed the arenas and paid a lot of money to see what would happen next. In short, boxing was a very lucrative business among backers, trainers, managers, and promoters, all looking for an unbeatable but durable fighter. The longer the champion lasted, the more money everyone around him made. As millions followed boxing contests and placed bets on their favorite fighter, a champion (even a contender) was not only a known celebrity for the adoring public but also a commodity who generated a good income for those connected to him.

Champions would defend their titles only if their managers approved the opponent and if the money was right. They fought only a few times a year, trying to keep a reign as long as possible without risking the crown. While a champion was the ultimate winner, a contender was a high-ranking boxer who might end up fighting for the title. To get there meant following a complicated maze dictated by the financial interest of managers, promoters, and backers, who looked at the champion as a source of making a lot of money. In fact, investors could buy shares in a champion's portfolio.

To regulate such a chaotic industry was a must for authorities. In doing that, the New York Athletic Commission and National Boxing Association competed to name the national and world champions. Because the entire system became so secretive and so against contenders, the New York Boxing Commission ordered champions to accept a challenge after six months of holding a title; otherwise the title would be forfeited. Any challenger had to be approved by the Commission and had to put up a $2,500 bond as proof of his intention to show up for the fight. No champion was allowed to box in any other state unless he honored a legitimate challenger first. "Non-decision" fights did not count as a challenge. The new law was issued after bantamweight title holder Joe Lynch refused to meet Carl Tremaine of Cleveland, and lightweight champion Benny Leonard turned down challenger Sailor Friedman of Chicago.

By March 1923, as reported in the Fall River *Evening Herald*, two champions, the featherweight Johnny Kilbane and the middleweight Johnny Wilson, "lost their status as champions as far as New York State is concerned, by failure to comply with the challenge provisions of the boxing law." In other words, champions had to fight more than twice a year to defend their title. But Kilbane argued that he had turned down a $40,000 offer, which was not large enough to justify a fight, and after all, he had never applied for a New York boxing license. The great Jack Dempsey agreed to meet Harry Wills from New Orleans, but the match kept being postponed because no promoter wanted to be involved with the colored boxer from the South. After the fight was sponsored with $350,000 by a wealthy industrialist and a contract was finally signed, Wills was still denied the title fight, and he kept the $50,000 defaulting fee, the most money he ever made in a one-shot deal, this time without putting the gloves on. In the same context, the National Boxing Association rejected the challenge of Jess Willard, who was found not fit to meet Dempsey for a title fight already proposed by promoter Tex Richard to take place at the famous Boyle's Thirty Acres arena he had built in Jersey City. Millions of dollars were lost by boxing entrepreneurs because the price was not right for striking a deal or putting up with bureaucratic red tape. The mild economic crisis of 1921–1923 was bad for industry but good for the entertainment business: unemployed and desolate people crowded movie theaters and sports arenas to escape the depressed reality for a few hours. Amusement parks and boxing events became part of the American landscape.

All of this was happening when the teenage Lebanese immigrant Nageeb/ Nagib Hashim began boxing under the name of Joe Grimm. As he listened to the radio direct transmission of the Dempsey–Carpentier fight, Joe knew he had found his mission in life, but there was one important drawback: Dempsey was a heavyweight, almost twice the weight of Joe, who was a bantam. The heavier the fighter, the more money he made, because the public loved to see supermen demolishing each other. On the other hand, the lighter boxers packed amazing speed, hard punches and great skills into a show that made the audience jump up on their seats. Furthermore, smaller boxers were numerous and therefore offered a large number of challengers for more titles, enriching the variety of pugilistic shows, and thus providing the quantity and quality desired by the public.

Joe Grimm was one of them, but unlike Dempsey or other champions who began by using their fists to protect their rights and be feared in their neighborhoods, he never threw a punch in anger. He also was not in a position to receive offers from top managers and promoters. For the time being, Joe, like thousands of other boxers, was following a dream while making little money. He was not worried about the world title but was rather focused on winning his next fight, where hopefully a promoter would notice him. With that humble but burning spirit, he diligently trained and kept walking out of the ring as a winner. Spectators and sports writers loved him, and Joe knew how to reward his admirers with one knockout after another. That reinforced his belief that he was on the right track. His brother Mike was a huge supporter, believing that Joe was "right on the money," at least as long as he kept winning. With Bobby Tickle and Mike in his corner, Joe Grimm was a perfectly oiled little wheel that kept moving the huge machinery of boxing, the ultimate sport in which one might become too injured to come back to fight again or even might not leave the ring alive.

Chapter 6

The Gentleman Boxer

Throughout his childhood, Joe had tried to help his family. A middle child in a large and poor family, he was well aware that everyone's contribution helped. Like some of the other Lebanese kids, as well as Italians, Portuguese and other immigrants, Joe joined the Boys Scouts. To him, this was one sure way to become a "real American," and he dutifully collected one merit badge after another. He loved sports but his small frame, short legs, and flat feet were little help when it came to running, high and long jumps, throwing events, basketball, soccer, volleyball, and the like. He probably could have been a gymnast if he had had a good coach: he could do sets of fifty push-ups, twenty chin-ups, and sets of one hundred sit-ups without interrupting his normal breathing. Pound for pound, he was by far the strongest Scout with the most stamina.

As most of the boys did at that time, Joe quit school after graduating six grades and worked at the mills, but he always felt that he could do better. With his inclination to be a leader and a loner instead of a member of a team, Joe found boxing to fit him like a glove and put all he had into it; he never regretted that investment. The strict discipline at home and at the Boy Scout organization prepared him for the hard training, and he diligently followed the coach's instructions. Advancing through the ranks at Camp Noquochoke, the Lebanese teenager kept boxing, scoring one victory after another. The Boy Scouts and boxing activity were a happy combination for Joe, as indicated in the *New Bedford Standard Times* on January 19, 1923:

His strongest rooters are the Boy Scouts, Joe being a

member of Troop 14, in the capacity of assistant scout master. For seven years, since the organization was formed, he has been a member passing from the tenderfoot stage to one of the most important positions in the troop. Whenever Joe Grimm is billed to appear, the whole army of Boy Scouts is interested.

Indeed, Troop 14 was in the audience for all of Joe's local fights, standing on their chairs and screaming their cheers. Not to let them down was Joe's new duty.

Many prizefighters of the time had criminal backgrounds. They had served time in jail or in juvenile correction institutions; they came from the ghettos and were gang members and brawlers. Violence was a part of their daily lives. They were either born with a killer instinct or they acquired it from their tough neighborhood. It seemed that the angrier and hungrier they were, the more motivated fighters they became. For them the decision was simple: why not fight in the ring and make some good money instead of fighting on the street for nothing? Most boxers, Joe among them, came from blue-collar backgrounds. Many were immigrants or their children, seeing in boxing the opportunity to make more money than they could get by working in the mills or on a factory line. No formal education was needed to step in the ring, where anyone with stamina and willpower had a chance to win. They might even have a crack at fame, as many did before them.

Joe, on the other hand, with not a single mean bone in his body, did not fit that description; he was a compassionate and kind teenager whose only "gang" was a Boy Scout troop. Even in the ring when he transformed into a fearsome fighter, he was respectful.

When Tickle began to train Joe, he noticed how pleasant it was to work with him. A Fall River newspaper sports columnist concluded a long article about Joe with the statement, "Grimm is an easy boy to handle, being faithful to himself." Tickle adopted a stance and a fighting style that suited Joe's natural abilities, including his flat feet. He was still a raw fighter, but he kept winning—by knockout, no less. He studied other boxers and learned from them how to strategically make the best use of his personal style. His notable determination led one reporter to point out that "Grimm was cool and collected." Columnists called him "one of the toughest bantams," "the clever bantam," and the "Jack Dempsey of the bantams." Certainly Joe had a distinctive fighting style, and definitely, he had a pair of KO fists.

But there was another nickname that gradually took over and stuck.

Joe loved to dress neatly, and, with barbers in the family, his hair was always perfectly styled. Spectators loved his charming and confident smile, and they joined their cheers with the enthusiastic Boy Scout supporters. When Joe was fighting, it was one of the rare instances when people bet on the "good guy" and not on the tough bully who usually was expected to win. Sports writers at the Fall River and New Bedford newspapers noted all of this, but what especially impressed them was that Joe would never pummel a guy who was already defeated or on his way to drop on the canvas. "He is a young gentleman and will never take unfair advantage of an opponent," wrote one reporter. Another commented that Joe was "the most likable youth in the game." In all of his fights Joe never delivered a low punch or other illegal blows and never fought after the bell. He always followed the referee's calls. It didn't take long before everyone was using a name that fit Joe alone: "The Gentleman Boxer."

Almost one month had passed since Joe's last fight. Then, on April 24, he met Sam Kilroy of New Bedford in his hometown arena, filled with more than one thousand noisy spectators, eating, smoking, and betting, as usual. It was an unofficial fight; Joe considered it of little importance and trained sporadically for it. He underestimated his adversary and confidently stepped into the ring amidst the wild ovations of his fans, screaming, "Do it, Joe!" and "Do it again!" It was the opening fight of the main event, and, after many announcements and other ring rituals, the bell signaled the beginning of the first round. With the cheers spurring him on, Joe sped to the center of the ring, ready to take Kilroy down quickly and reset his winning string record. But what he encountered drastically upset his fighting plans: from the first exchange of punches, it was clear that Kilroy knew how to avoid Joe's determined charges. Not only that, but Kilroy was able to rush Joe against the ropes, forcing him to defend against fast jabs thrown from a distance. There was no doubt that Kilroy had observed Joe fighting many times and had trained accordingly, sparring with fast and heavy punchers in his gym.

What the Bedford guy did from the beginning to the end of this bout was to make it difficult for flat-footed and slower-moving Joe to trap him in any ring corners or engage him in head-to-head battle. Each time Joe tried to use his formidable left hook and right cross or to launch an assault, the taller Leroy avoided it and ended up being the one in charge, shoving

Joe around with long, punishing jabs. Round after round, it was the same frustrating scenario for Joe, who could not deliver his winning punches. He was learning the hard way that he could take a lot of leather that mounted winning points for his rival. "Brother, kill him, not me!" shouted Mike in Joe's ears during the breaks. Tickle, massaging his neck and shoulders, firmly said, "Smash his guard and his chin!"

Nothing Joe tried seemed to work. Then, in the last round, Joe shook up Kilroy with a few piercing blows to the body, and the crowd went wild. Apparently at least one blow hurt Kilroy very badly, because he wobbled and retreated. Finally, here was the moment for which Joe had been waiting. He went in for the kill, charging like a brawler with both fists as the bell sounded the end of the fight. Joe froze in midcombination, and Kilroy collapsed. He was disoriented and needed to be led to his corner, where he dropped on the floor next to the stool. The crowd went crazy with frustration. The fight was over, but the judges disagreed with the audience. Referee Ralph Tickle (the brother of Joe's coach) went over to Kilroy, still sitting on the floor, and raised his arm, declaring him the victor.

Joe was devastated. He had lost against someone he hadn't considered a real opponent. It was a lesson in humility that taught him that every fight was equally important to train for. As he left the arena, he heard the crowd booing the decision and saw fans trying to make him feel good. But Joe knew that he had lost for one good reason: Kilroy had wisely strategized his fight and won. Unlike other times, Joe went straight home, without returning to the stands to mingle with his Boy Scout fans.

Back in the warm kitchen that smelled of cooking food, sad Joe handed his father an envelope with only $25 in it. The old man smiled and, raising his bushy brows, teasingly said, "It looks like we'll never ride that Model T after all!" Mike quickly responded, patting Joe's back, "Next time we'll do better than that! Right, Joe?" Joe smiled and nodded his head a few times with a sigh.

Joe not only recovered from the defeat, but to his surprise, he became even a bigger hero in the eyes of his fans. Everyone at the barbershop agreed that, in fact, Joe had won against Kilroy by another knockout, and that the victory was stolen from him. He felt so good about the new twist that he began training harder and harder in Tickle's gym. The *ta-ta-ta-ta-ta-ta-ta* of the speed bag never sounded more rhythmic and faster, and the hundred-pound punching bag took even harder hits from Joe. He jumped rope at an increased tempo for five minutes in a row, worked with elastic bands, and, most importantly, sparred more than ten rounds with heavier or speedier stablemates. He trained one-to-one with Coach Tickle, who made Joe memorize sets of punching combinations and how to use them, always focusing on his half left hook and right cross. It was crucial to fine-tune these hitting reflexes so they were automatic when the opportunity arrived to use them. His flat feet were not an asset for fast moving around an adversary, but they did plant him on the canvas in a solid position that gave him good balance from which to throw or absorb punches.

Joe was all pumped up when Tickle told him he would be fighting Young Dawson again on May 19. Wearing only shoes and boxing trunks, he began running again from home to the gym at Towers A.C. and back, sometimes taking a path along the water while enjoying the beautiful spring weather. Four days before the fight, a cold rain caught the runner, and the next morning he woke up with a sore throat and fever. Tickle wanted to cancel the fight, but Joe assured him that he was ready to battle Dawson.

By the day before the fight, Joe's cold was worse. During the weigh-in he felt so light-headed that Mike had to steady him before he stepped on the scale. Joe was four pounds less than the required 118 pounds, whereas Dawson had pushed himself to lose a few pounds in order to make the category. Joe was feverish, his muscles ached, and his eyes itched, but he continued to reassure everyone that he was just fine and "ready to mingle." His mother did not believe him. Since he was determined to fight, she did her best to push the cold out of her son before he went into the ring. She made *za'atar* tea, using Lebanese herbs and spices mixed with honey. Joe sweat a lot as he drank the hot brew. After that, sleep was all he could do until the next day.

The Fall River Casino was again packed with smoke and fans who wanted to see Joe fighting. As soon as he entered the ring, he was welcomed by the chorus of cheers from Troop 14. The sound triggered an adrenaline rush for Joe. Revived and smiling, he threw a few punches of reassurance toward the happy spectators as Dawson entered the ring. The two fighters stood on the left and right of Referee Billy Gurnett, who recited instructions with the same impossible end, "Good luck to both of you." Joe was visibly smaller, if not frailer, and some of the spectators were heard wondering if Dawson cheated on the scale. But he had not—he just looked bigger and stronger than sickly-looking Joe. The bell announced the opening round.

Joe, still feeling light-headed, stepped into the middle of the ring; his eyes, burning with fever, pierced Young Dawson, focusing on his chin. His well-aimed intimidation was having an effect: already Dawson was not looking so confident, as he believed that slow-moving Joe was preparing for a surprise that could take him down. On the other hand, Joe reminded himself not to underestimate Dawson, who prudently danced around the floor to evade Joe's exploratory jabs. The audience was fired up, sitting on the edge of their seats, whistling and cheering for both fighters, anticipating something spectacular happening at any moment. Joe set the pace, and the round continued with both fighters testing each other and neither landing a big punch.

Throughout the next three rounds, Joe delighted the audience as he showed off some fancy moves that made Dawson dodge and duck, keeping his gloves protectively close and missing each opportunity to strike back. So far he was allowing himself to be outboxed—or better put, outfoxed. The fight was so entertaining that the public didn't object to the uneventful pace. Moreover, the judges had already made up their minds that Joe was the better fighter. At each break, Coach Tickle smiled and advised Joe to continue with the same tactics. Mike, more aware of how ill Joe had been just the day before, asked if Joe wanted to quit. It's very possible that Mike had bet against his brother for this match, knowing his condition. But Joe had no intention of deserting the fight.

By the sixth round, aware not to waste himself without good results, Joe launched a full-scale attack. It was so sudden and so well-done that the crowd stood and pumped their fists toward the rafters, screaming, "KO now! KO now!" Joe machine-gunned his punches with all the vigor he had left, but it was not enough to drop Dawson. To the contrary, Dawson immediately realized how little power was left in those punches, and he fought back with such severity that the audience grew quiet, now fearing that Joe might go down. But it was too late for that. The bell ended the fight, and both boys were glad to hear its final sound. Joe had succeeded and won by decision. Dazed by a recurring fever, he went home with his winnings of $35 and collapsed with exhaustion.

It was certainly good to win again, even by points, and days later, Joe felt more confident and healthier than ever. He asked himself if all that sickness was not in fact a case of stage fright induced by the lost bout. Regardless of the cause, he had learned another valuable lesson: a fight can also be won in a smart way, not only by demolishing the opponent. He went back to normal training and could not wait to fight again. The opportunity came when it was announced with many whistles and bells that Jimmy Dime, the bantam champion of the state of Maine, would be his next adversary. The match took place on May 26 inside the same Casino with the same audience, who had begun to wonder if Joe was ready to battle a real champion. In the dressing room, the homeboy got laced into a pair of brown gloves by Tickle, while Mike asked his brother if he was in a position to win. Joe, who had seen the champion train the day before, answered, "I'll do better than that!" Mike rushed to place his sure bet.

When Joe stepped into the ring, the floodlights showed a determined young man who could not look better fit to fight. From his reassuring smile, perfectly parted hair, and feline moves, he radiated utmost confidence. With that attitude he began the first round amidst a hurricane of whistles and screams. Dime, who knew little about his rival, attacked first with many solid and well-placed blows that took Joe by surprise and forced him into a clinch.

Even from that "embrace," the Maine boy kept on hacking at any opening he could find, including rabbit punches behind Joe's head and neck. They were illegal blows ignored by Referee Bouchard, who pushed the boys apart. But they collided again and again, as Joe was painfully hit a few times in the kidney. They kept wrestling along the ring ropes until the referee stepped between them and finally warned Dime about his sneaky hits. For the remainder of the round, the two kept chasing each other back and forth, trying to adjust their salvos and find weak spots in the other's defense.

When the bell sounded, Joe sat in his corner so abruptly that Tickle asked if he was hurt or sick. When Joe shook his head, the coach almost screamed, "Then go out there and fight like a man!" Mike encouraged him with a disciplinary slap on the face, "Stop playing around!" and Joe was ready for the second round. "Come on, Joe, what's the matter?" yelled the crowd, obviously unhappy with his performance. Even the Boy Scouts were quieter than usual.

The second round was more or less a duplicate of the first, except that Joe tried unsuccessfully to initiate a few attacks that ended once again in clinches. He ducked some powerful punches that could have done a lot of damage, but as hard as he tried, he was not able to take control of the fight. His power punches were smoothly evaded, as his rival countered and cancelled Joe's bold actions. Dime was a semischooled boxer who fought almost like a brawler or a street fighter. To his merit, he proved to be a versatile fighter who could punch even if he was off his feet. In other words, he was highly unorthodox and unpredictable. So far, the fight was mayhem, and the public began to grow restless, feeling the limitations of their local hero. Suddenly Joe opened another assault, only to eat a devastating right to his neck that caused him to black out. Instinctively, he hugged Dime until the bell saved him—just in time. By now, the spectators had lost trust in Joe.

Mike rushed to pour icy water on his head; fanning the towel for more air, he looked into his brother's eyes and said with a smirk, "What are you now, a dancer?" Shaking his head, Joe caught a glimpse of his fans and realized they were puzzled by what was going on. The bell had barely finished sounding, and Joe was back in the center of the ring with a determined look on his face. His firm stance drew a startled look from Dime, who was still sitting in his corner chair. Sudden cheers with his name motivated Dime to all-or-nothing action, and he charged Joe with a ferocious two-fisted attack. Joe waived the danger with a lateral move and crashed Dime's chin with his right cross. As Dime tried to regain balance, he turned his head to the left, enough to receive a second hit from Joe's half hook. Dime dropped on the floor like a pancake. It was the shortest and the most efficient one-two combination Joe ever threw. One second later, the public exploded in delirium that was sustained for a whole minute: their Joe was back! "Grimm sent his opponent to the floor a couple of times and then finished him for keeps," wrote one ringside reporter. Referee Bouchard held Joe's right arm high, confirming another knockout victory. Joe grinned at his fans, including the wildly screaming members of Troop 14. He was a winner again!

That night Mike delivered an envelope with $50 to their father, who proudly twisted both ends of his mustache. Mike looked very satisfied; he had made much more with his betting on the unlikely KO. It was hard to believe that little Joe, who was so gentle and soft-spoken, was such a fierce fighter.

The following day Mike accompanied Joe to a photo studio, where a professional photographer took a picture of the youngster in his ring gear, including his white trunks with a JG monogram. Publicity photos were also taken of Joe in his Boy Scout uniform, with and without the hat. Mike ordered numerous duplicates, which he presented to the sports editors and boxing reporters at the area's newspapers.

CHAPTER 7
FIGHTS AND MORE FIGHTS

By the early 1900s the most popular sports in Fall River were bowling, baseball, boxing, and a sport little known by most Americans at the time, soccer. The confluence of immigrants who fanatically loved soccer —British, Portuguese, and others—made it a big attraction in Fall River and neighboring New Bedford. The cities had numerous teams whose members were selected because of their nationality. Often the teams were sponsored by the mills' owners, who were not only fans but also benefactors. The most successful teams had players selected not because of their ethnicity, but for their merit, like the Fall River United Team, which won the American Cup five times in a row between 1888 and 1892, and the 1917 National Challenge Cup. Now, four years later, the city team had qualified for the American Soccer League. Still, soccer was not lucrative for anyone.

The sport that did bring in the money in Fall River and New Bedford was boxing, and Joe Grimm was a part of it. His next fight was on June 2, 1922. It was a rematch against Sam Kilroy, who had defeated Joe in April by a disputable decision that infuriated the spectators. Now they all came back to the smoke-filled Casino to witness Joe punishing the New Bedford guy for his unworthy win. The arena ended up being overpacked, because Kilroy's fans wanted to see their boy teach Joe a lesson that would settle once and for all who was a better fighter. The betting was heavily split, and many counted on a draw. The tension could be cut with a knife. As soon as Joe appeared in the ring, his former Boy Scout troop led the ear-piercing screams: "Down him, Joe!" Joe smiled and threw a few fast punches toward the crowd, who responded with whistles and shouts. Kilroy also attracted roars from his supporters. "Remember, you have to win!" hissed Mike, who had put a lot of money and trust on that prediction. Joe nodded as the bell sounded. The fighters walked to the middle of the ring and touched gloves.

Just like the last time, Kilroy began to throw jabs, dodge, and duck, aiming to outsmart and out-slick Joe. Anticipating a tough fight, Referee Ralph Tickle rolled up his sleeves as he tried to keep up with the fast pace in the ring. Obviously, Kilroy had a well-planned battle in mind and was determined to stick to it. He did very well until Joe suddenly stepped inside and, faking with a hook to the body, sent a crushing right cross to the chin. Kilroy took a dive to the canvas and stayed there, like he was being held down by the roar of the spectators. The referee began counting, but at eight, the diver jumped back on his feet and continued his routine to keep Joe away. It didn't work. Joe began bobbing and weaving his way close enough to throw powerful uppercuts to the body and chin. Again Kilroy was flat on the canvas. The crowd went crazy! The screams of "Drop 'em, Joe!" seemed to wake up the fallen guy, who bravely stood and began diligently jabbing. But moments later he was caught in a flurry of punches, and one of them hit his jaw. Down he went. Again, he got up. But Kilroy was caught off guard by Joe's fists, and a second later he was rolling on the canvas. The bell announced the end of the first round, and both boxers went to their corners. Joe, winded, refused to sit down, and Mike pumped air with the towel while Coach Tickle wiped his face with icy water and said, "The kid is tough. Don't take a risk. Just win the fight."

In the next rounds Kilroy gave Joe a harder time. He danced around, trying to score from a distance and forcing Joe to chase him all around the ring. Even when Kilroy was cornered, he managed to escape Joe's lethal punches. Remembering the last fight, Joe launched a decisive assault in the middle of the last round and hit Kilroy with everything except the ring poles. But his opponent absorbed each punch and even scored some points for himself. Joe's fans had stopped yelling for another KO—it was pretty clear that wasn't going to happen. Looking at Mike and Tickle, who clearly showed one minute left, Joe charged again. By bending and slipping below the incoming punches, he machine-gunned a long combination that raised the entire audience to its feet. Kilroy was hanging on the cords, practically held up by Joe's punches, when again the bell rang. Joe went to his corner, while Kilroy was helped to sit in his chair. It was over. Joe won by unanimous decision, which brought him $45 and a repaired reputation.

❖❖

The summer that followed was quiet. Joe worked a lot in the barbershop and trained sporadically, because no fights were scheduled for him. For that matter, not too much boxing was going on. Many mills and factories had reduced working hours because of the sluggish economy. People were uncertain about their future. A good card scheduled for the cycledrome on August 29 attracted only some three hundred spectators. The main fight of the hot, late afternoon was between veteran boxer Al Shubert and Charley Manty, both of New Bedford. At the last minute it was canceled because Shubert was overweight. This put the spectators in a foul mood, and they loudly showed it. Yet, they quickly forgot about it once the opening fight started. Joe Grimm gave them the kind of fight that had everything an audience wished for: a well-matched contest that went to the last round, the drama of changing winning prospects, his one-sided KOs that refused to materialize in a final knockout, and bell rings that came right in time to save a doomed fighter.

That doomed fighter was Jimmy Wilde from Taunton, a city north of Fall River, who began the first round full of confidence. In the beginning he dominated Joe, who just could not pace himself and adjust his punching range. What happened is best described by the local paper:

> In the sixth Grim started Wilde on the go with heavy rights to the body and then socked both hands hard to the jaw, Wilde being all but out when the round ended. In the seventh Grim slipped through two sharp right uppercuts to Wilde's jaw, and the recipient was on the floor taking the count when the bell saved him. The count was half finished when the bell rang.

> Wilde attempted to keep on his feet in the eight by rushing and clinching, but Grim fought him off and continued to deal out punishment. He finally copped Wilde on the jaw with a right, and Wilde, although he stood up under the punch, slumped to the canvas a second later, after Grim had swung for his jaw and missed. Wilde took the count of nine, and got up again, only to be floored shortly afterward. This time the referee sent him to his corner and gave the fight to Grim.

> Joe won by a technical KO and "handed Jimmy Wilde a fine lacing," concluded the paper.

An hour later, as he was leaving the cycledrome, Joe was stopped by a middle-aged gentleman, distinguished looking and well dressed in a double-breasted pin-striped jacket and white pants, carrying his panama hat in his hand.

"So, you're the kid who pulls the fast ones!" The man smiled. Seeing Joe's puzzled face, he continued, "My name is Charlie Doessereck, and I'm a boxing manager and promoter in New York and New Jersey. Here's my card in case you need representation. Keep up with the good fights. We'll meet again. Good luck, kid!" Without knowing it at the time, Joe had made the best connection of his career. He rushed to show the card to his brother. Mike looked at it, beautifully engraved in Gothic letters he could hardly read, put it in his pocket with the money envelope, and shook his head. "Not a word to Tickle. I'll take care of this."

In October, Joe went to Providence, Rhode Island, to meet Heim Schwartz in a six-round fight, "a curtain raiser" intended to warm up the crowd for the star bout featuring Harry Greb and contender Larry Williams. That was the first time Joe fought outside of Massachusetts, and Schwartz was a different fighter from everyone he had met before. Basically he was a smart guy who anticipated incoming trouble and did whatever he could to avoid it. Even though Joe punched Schwartz all over the ropes during round after round, he couldn't pin Schwartz down.

Unlike others, Schwartz did not attempt to wrestle or to hold on until the referee stepped in; his hug was long enough to diffuse the efficiency of his rival and make him lose the momentum. He not only disengaged with swift ease, but he also successfully threw back sneaky punches at frustrated Joe, who kept missing one decisive blow after another. Regardless, Joe did keep winning each round, but Schwartz continued to escape KO punches, even when he was seriously nailed in the stomach. Joe learned a valuable lesson from this fight: if a guy did not want to be knocked down, he was not going down, regardless of what his opponent did.

So, Joe won an inglorious fight, collected his $50, and went back to the arena to see the Greb–Williams fight. Joe watched the fight, following each move of Harry Greb, who provided nonstop pugilistic action with a blizzard of punches that came from all angles and directions, landing flush on Williams's body and face. From that evening on, each time Joe approached the ring he reviewed Greb's style in his mind.

Two days later, on October 29, Joe met Young Dawson for another rematch in New Bedford. Dawson, who never knew about Joe being sick in the last fight, was in a murderous mood and believed he could win this time. Billy Gurnett was the referee again. It was an uneventful fight that Joe won by unanimous decision.

⋇⋇

The winter of 1922–1923 made it difficult for Tickle and his boxers to come often to the gym. Joe's only training was to shovel the snow in front of his house, the barbershop, and the church. Then, on the afternoon of January 17, Coach Tickle came to the barbershop and asked Joe if he could fight the next evening against Charlie Baxter of Pawtucket; Baxter's scheduled opponent, Georgie Murray, was sick.

The matchmaker and the promoter of the event were desperately looking for a last-minute substitute and, finding none, called Bobby Tickle, who rushed from his dairy shop to find Joe. Tickle was excited because Joe's participation in this fight, regardless of how he scored, would automatically enter him in the New England semifinals, giving him a shot at the title. Mike asked for an extra $20 bonus and agreed for Joe to fight Baxter, who incidentally was in top shape and a far more experienced fighter.

Without losing any time, Joe left to weigh in and gather his boxing equipment for the next day. He made it to the Casino before another snowstorm began, and while in the dressing room, Mike asked, "What do you think?" Joe took a deep breath. "Give me two weeks training, and I can beat Mr. Baxter!" Obviously, after seeing his rival, Joe was aware that this could be the most difficult fight of his career. "Forget about that. Are you going to win or not?" Joe smiled and looked at Tickle, who also smiled. "We'll see!" So Mike bet on Baxter.

It was one of those evenings when one stepped from the freezing cold, snow-covered sidewalk, into a large, heated public space, flooded with lights and suffused with the smell of sweat, cigarettes, cigars, fried hot dogs, and steam-boiled sauerkraut. It was a party-like atmosphere with everyone talking and having a good time, when Joe slipped through the ring ropes. The crowd, which did not expect to see him, erupted with long ovations. His adrenaline pumped accordingly, and immense pride kicked in. Not even properly trained, Joe never had felt better in his life. At the sound of the bell, both rushed to bump gloves one more time. The fight began in a surprisingly friendly way.

As expected, the first round consisted of cautious exchanges. Baxter tried different fake moves to see how Joe would react, but he was "too cool and too good to fall for the trick." By the fourth round, "it was a battle worthy of a championship," the ringside reporter from the Fall River *Evening Herald* wrote. He continued,

> They boxed a minute or so when Grimm landed a steaming right to Baxter's jaw and the Rhode Islander's knees sagged for a moment. The crowd came to its feet, but Grimm failed to follow up his advantage. Baxter came back like a streak, but Grimm held his head and Charlie missed badly. The visitor missed more shots last night because of Grimm's cleverness. Baxter closed in and crashed a left and right to Grimm's head and jaw, but the local youngster was mixing at the bell.

Baxter was fighting at top speed in the fifth, hooking some solid socks into Grimm, but Joe's left hand was raising havoc with Charlie. Grimm stuck it out repeatedly into Charlie's face, with a solid sting behind it. The sixth was another great round for Grimm. He carried the fight right to Baxter and worked a pretty inside right that bothered Baxter. In a breakaway, Baxter clouted Grimm before they were apart and the crowd booed him. Grimm whipped a right into Baxter's jaw that straightened the Rhode Islander up and took a right hook in exchange. They mixed it furiously and when the exchange was over, Grimm had held his own. Baxter was swinging like a gate and missing, but when he did land they were solid smacks and were telling on Grimm, whose condition was not any too good because of the lack of training. Grimm had Baxter worried in this round and up to this stage it was Grimm's battle. Condition told in the next two rounds. In the seventh Grimm worked both hands to the body and Baxter was having a hard time fathoming his attack. Grimm shot through opening to the jaw and face and stood what he received in return like a major.

In the eighth Grimm was tired and Baxter's advantage earned him the decision in this session. Grimm was a very little youngster and was satisfied to rest on his achievements in the last round, which was excellent judgment. It was a whale of a bout and Joe Grimm jumped right into the semi-final ranks immediately.

Joe's taking on the fight with such short notice made a deep impression on the spectators and the press. The next day the newspaper ran a headline in bold letters that read: "Grimm Puts Up Wonderful Fight But Loses to Baxter." In the opinion of everyone who witnessed the fight, Joe should have been declared the winner.

Two weeks later, on February 2, Joe had another fight, this time with a fellow Fall River boxer. Young Barry had been long absent from the boxing scene, but he made a strong comeback by defeating George Vanderbilt, a tough aspiring scraper in the bantam category. From the first bell, Joe had taken a strong lead, and Barry was the unlucky target for many of Joe's combinations of stiff punches. It wasn't too long before his half left hook found Barry's jaw, and Barry went down like a tree falling on the ground. Referee McCarthy began counting very loudly, moving his right arm up and down with each passing second. The humiliated Barry managed to get up and fought back in a hammer fashion until it was Joe's turn to hit the floor, to the total silence of the Scouts and his other fans. They had never seen Joe down! Joe sprang back on his feet before McCarthy had the chance to begin counting. Regardless of whether it had been a slip or not, the shock of being floored was visible on Joe's face. More than that, he soon discovered that Barry was an excellent inside fighter—a boxer with a style equal to Joe's.

For three rounds in a row, Joe led the fight and prepared the stage for his crushing half left hook and right cross. Suddenly, during a close exchange of rapid blows, a piercing burn in Joe's left eye brought tears and salty saliva in his mouth. Not noticing anything wrong, Referee McCarthy made no attempt to stop the fight. Back in his corner, Joe bent over with pain, and Coach Tickle hardly could open his eye that was badly thumped. He washed the eye and put ice on the eyelid, but Joe began his fourth round with one-eye vision. He fought as energetically as usual and did everything to salvage the fight, but he kept missing clear shots that normally could have floored Barry in no time.

Soon Barry took over the fight, relentlessly issuing powerful blows that Joe randomly avoided only because of good reflexes. In the last round Joe "went for the kill," as advised by Tickle and Mike. Catching a strong second wind, Joe forced Barry to cruise along the ropes, exhausted and confused by the new turn of events. When the bell stopped the fight, Joe's face and chest were covered in blood, the blister above the eye now cut open. He had never experienced this before. The decision went to the North-Ender. This "was not altogether in accordance with the wishes of the fans, yet for one thing, Barry made the fight," wrote the *Evening Herald News* the next day. Thus Joe failed to qualify for the final and, collecting his $30, went right back into the arena to witness the main fight of his superior competitors, Midget Smith of Harlem and Mickey Delmont of Newark.

The next day Mike came with a pile of local newspapers featuring Joe's picture in a boxing stance, wearing his monogrammed white trunks, black ring shoes, and punching gloves. In the lower left corner there was an oval portrait showing Joe in his Scout uniform, captioned: "Joe Grim[m], Clever Local Bantamweight—Insert, Joe in Uniform as Assistant Scout Master." Above the pictures, in large bold capital letters was written: "East End Youth Shaping Up Like Real Artist in Ring." The headline of the article was also bolded in majuscule letters: "Scout Grim[m], Coming Champion." Many of Joe's personal and boxing accomplishments were noted in another title, "Assistant Scout Master of Troop 14 One of the Most Promising Bantams in This City—Has Fought Some Sensational Battles."

Ironically, the newspaper article opened with a mention of the recent "two sensational battles with Charles Baxter of Pawtucket and Young Barry of this city. Both decisions were hairline, and against Grim, but the difference was so little, ring followers immediately jumped to conclusion that Joe Grim is the real class." It continued, "Then again, Baxter and Barry are at the height of their careers, while Grim is just coming." A few lines farther, the reporter made it clear that "whenever Joe Grim is billed to appear, the whole army of Boys Scouts is interested." There was some biographical information and a long list of boxers Joe had defeated recently. At the end of the piece, manager Bobby Tickle was quoted: "Joe Grim has come along fast," and he is "the coming bantamweight champion of New England." The only problem was that Grim was spelled only with one "m."

Ignoring the typo in his brother's fight name, Mike clipped the article very carefully and mailed it to promoter Charlie Doessereck in Bayonne, New Jersey, with a personal note that read, "If you are interested in my brother, let's meet and talk." Then, turning to Joe, he smoothed his pencil mustache with his fingers and smiled. "We're making news!"

The article made Joe feel so great that he seemed to recover from his defeats the moment he read it. Besides, Coach Tickle and brother Mike already had reassured him that he was the best, so he began training hard for the next fight against Jimmy Bergen on Friday, February 16, 1923. When Joe appeared in the ring, Troop 14 yelled a rhythmic "Here is Joe! Our Joe!" He bowed, gloves crossed upon his heart. With two matches lost in a row, he was determined to fight like never before.

That determination was brutally stopped when the other boxer opened the fight with a powerful left that landed right on Joe's wounded eye. For a few seconds he went blind with pain and punched aimlessly to keep Bergen away. A long sigh of disappointment reached Joe's ears. Once again, their hero had taken a horrible blow that could ruin his career. The end of the first round did not look good for Joe, as another large blister full of blood covered his eye, forcing him to fight defensively. At the break Tickle applied a bag of ice to Joe's swollen face, while Mike, fanning the towel, whispered, "You aren't going to take a dive, are you?" Joe shook his head as he gargled icy water and spit in the pail held by Mike. He took a few deep breaths and pushed the stool away, ready for the next round.

At the bell, the overconfident Bergen stepped right into Joe's half cross, and his knees buckled. Joe knew what would happen next and did not follow through as any other boxer would have. There was no need for extra punishment. Calmly he waited for the Maine boxer to go down. The public and judges also watched the slow-moving doomed boxer with the same interest. What they saw next was Referee Kid Oscar walking alongside dizzy Bergen, who kept turning right and left, knees melting, trying to reach his corner. The referee brought him to the center of the ring, where Joe stood, and after shouting "Box!" he stepped back. Apparently Bergen had recovered; he sent a few long jabs to Joe, who for a while did some good sparring with his rival, who believed himself to be out of danger. In the meantime, Joe's blister burst open, and blood gushed down his face and chest.

Encouraged, Bergen got the idea that he could win and launched a careless two-fisted attack aimed at the blistered eye. Joe slipped under the flying mitts and hooked Bergen's liver with a snappy left. The guy bent over holding his belly, mouth open, ready to vomit. He again wobbled helplessly and breathlessly toward his corner, followed by the referee, who expected him to fall. So did everyone else, who wondered why Joe didn't finish him off. But he didn't, and the gong terminated the second round as Bergen was helped to sit on the stool.

An agitated discussion took place in Bergen's corner, and he got up to leave the ring. His assistants pushed him back onto the stool. The guy became furious, and punching his way out the ring, he headed to the dressing room while the audience laughed and joked at his expense. "Hey, Bergen, you wanna be home earlier?" Joe and his corner watched the whole thing in disbelief; they had never witnessed a boxer abandon a fight like that and walk out of the ring. Joe even wanted to go after the guy and convince him to come back, but the referee took his hand and declared a win by TKO.

Back home, Mike delivered the envelope with $50 to their father, while their mother shook her head, dampened a cloth in herbal tea, and gently applied it to Joe's face. "Look at you. Look at this blood. This is no good. No more boxing!" But Mike sat down next to her and patted her shoulder. "It's nothing! Come on, look at Pop counting the money!" The next day, Joe was the talk of the city. The sports reporters agreed that Joe was a rarity in the sport. Indeed, "Gentleman Joe" was the way to describe "the clever bantam" who never despised his rival or went for overkill.

CHAPTER 8
AN ERA OF MANY NAMES

The 1920s, when Joe Grimm's pugilistic career began, would initiate an era that came to be known as the Golden Age of Boxing and the Golden Age of Bantams, among many other names. America was departing from semi-Victorian morals and values and was looking for its own identity. The GIs victoriously returned from the war in Europe and found a country different from the one they had known. The most striking novelty was the vast presence of automobiles. Henry Ford had introduced the Model T in 1908. By 1921 he had sold five million affordable cars, most of them on payment plans. The affordability of the "universal automobile" had hooked middle-class Americans, who quickly became dependent on what years before was a circus curiosity. The individually owned motorcar facilitated commuting to distant jobs. The "sex chariot" also changed the dating rituals of the young generation. Very soon, the car became part of the good life, making it easy to be independent, visit others, go on a picnic or to a fair, see a movie or play, or go to a circus.

One of the most popular new destinations was the ballpark and the cycledrome. There one could watch sports events, have a snack or meal, and, at the same time, place bets on bicycle and motor races, boxing, and wrestling. By rooting for a favorite competitor, one could loudly express an opinion and let go of anger and frustration. Plus it was just great fun. For a twenty-five–cent entrance fee one could be entertained for hours, see celebrities, and be part of a happy society.

Rapid industrialization made it possible for one-half of the American public to urbanize and adopt a different way of life—a city life, with electricity, the radio, telephone, central heating, indoor plumbing, and easy access to shopping around the corner. Houses and apartments were loaded with appliances and everything else one needed to live comfortably. The business of producing new luxuries took on giant proportions and hired millions, including 800,000 immigrants who came to the country in 1920 alone. Greed allowed fraudulent investors to prosper, and a Ponzi scheme promised a 50 percent return in ninety days for each dollar invested. Forty thousand hopefuls—or, better said, hope-fools—lost $15 million as the financial lure collapsed, just like the Florida bubble that guaranteed that land bought immediately could be resold for fifty times as much. Out of this debacle came the saying, "Too good to be true," a lesson from which nobody learned anything. American greed remained stronger than reasoning, feeding speculators who promised everything and delivered very little. Because of them, countless deals took place in the get-rich-quick era, bringing only grief and financial chaos to the ruined gamblers. Yet, the capitalistic lesson that greed was good optimistically lingered on and produced spectacular enterprises.

Unfortunately, with the war over and its industrial demands drastically reduced, one-third of the factories closed their gates, 453,000 farmers lost their land, and some 100,000 people and businesses declared bankruptcy. This revived Puritanism and led to the Emergency Quota Act, intended to protect the racial purity of America by restricting immigration to 3 percent of any nation. Determined to reinforce white supremacy, the Ku Klux Klan reached it largest membership ever. Chinese and other Asian people were not admitted into the country. Colored people were segregated and could not vote; furthermore, only the "colored" who had special talents were accepted, mainly as entertainers, by the white society. Bessie Smith and Louis Armstrong might enter a club through the kitchen, but they could not eat next to the white customers. Still, they were household names and very well liked in the era of experimentation, when all arts flourished.

The resourceful American people overcame the temporary economic crisis by adopting a new style of living: consumerism. Just about everything was disposable, beginning with Gillette razor blades and including cloth, furniture, and cars. The race to keep up with the Joneses and the need to stay abreast of the newest fashion defined the new spirit of progress. Installment plans were the way to afford all the "necessities" that no one had heard of months before. The traditional "a penny saved is a penny earned" became the nonsense of the past. Suddenly, debt was good because it enabled people to get what they could not afford otherwise. *Enjoy today and pay tomorrow* was the concept of the good life for a society of "to have" and "have more." Leisure time and the American can-do-anything attitude again put factories to work, overtime.

The only dark cloud that shaded the live-free era was Prohibition, a government abstinence act intended to cut down on violence, the sickness of intoxication, and low morals, all stimulated by the evil of alcohol. It was a "dry crusade" rooted in the church and carried out by puritans who saw drinking as the most destructive enemy of American society. The noble movement backfired in unexpected ways when the illegal businesses of bootleggers grossed $2 billion a year. Countless addicted drinkers went blind or died from consuming "bathtub gin," "monkey rum," or liquor made of medicinal alcohol and embalming fluid. A $20 investment in making liquor could bring a profit of at least ten times more. Unlicensed speakeasy saloons mushroomed all over America, and gangsters stepped in to control and monitor the lucrative underground business as political corruption kept brewing. Bribery was rampant at all levels of official administration. A federal agent who let an illegal operation go untouched could make in one "deal" half of his yearly paycheck. With a supply of 800 million gallons a year, mostly flooding in from Canada, the booze was more abundant, and cost more, in the dry era than before. And with more than 280,000 distilleries in the United States, the Noble Experiment was doomed to fail. Prohibition turned into "profit-bition." In no time it reached a lucrative zenith with the illegal production of moonshine.

The entertainment industry benefited the most from this mini-economic crisis that encouraged the unemployed to become addicted movie watchers. To be entertained was the new way to spend free time, and movie moguls from Los Angeles made sure to provide plenty for the silver screens that attracted 35 million spectators a week. New movie houses were built to feature the latest comedies and dramas just released from Hollywood, the mecca of the movie business, where, in 1923, a three stories–high advertising sign was erected on the hill with that same name. Beverly Hills became the address for movie stars and an instant tourist attraction. Rudolph Valentino, an Italian immigrant riddled by debt he never paid back, personalized the American dream, advancing from being a tango dancer to a movie idol and becoming the decade's Great Lover. More than thirty thousand women worshippers attended his funeral in August 1926. Mary Pickford, raised in an impoverished Canadian family, became an idol, in seven years going from making $40 a week to $40,000 a week. The message from Hollywood was as clear as the stories in their movies: anyone who dared could make it big in America, the land of all possibilities and opportunities.

Besides Hollywood and the Great White Way, American arts produced remarkable painters like George Bellows, who immortalized on canvas the moment when Dempsey was thrown out of the ring by Firpo during the 1923 heavyweight championship fight. Literature was enriched by William Faulkner and Francis Scott Fitzgerald, who reflected the era of abundance by describing the ultimate social climber, Gatsby. Ernest Hemingway was such a boxing lover that he settled a dispute with the Canadian writer Morley Callaghan in the ring at the American Club in Paris. Fitzgerald was their timekeeper. Many other notable writers emerged during the publishing boom that became an industry in itself.

The Jazz Age made its debut in New Orleans as Negro blues, and by the 1920s it had made a huge splash in Chicago, New York, and other major cities, with the vivacious sound of optimism. It introduced the Swing Era along with the equally dynamic Charleston dance that would have major effects on fashion, nightclub settings, nonconformist behaviors, relationships, and morality.

Linked to the Charleston was the new word "flapper," describing a young socialite woman with short hair (mostly jaw length) covered with a bowl hat, wearing a shapeless short dress (revealing the knees!), covered with long fringe, and draped with long strings of beads—the fringe and necklaces swinging wildly during the wild moves of the dance. It was a dance during which, for the first time, a man was not needed to lead the woman across the floor. The flamboyant flapper often wore heavy makeup and acted like one of the boys—slouching casually on a chair, smoking, drinking prohibited alcohol, openly flirting, and yelling in public—definitive proof of the new freedom for womanhood.

Women gained the right to vote and more and more freely expressed their needs and thoughts. While at one time wearing a swimming suit at a public beach got them arrested, now in the torrid twenties, a one-piece swimsuit was acceptable. It went one revolutionary step forward, and in 1921 the first American beauty pageant was held in Atlantic City. The next year the Miss America contest of half-naked beautiful, healthy white women became an American institution.

In a short few years, Americans were known abroad not only for their chewing gum habit, denim jeans, and cowboy movies, but for cars, Hollywood productions, jazz and the Charleston, fashion and feminist ideas, and most of all, dominating all sports, with world boxing champions in each weight category.

By the year 1923, gangsters, wearing custom-made silk suits and diamond rings while toting Thompson machine guns, practically ruled the big cities. Intriguing dangerous characters with names destined to become legends, like "Bugs" Moran, "Dutch" Schultz, "Lucky" Luciano, and "Scarface" Capone, became the new heroes of the Lawless Decade. While the mafia business flourished, legitimate American business suffered from overproduction, and during 1923–1924 a mild self-adjustment recession hit the nation that had become used to living well. Once again, the large influx of immigrants was blamed, leading to the passage of the National Origins Act, which reduced the immigration quota of any nation to 2 percent. As a result, only 141,000 immigrants entered the country in 1924; Asians were still banned. The KKK reached a record five million members united by the motto, "Native, White, Protestant Supremacy!" President Coolidge decreed that "America must be kept American!" Millions of American patriots claimed "America First!" Because of the victorious Bolshevik Revolution in Russia, many communists and anarchists like Emma Goldman and Alexander Berkman were expelled from the United States. Jazz was banned by the Lutheran Church, and conservative groups wanted life to go back to more traditional roots. Still, at the $100,000 funeral of assassinated mobster Dion O'Banion, a crowd of fifty thousand paid their respect.

Regardless of political turmoil, American business found new directions to extend and prosper. The lure of becoming rich turned almost everyone into an inventor who rushed to patent his discovery. In 1923 Clarence Birdseye of New York, who used to stuff animals, invested $7 in experimenting with frozen food and sold his business six years later for $22 million. Grocery chain stores like A&P reached fourteen thousand locations, and Sears Roebuck and Co. used a mail-order catalog to sell just about everything. In 1924 the Macy's department stores, founded by a whaler with the same last name, inaugurated the first Thanksgiving Parade in Manhattan, combining prosperous business with ardent patriotism, under the umbrella of huge promotional wit. Macy's main competitor was Frank W. Woolworth, who, after growing up as the son of an impoverished farmer, succeeded in constructing the tallest building in the world, as well as owning a chain of popular merchandise stores. Both were a testimony of the boundless opportunities America offered. As the country began to switch from coal to oil and to electricity, countless businesses took off and prospered.

Consumerism continued and, with it, massive production, massive employment, massive entertainment, and massive worship of heroes. Some of the latter were remarkable athletes in each sport, marking the 1920s the Decade of Heroes. The competitive American society enjoyed watching sports competitions, and boxing was the epiphany for distinguishing a hero from a loser. It created the idea of a temporary "underdog" who "made a comeback" and "upset" the champion when proving victorious, as well as the concept of a challenger and of the final contender for a title fight.

Joe Grimm was one of those undefeated athletes who became a local wonder; implicitly, his fighting skills became a commodity in demand. Thus he began winning money to help his struggling family, who now moved to a better house in a better neighborhood on Bedford Street in Fall River. If emancipation was the key word of the tumultuous 1920s, Joe noticed the sign of progress in his new home, when the wooden floors of the kitchen, hallways, and bathroom were covered by the new revolutionary product, linoleum. It was a plastic sheet designed with blue and white squares, easy to clean with a broom or a wet mop. Soon, a hot dispute took place between Mike, the family doer, and his parents over the purchase of a secondhand Arctic refrigerator, but the old trusted icebox stayed under the crucifix. The radio was also ruled out, because was it was too expensive and not necessary. The electric press iron and vacuum cleaner were disregarded for the same sound reasons.

However, a secondhand black boxy Victrola gramophone, bought by Mike from his winning-bets money for less than half of its original $60, was triumphantly installed by him in the family room and cranked so they could all listen to a disc record with a fox terrier picture on it. The sound came from the opened little doors underneath the record player. A melodramatic song, interpreted by a highly emotional tenor who kept imploring, "Oh, Rosie, I love you," was an instant hit with the family. Mother and girls cried, but the mood totally changed with the next record. It was the Charleston, with sound that ripped into the room with the instigating rhythm of drums, piano, trumpets, violins, and guitars. The girls tried to dance it under the confused and disapproving eyes of the Hashim parents. To make up for his mother being upset, Mike spent $25 and bought a brand-new Standard

Rotary sewing machine, beautifully decorated with gold leaves. The modern gadget improved the clothing of the Hashim children and helped the family save money.

For the Hashim family, entertainment was socializing with other Lebanese families after church on Sunday. They all spoke their native Arabic, and showing off their well-dressed and healthy-looking children was a great joy. The family was not poor but still lived in a rented house and did not have a steady income. Louis, the barber, was twenty-five, and he was looking to get married, as were his sisters Edma and Emma; all were looking for a good match in the Lebanese community, or with someone who had come from or had roots in the old country. So far, the Roaring Twenties had little effect on the life and thinking of the Hashims. The motto of the parents seemed to be "No change is a good change" and "Any debt is bad." Spending above their financial means was not the Hashims' idea of prosperity. The ingrained family values, based on church teachings, were stronger than any temptation of the glamorous era.

But like it or not, many things around them changed, even as their old world lingered. Among the last vestiges of the earlier era was the horse-drawn streetcar, still used for public transportation in Fall River. Trolley cars running under the electric cables were becoming increasingly popular on Main Street, now too small to offer enough parking spaces to all the cars that flooded it. Newly designed houses went from farm style to colonials with attached garages. The textile industry in the Spindle City still employed tens of thousands of workers, and apparently business was as strong as always. However, the population was split between the old generation of immigrants and their children and grandchildren. While the first physically lived in America, their hearts were in their former countries. The second and third generations wanted to be part of the new land and its culture. Young and curious, they did not want to miss anything that the restless era so generously offered.

On the other hand, the locals could look more modern. Mike learned how to cut women's hair in a bob, for which the charge was three times more than a regular man's haircut, and that meant double the tip, as well. Local girls with hand-beaded dresses sat in his barber chair before going in a group to dance at the Armory. There, the girls mostly danced among themselves but openly flirted with the boys. For the first time emancipated girls picked the boys they liked—and refused to dance with or date those they weren't interested in. Saturday evenings were usually reserved for ballroom, when the youth of Fall River danced the foxtrot and waltz, since the tango was too intimate and the Charleston too wild and indecent. Friday and Saturday evenings were perfect to go to the movies, and Fall River had ten theaters from which to choose.

The Casino on Morgan Street was a well-established entertainment center, operating since the last century. The huge brick cubical building held just about every form of political rally, as well as social and sports events. Here was the arena where Joe confirmed most of his boxing abilities. The old Casino could still host artistic events, like America's Famous Boy's Band from St. Mary's Industrial School of Baltimore, Maryland, on Wednesday, November 19, 1924, selling tickets for one dollar each. But the mammoth building did not have the facilities for showing movies or staging vaudeville acts and classical plays, nor could it offer proper ventilation or plush seats. So, to keep up with the sophistication of the amazing era, a modern theater was built adjacent to the Casino, with an entrance in ornamented marble sections facing South Main Street. The rest was a red-brick building with a modern interior that combined the best of art deco and classical looks. It was called the Capitol.

Its magnificent street entrance led to a long walk with floors lined with black and white marble squares bordered by dark alleys, and green-painted walls with fake windows; electric bulbs framed colorful posters of the past and future film attractions. Above the second entrance, bright neon letters announced the name of the performance or performers. The exterior glamour set the tone for the luxury of the spacious oval foyer with black leather sofas lined up alongside the walls, facing the main column whose base was cushioned with similar seats. The largest mirror in the city, eight feet by fifteen feet, made the foyer look much larger and even more brilliant, as it reflected the clapboard-like walls and the ceiling, with its shiny metallic finish that matched the mosaic floor and the elegant side doors.

Two large doors opened into the theater, whose elegance and lavish decorations were breathtaking. There was a massive balcony that hung over half of the main seating area. Attached to the bottom of the balcony were ten large, round, electric fixtures that, with two palatial chandeliers, provided lighting that gave the high ceiling and molded walls the look of an impressive temple. The 1,600 well-cushioned seats were attached to the floor that slanted toward the imposing stage with rounded upper corners and a large decorated frame that matched similar decorations from the ceiling and walls. A front velvet curtain opened to reveal a spacious opera stage that ended with another silk curtain that covered the two stories–high silver screen. The entire theater—with its marble, mirrors, mural paintings, and art deco glitter—spelled a true American Renaissance style and added credit to the tasteful era of the twenties. The people of Fall River who had supplied the finances, artistry, and manpower for the construction could not be more proud of their modern Capitol Theatre, a main nouveau chic attraction for locals and visitors, as well.

The city's rival, neighboring New Bedford, was determined not to come in second when it came to modern changes. After all, when Fall River was "nothing," the Whaling City was the leading center of the once-important whale industry; it took a setback when animal oil was replaced by petroleum fuel. In time, New Bedford acquired its own textile mills, where mostly Portuguese dwellers labored. They claimed to be better at stitching, dressmaking, tailoring, and sewing, because they worked primarily on white fabrics, which would show error far more easily than the more common colored fabric. Admittedly, Fall River had more looms and mills, but it was New Bedford's population that increased by 10,000 people to 121,000 in 1924 (most having left Fall River because of its higher unemployment rate). New Bedford was immensely proud to claim the oldest operating fire alarm system in the country. The Whalers had a monumental Custom House dating from 1836, the oldest in the United States, a solid reminder of a proud bygone era. They felt that their library (once a city hall) was more beautiful and better built than the one in Fall River; in truth, both majestic temples of books and archives looked almost out of place in their blue-collar surroundings.

Many old cultural and social establishments continued to serve the population of New Bedford, like the Orpheum Theater, but the most impressive venues were the Bristol Arena and the cycledrome. The Bristol Arena was a new multipurpose indoor space with four thousand seats. It was located in the center of New Bedford and became known as the Madison Square Garden of New England. It guaranteed spectacular fights, because the packed audience provided a good purse. The fistic events held there were the main reason for the prolificacy of the city's many good boxers. The city's cycledrome was the largest open arena, holding six thousand spectators. Inaugurated in the middle of 1921, it was designed with bicycle races in mind. It had an elliptical wooden track, one-quarter of mile long, formed by two opposite flat straight lines connected with 180-degree raised bends. In many ways, it was reminiscent of an ancient Greek Olympic stadium but with bicycle and motorcycle races and relays providing the competition. The infield was a large area that could accommodate a circus rink or a boxing ring with enough space around it to place an additional 1,500 spectators who paid one dollar to be closer to the action, versus fifty cents for the bleachers. The construction was duplicated on a larger scale by the same entrepreneur, former bicycle racer Charles Turville, in the city of Providence. When it opened four years later, it was called the "mammoth bowl," because it was the largest bicycle track in America. It could host a thirty-mile race, football games, and major boxing events in front of 13,000 spectators. Joe Grimm won many fights in all these above-mentioned arenas.

At the same time, all over America, some twenty thousand similar new theaters and other entertainment establishments were built in granite and terra-cotta, all finished in gold and bright colors, glittering under strings of electric lights. This was the era of sugarcoated plays, elaborate vaudeville, popular musicals, and other live shows performed inside lavish architecture called the Belasco style. It consisted of compressed luxuries of art deco and Greek style, with sharp geometric lines, glitzy decorations, lots of chrome and mirror elements, enhanced by a sophisticated lighting system. Expensive and elaborate Wurlitzer organs provided the musical background to accentuate a romantic kiss or a cavalry charge shown in the silent movie, as well as playing for choir formations and patriotic plays. Yet, when the theater hosted a boxing event, the same rather nostalgic place suddenly changed: the idyllic setting where crying spectators identified with heartbreaking melodramas became a violent gladiatorial arena where the audience cheered for spilled blood. Obviously the progressive twenties changed many material things that had unexpected effects on human behavior and led to what was called a "ballyhoo" attitude toward life. The new phenomena triggered the American style of La Belle Époque of enjoyment and prosperity.

Chapter 9

Winning and Losing

The spring of 1923 looked very promising for Joe when he met Georgie Vanderbilt on March 14 at the Casino in an eight-round preliminary match. Vanderbilt—or "Vandy," as he was called by his friends—was a robust fighter with a good record. One year before, he had lost by a narrow margin in Providence against Charley (Phil) Rosenberg, the future world bantamweight champion. Vandy had many fans, because he was a native of Fall River and also because he had a unique promotional vaudevillian gimmick: he always entered the ring wearing coattails instead of a robe, with a shiny top hat and an elegant cane, pretending to be a gentleman invited to fight. So Vandy, who was six years older than Joe and more experienced, was the reason Mike entered the dressing room to announce that betting was two-to-one against his brother. Mike poked all his fingers into Joe's chest. "If you win, I'll give you half!"

Minutes later when the announcer introduced the two rivals, the cheers clearly showed who was the favorite—the cocky Vandy. The first-round bell sent the eager punchers against each other in full force, and Vandy laid a powerful left right into Joe's chin that stunned him into a clinch, where he received another lightning left in the jaw. The last impact seemed to wake up Joe, who then swung his left hook into his rival's jaw. For a second Vandy went blank. The entire audience was up in their chairs, and a storm of encouragement threw the fighters into a close jackhammer exchange. Pressed with stiff punches, Joe emerged with a bloody cut above his left eye. The spectators reacted with a long "Aaaahhhhh," considering Joe to now be on the losing side of the ring. It happened so quickly that Referee Donnelly didn't see if a head butt, the glove laces, or a tough punch was responsible for the injury, and he let the fight go on. Blood was draping Joe's eye, and he tasted it on his lips. Quick to exploit the damage, Vandy directed all his blows to the injury, while Joe tried to steal time until the end of the round.

Coach Tickle was glad he had brought his leather medical case, from which he pulled out a bottle of alcohol that he splashed on a large cotton ball and swabbed the wound, making Joe jerk from the pain. Next he took a silver coin from the vest pocket and pressed it against the bleeding cut. Then he scooped sticky Vaseline from a small round jar and generously pasted it over the laceration; the bleeding stopped. Mike poured icy water on his brother's head. Joe grabbed the bottle, rinsed the blood from his mouth, and spit in the bucket. The coach wiped his boy with the towel, and the bell rang again. "Get him, Joe! Get him, Joe!" the troop was chanting when their leader got up from the chair and saluted them with a reassuring extended arm.

Confident Vanderbilt was determined to end the fight, but instead he was struck by Joe's formidable combinations, including the left hook and right cross in the jaw that put a glassy stare in his eyes. The troop went ballistic, and Mike yelled from the bottom of his lungs, "Go for the kill!" Joe unleashed a determined attack that ultimately kept his rival on his feet against the ropes. Somehow, the half-conscious Vandy found the energy to swing a wild left from the floor into Joe's face. The public went silent for a moment, waiting to see what would happen next. Referee Donnelly kept switching his attention from Joe to Vandy, expecting one to drop on the canvas. It looked like whoever stood up would win the bout, yet both continued to fight with vengeance until the end of the round. Joe slammed into his chair, hearing Mike begging, "Brother, go for the kill, not to be killed!" Coach Tickle confidently said, "He's finished, keep attacking," while adding more grease to the eye wound. The bell rang.

In the eighth round, Joe's left hook found Vandy's jaw; a second later the boy was crawling on all four toward the ropes. The referee stopped his counting at eight, because Vandy was up on his feet and ready to continue. The final bell ended his ordeal. "The decision went to Grimm by a city block," wrote the *Evening Herald* the next day, praising Joe's efforts. Vandy left the ring resting on his seconds' shoulders, who also ingloriously carried the tails, hat, and cane. Later Joe entered in his record book, "Beat him real bad. Betting was 2 to 1 against me." He had earned another $50 for the fight.

Joe's next ring appearance came in the middle of April against Charlie Baxter, who believed he was a better boxer than Joe, based on the decision for their last fight. Sure of himself, Baxter immediately threw his entire arsenal at Joe, including his signature fake shoulder moves. He was determined to end the fight quickly, but Joe had his own agenda and turned the aggressive Baxter into a steady target round after round. Far from getting tired like the last time, Joe pressed forward for a knockout, but Baxter was still a powerful opponent with a strong jaw and endurance that could digest incoming punches. Baxter fought like a possessed man to the end and returned many counterpunches. This time, though, Joe received the unanimous decision and succeeded in wiping the smile of victory off Baxter's face. The Boy Scouts and the rest of the audience were jubilant. So was Joe with his $45 and Mike with his sure winning bet.

The following month, in a main event fight in Fall River's Casino, Chick Suggs, the bantam and featherweight champion of New England, lost against a formidable opponent from New Jersey, Irish Johnny Curtin. The manager and promoter of Curtin was the well-known Charley Doessereck, who spotted Joe around the ring and greeted him with a cheerful "Aren't you the hotshot kid with all those KOs in a row?" He added that he was following the good progress Joe was making. Then he shook Joe's hand and, smiling, said, "Who knows, one day we may join forces." Looking at the youngster's large hands, Doessereck added, "That fist might one day land a million-dollar punch!" Joe smiled and the promoter added, "That smile too!"

Drunk with happiness, Joe went home and told Mike what happened, adding, "That's the second time someone has said that to me! Maybe it can really happen!" Mike nodded and then frowned as he asked, "Did he mention the letter I sent him?" Joe shook his head no. "What a creep!" Mike responded. A week later, Joe fought the ambitious Young Larabee for the third time and defeated him on points in a routine fight he dominated from beginning to end.

Three uneventful summer months passed for Joe until August, when he faced the good-looking Tony Thomas, a novice from New Bedford. Joe believed this fight would be another sparring session that would end with an easy knockout. Indeed, in the first two rounds Joe looked like a mitt artist toying with an ambitious debutant. Joe kept piling up points while looking for the best opportunity to floor his opponent. All was going well until the third round, when Joe was the one who collapsed! His right calf muscle was twitching with charley horse spasms. Referee Flynn stopped the fight while Joe moaned and shook with excruciating pain. A physician rushed to examine him, and Coach Tickle was allowed to massage the leg. Mike applied an icy bottle of water to the jolting muscle. The judges asked Joe to quit, but he refused; limping, he went to his corner to recover.

The fourth round began with a different Thomas, who took advantage of the situation and pummeled Joe into the ropes. As described by a ringside reporter, his wild attack ended by bullying limping Joe, who was pushed "through the top and middle ropes with Thomas on top of him. The pair crashed to the floor a good four feet below, with Grimm landing on the back of his head. He was temporarily stunned as the result of coming in contact with the floor. The two scrappers were pushed back into the ring and Grimm insisted upon continuing." The spectators were on their feet, screaming opinions about the fight decision. The next break allowed Joe to recover. Tickle pulled a small bottle of ammonia out of his medical bag and held it for Joe to sniff. He was still dizzy from the fall and in pain not only from the leg cramp but now also from Thomas's merciless wallops. Oblivious to his many injuries and pain, Joe went through the fifth, sixth, seventh, and eighth rounds with stoic determination, as his blows turned into pats. "At least don't take a dive!" Mike encouraged him during the breaks.

The ninth round brought a new twist to the awkward fight. Joe seemed to recapture his usual style and began to administer a rich assortment of punches that made the audience leap on their feet and had the Scout troop cheering at the top of their lungs. Joe also dominated the tenth round, but according to the same reporter, "his blows did not appear to carry the same sting to them as on occasions in the past." Joe was just about to win, but it was too late to compensate for all the lost rounds, and Thomas received the decision by points. The announcement triggered a loud protest from the spectators who had hoped to see at least a draw decision.

After the terrible fight, Joe came home with $20 and Mike with empty pockets. One thing was crystal clear to both: lack of training and overconfidence guaranteed losing a fight. All in all, boxing was a very dangerous sport if not treated with proper respect. Joe went back to the gym with renewed determination, just in time for his next bout, facing Johnny Dias, who also lived in Fall River and was so far practically undefeated.

This fight was greatly anticipated by boxing fans in Fall River. It took place on September 28, and Mike bet even more heavily than usual on his brother, because the odds were against him. When they entered the ring, both boys looked like picture-perfect boxers. The audience was tense with anticipation as the bell sounded. Joe was the first aggressor, punching hard and accurately, forcing Dias to use his excellent footwork to escape dangerous entrapments and making him defensively punch his way out of uncomfortable moments. In the second round, Joe used his best rapid-fire shots to Dias's body and head, raising the audience off their seats as they screamed and cheered. Quickly Dias switched gears and kept his determined rival at a distance by firing efficient long shots. Each time Joe slipped under the striking gloves, he scored big with solid uppercuts, until the bell retired the two battling bantams to their corners.

Dias opened the third round with a wild right that landed on Joe's ear, so it "blossomed out a cherry red," after which the fight broke loose, both boys giving and taking blows generously. When locked in a clinch, Joe broke away with many well-aimed shots that thrilled the fickle audience, which screamed support for whichever boxer was punching the hardest. The next round was dominated by Joe, who successfully launched a flood of combinations to Dias's head and body at close range. The fans cheered his skillful effort as he won the round. In the fifth, both slowed down a bit. Finding an opening, Joe threw a right so strong and fast that when it missed, he spun halfway around, exposing his jaw to a well-placed right from Dias. That punch staggered Joe, who slowed down and could hardly wait for the bell to ring. The one-minute rest that followed was enough for Joe to fully recover, helped by his corner seconds.

Dias believed Joe was finished and took the lead in the next round, only to be counterpunched into the ropes and hit again and again by left hooks that made the audience scream for a KO. Dias was still standing, and surprisingly, the bell found him with both hands working like a windmill. So far, Joe was ahead with points. In round seven, Joe continued to force the pace, and Dias was pelted with many combinations. The tired boys were so tangled that it became hard to judge who was hitting better.

The eighth round belonged to Joe, who excelled in scoring to the body, while Dias worked to keep his head covered and avoid a KO. When he could, Dias responded by engaging in "a little catch-as-catch-can stuff in the milling," as the newspaper reported. Frustrated, he used the heel of his glove to injure Joe, but the blows glanced off his head. In the ninth round, Dias engaged in a major assault and forced Joe to be defensive, and it didn't look like Joe would score that KO. The last round began with "Lick him, Joe!" shouts from the Scouts, but Dias was "just as fit as he appeared in the opening session ... scoring with both hands to Joe's head and body." Joe was forced into a corner, but he "rallied before the close and sent over a couple of good wallops" that could have led to a KO if the bell hadn't stopped the fight.

"It was easily the best fight of the evening and though the decision did not prove popular yet each fighter was accorded a fine hand as he left the ring," wrote the *Evening Herald* the next day. Another local paper headlined its coverage: "Grimm Loses the Decision," adding in the subhead, "East Ender Outpointed and Outfought Johnny Dias In Feature Bout At Casino Last Night But Officials See It Otherwise." In the end, "the decision in favor of Dias was a shock, but it is one of those things that happened every once in a while," the reporter wrote. But "fully 90 percent of the boxing fans present were of the opinion that Grimm had won the fight."

Joe himself had no doubt that he won and wrote in his little notebook, *"Won over Johnny Dias; robbed out of decision. Gamblers won"* (his italics). Obviously, brother Mike lost with his bet, and Joe made only $25. Worse yet was that after the fight, Chick Suggs was invited into the ring to promote his appearance the next Friday night against either Abe Attell Goldstein or Terry Martin, both elite contenders for the bantam title. That meant Suggs and his manager, Dave Lumiansky, witnessed the fight and saw Joe losing; Joe's pride bled a lot.

The Casino owner knew that the Dias–Grimm controversy was a golden opportunity for big crowds and money, and one month later the boys were back in the ring for another ten rounder inside the arena, overpacked with spectators, and air filled with smoke. The announcer introduced them during a small lull in the hubbub. Back in the corner, Mike slapped Joe's face and whispered, "Put him down and fast!" Coach Tickle stood by Joe's side, staring at Dias.

At the bell, Joe determinedly walked toward Dias, knowing well that a knockout could not be contested by anyone. With that intention in mind, he began to stage his proven half left hook and half straight right, but Dias displayed his customary slam-bang aggressiveness, and one round after another passed in his favor as he kept delivering distant and easy punching points. The audience still cheered for Joe, but what they saw was trim and fast Dias handling all Joe's attacks advantageously. Nonetheless, as the ringside reporter wrote in his next-day's column, "Grimm shot over his short right into Johnny's head repeatedly and it shook Dias up each time it landed."

So far, it was a clean fight, with both scrappers being cautious, interspersed with some holdings and hitting after the break by Dias. Urged by his corner, Joe delivered showers of ambitious punches during rounds five, six, and seven. But Dias had no problem absorbing them as he glided around with remarkable footwork. Those were Joe's best rounds, after which "Grimm was slow and not half so good as he appeared in their first meeting … while Dias was as fast as he started," wrote the same reporter from the *Evening Herald*. Moreover, Dias forced Joe across the ring numerous times, and in the ninth, "Grimm slipped to his knees in the scrimmage." He jumped right up, but little could be done to win in the last round.

To everyone's dismay, the newspaper's headline was short and to the point: "Young Dias Beats Joe Grimm." The paper announced that Dias qualified to meet Young Carney the following Friday in New Bedford, when also Jimmy Wilde would fight Young Falvey of the same category. Joe took a big step back. To avoid the treacherous bantamweight contests, Red Larabee, Young Mack, and others, preferred to fight in the next heavier category.

Eager to recover his betting money, Mike urged Tickle to book his brother for the next Thursday event against Young Barry, who had defeated the badly injured Joe back in February. Barry was so dangerous that many boxers hesitated to meet him in the ring, but Joe was ready and willing to fight him again. For eight rounds, witnessed by all his adversaries who were present in the audience, including Dias, Grimm performed spectacularly and was almost deadly in the ring. Joe knocked out Barry's front teeth, opened a cut above his eye, and gave him a beating to be long remembered. Yet, because of Barry's incredible stamina and willpower, Joe could not score a knockout; still, he won the eight-round fight by unanimous decision.

A week later on November 2, Joe almost took out Tony Carney in the first round. Carney actually proved to be a good schooled fighter with an unlucky chin. After all, he had defeated Johnny Dias a year before. This time he went toe-to-toe for a few rounds with Joe but was outboxed in the final rounds. Carney lost by points. The local newspaper called Joe's revival the "wearing the former king of the local bantams."

Sure enough, Joe was scheduled to meet Henry Ford of Boston, a well-known fighter who, in October 1922, also fought in the opening bout for Larry Williams and Harry Greb, now the American light heavyweight title holder. Certainly Ford was the most important boxer Joe had met so far. The bout took place one year later in the same place where Greb won, at Marieville in Providence, where Joe again faced an audience that had no reaction when he was introduced as the "Dempsey of Bantams." Obviously, only a few had heard of him. From the beginning, the two equally aggressive boys set up a fast pace to ensure a lead and gain respect. Ford was an experienced fighter who knew how to use his height advantage to throw punches from a distance, which Joe blocked or dodged with partial success. Told by his corner that the fight was even and that he must do something, Joe began the fifth round by hammering at Ford's body, scoring many points of his own. He was surprised that his most powerful hits did not make the expected dent. This was mostly because Ford moved with the blow—his main defensive skill.

But Joe gamely stood ground and increased the storm of punches as the last rounds expired. When Referee Fennell raised Joe's arm as the winner, Joe looked at the rather nonchalant audience, which seemed to care little about the result, waiting for the clash of the main eventers. A record payment of $75 made him feel better about himself and what he was doing.

Joe ended the year of 1923 with two more surprisingly tough fights provided by two boys from Fall River—Joe Pete and Red Barnet, whom he had defeated before. Pete the North Ender returned to the ring after a long absence. His style was rusted, but he was still, as a sports reporter noted, "one of the toughest bantams in this vicinity" and was sharp enough to give Joe the East Ender a difficult time. But Joe's recent fighting experiences prevailed, and he soon took the lead as he "outhit and out boxed the North Ender," who was pounded over and over. The report in the local newspaper was headlined "Grimm Wins Hard Fight," with the subtitle, "East Ender Shows Improvement in Beating Joe Pete." The reporter concluded the article with "Grimm made his best appearance in many months." In the same event,

Johnny Dias hardly outpointed Red Barnett, a former bantam champion of New England, who actually severely beat Dias only ten days before.

A month later, on December 14, Joe entered the ring to face Red Barnett, who wanted to recover his fighting dignity and, for the first two rounds, "was traveling at top speed" (as noted by a sports writer) and scored valuable points. At the break, Mike poured icy water over his brother's head and asked through clenched teeth, "You won't lose the last fight of the year, will you?" Joe shook his head as Mike slapped him on the shoulders. "Then let's make some money!" In the third round, Joe began his assault, delivering a blizzard of punches that sent Barnett in reverse all over the ring. In one instance he stopped in a corner where he hit his head against the ropes joint. Even though Referee McCarthy did not interfere, Joe dropped his gloves and waited for the dazed Barnett to walk around and regain his fighting stance. Mike couldn't believe his eyes and cried hoarsely from the corner, "Finish him!" Joe ignored him. Forced to fight in defense, the dazed boy still threw powerful punches, and one of them spun Joe around, drawing a long "Ahhhhhhhhh" from the audience. At the break, Mike cried again, "Put him down!"

This was more easily said than done, because Barnett's injured ego changed him into a violent fighter who hit so hard that he kept spinning Joe around. Upset by how the fight was going, Joe took charge and, as the boxing columnist wrote, "did most of the forcing in the closing rounds and he scored heavily to Red's body and head." Overpunched and overpowered, the bruised Barnett ran away from a KO and found himself partially thrown outside the top rope. "Kill him!" again screamed Mike with a hoarse voice, joining the audience. But Joe waited for his troubled rival to bring his body and head inside the ring, and resumed the fight. Again "Grimm slashed him with a left hook," and only the bell saved Barnett from a disastrous knockout. Mike was beside himself, witnessing how his brother lost one occasion after another to floor Barnett, who certainly showed no gratitude. After the final round was dominated by Joe, Referee McCarthy raised his arm and shouted the unanimous decision, "And the winner iiiisss, Gentlemaaaan Joooooeeee!" Rising to their feet, the public roared their approval.

Both fights brought exactly $110 to the Hashim family for Christmas, and an untold amount for Mike. But more importantly, the local newspaper came up with a list of the three most promising fighters around—namely, the junior lightweight Johnny Wilson, Tony Thomas (both of New Bedford), and Joe Grimm. Their pictures appeared under the largely bolded title, "Three Coming Champions," with Joe in the middle, described as the "hard hitting bantam of Fall River." After church that Sunday, everyone congratulated Joe.

CHAPTER 10

WHEN BOXING WAS KING

Image was everything in the Roaring Twenties. The way one looked could reflect success, prosperity, social achievement, and status. Anyone who was somebody wore the latest fashion, drove fancy cars, and lived in large houses. Smoking expensive cigars and drinking illegal booze were other signs of doing well. The ballyhoo was in a full swing as the advertising industry bombarded the public with products guaranteed to make consumers look just like the beautiful and healthy-looking men and women featured in ads. Sports became part of American consumerism. Competitive athletes flexing muscles made a lot of money and achieved stardom. Just looking athletic was a sure ticket to getting a better job, gaining entry to an elite saloon, being admired, and being assumed to be a good lover. In no time, sports heroes drew the American public to a new breed of idols.

Tennis and golf were believed to be the sport of relaxation for the rich and famous, but they became highly competitive when William T. "Bill" Tilden was unbeaten in national and international competitions. At the same time, Young Walter Hagen was the ultimate champion, acclaimed by some two million American golfers. The way the two heroes dressed was imitated by legions of club members who practiced the two noble sports. Tennis sweaters and golf pants quickly became trademarks of the Roaring Twenties. Hagen's success was easily measured when in 1926 alone he made $90,000. Tilden, who was independently rich, played as an amateur until 1930, after which he made half a million dollars during his professional tennis tours. Glenna Collet, who dominated the golf tournaments, was their famous feminine counterpart.

The sports hero who captured the imagination of "regular folks" was George Herman "Babe" Ruth, the pitcher for the Boston Red Sox and New York Yankees. He made $10,000 in salary in 1920 when he scored fifty-four home runs and a .849 slugging percentage, making him the most powerful hitter for the next eighty years. He pioneered the "live-ball era," fired the imagination of millions, and helped make baseball an American icon sport. After hitting sixty home runs, Babe's salary jumped in 1927 to $70,000 a year, but he grossed $250,000 from his endorsement, movie, and vaudeville appearances. His popularity was bigger than that of the president of the United States yet lagged behind that of Jack Dempsey and Gene Tunney after their second fight.

Unlike hugely popular baseball, football was mostly a college competition and strictly an amateur game that took place in front of an audience in the school stadium. However, it displayed quality athletes, one of whom was Harold Edward "Red" Grange. At that time some other football teams played sporadically; the best player would make under $150 a game. It was promoter Pyle who organized the first professional football tour after he made Grange an offer he could not refuse: play nineteen games for the Chicago Bears and pocket $100,000 cash. Before college he had earned $37.50 a week delivering ice blocks to customers. He was the first football superstar who graced the cover of *Time* magazine. Hundreds of thousands of fans went to see the "Grange Game," and scalpers sold tickets at a good profit. When Greta Garbo's salary was raised from $550 to $5,000 a week, Grange was paid $300,000 for his first silent picture, *One Minute to Play*. He then nailed a contract for a twelve-part talking movie serial titled *The Galloping Ghost*. Enormously popular, he was living proof that an average guy could become famous and rich.

While Grange played football in June 1924 in Illinois, thousands of miles away in Paris at the Olympic Games, another twenty-year-old American was collecting three gold medals in the swimming events. Four years later in Amsterdam he won two more gold medals. He was Johnny Weissmuller, who had emigrated as a toddler with his parents from Romania to Chicago. He signed a Hollywood contract to play Tarzan, earning him $2 million.

That was not the case for the legendary Jim Thorpe, who was stripped of his Olympic gold medals because of "shamateurism" rules regarding his amateur status. In the 1920s he played professional baseball, football, basketball, and even tried to act in movies, but "the greatest athlete in the world" never made big money. Affected by many personal problems, the frustrated Thorpe turned to alcohol and died penniless.

Eighteen-year-old Helen Willis won two gold medals in tennis at the 1924 Paris Games. Benito Mussolini was one of her biggest fans and invited Helen and her mother for a three-week tour of Italy. Once again, the maverick Pyle handled Helen Willis, and her tennis exhibitions proved to be a financial hit; Pyle took $24,000 following one such event in Madison Square Garden in October 1926. A true champion, "Queen Helen" had the unique distinction of a winning streak of 158 matches, winning 31 Grand Slams, including 8 single Wimbledon titles. She made $100,000 during a four-month exhibition tour in 1926.

The U.S. Open and other prestigious sporting events established legendary champions who delighted the public with their performances. But only so many tennis courts and golf fields were available for youngsters to perfect their game. Immensely popular baseball and football had many heroes and attracted millions who watched them play. To accommodate these enthusiastic spectators, giant baseball and football stadiums were constructed from New York to Los Angeles, and from Baltimore to Chicago. The huge gamble of spending the money on these structures would bring the investors major profits in time. It was the era of wonderful nonsense, when everything was possible when it came to making money.

Boxing was a different game: only two rivals competed, and often only one remained standing after a bloody contest. In spite of the brutal display of devastating punches, splattered blood, and remarkably physically fit men dropping on the canvas, the appeal of this aggressive masculine competition was increasingly huge. It addressed the ultimate question: who is the strongest and most feared man? For Americans, boxing contests were the continuation of the bygone Wild West, where a gun fight between two proud marksmen left one standing. Now it was an official confrontation, and the warriors were paid to practically kill each other. This was reason enough for boxing, before 1919, to be banned in most states as a kind of criminal activity that offended public morals and Christian values. Originating with bare knuckle fights that lasted for hours in back alleys, boxing was considered an ill-reputed sport, and wearing gloves did little to change its violent nature. Its spectacular savagery most closely duplicated life, which also came with brutal punches, giving it a unique appeal to the masses.

Many strong men from the circus and from other sports thought they could become successful boxers but failed; the sport was more brutal than they realized and demanded special physical and mental qualities. To be the strongest was not enough, as exemplified by Joe Rollino, who boxed under the name "Kid Dundee." Weighing 150 pounds, he could lift 635 pounds with one finger and bend a quarter with his fingers, but nevertheless he quickly discovered that to win a boxing bout required many other qualities. Another challenger was Wayne "Big" Munn of Kansas, a former college football star and a local wrestling hero, who believed his height and weight (6 feet 2 inches and 250 pounds) were sufficient to make him a good boxer. Prematurely compared with Jack Dempsey, he could not win even against second-raters.

Unlike in other sports or professions where bluffing worked hand in hand with skill as a way to achieve fame and money, boxing was an eliminatory competition between men who could absorb extreme physical battering. Illegal blows to the kidneys, head butts, and elbow jabs were not only painful but could be crippling, and hits by the movable thumb of the glove could blind an opponent. In the beginning, there was no mouthpiece, nor was there a groin cup, so these areas, too, were open to damaging punches. Having an impeccably dressed referee in the ring and respectable judges seated on the opposite side of it, monitoring the fight, did not dim the sheer barbarism in the ring. There was no three-knockdown rule, so a boxer could be downed again and again when he managed to stand up after a nine count. Nevertheless, the public was addicted to the legal savagery, and its appeal kept increasing with each new championship.

So, in the midst of this era of many names—when art and jazz were heralded alongside sporting events, when men and women danced the nights away, and stadiums were erected—boxing became not only legal in many states but a primary social event; the ring arena was the place to go for excitement, glamour, and unparalleled entertainment. Boxing created clear-cut winners. Best of all, an underdog could become a champion, worth a lot of money to a lot of people. Not only cities but also small towns throughout America had an arena for boxing events, which became enormously popular at all levels of society. Fierce pride was connected with each boxer when he rendered glory to his community and ultimately to the American nation.

Jack Dempsey was one of those who did both. He also put boxing on the front pages of newspapers and launched what became known as the Golden

Era of Boxing. He defeated Jess Willard in a hugely controversial fight for the world heavyweight title on July 4, 1919, in Toledo. The Dempsey–Carpentier fight of the century generated the first million-dollar gate in the history of boxing. It happened because more than 90,000 American fans came to see their hero battling the French hero. Dempsey's victory brought him $300,000 plus 25 percent of the movie rights. Some 85,000 American fans also got their money's worth watching how Dempsey demolished Luis Angelo Firpo, the hero of South America in what was believed to be "the best two rounds ever fought in boxing history." A record 120,557 spectators came to see the first Dempsey–Tunney fight, and the legendary Battle of the Long Count broke all previous money records with $2,658,660. Gene Tunney won again by unanimous decision and received exactly $990,000. Dempsey was paid only almost half of that amount for the heavy beating, a far cry from the $2.50 for his first victorious fight.

Harry Greb was another hero in the Golden Era of Boxing. He fought three hundred bouts covering three divisions for thirteen years, the last three of them fighting half blind. "The Human Windmill" was the ultimate warrior of all times and a man's man who filled each arena with people who wanted blood and guts. He was famous not only because he threw more punches in and outside the ring than any other boxer, but also for his expensive taste in clothes, his car crashes, and his thrilling escapades in the nightclubs, where he did most of his training, knocking down heavier men. Greb, the middleweight fighter, had the unique distinction of being the only boxer to defeat Gene Tunney, then the American light heavyweight champion, in 1922. In July 1925 Greb defeated the ambitious world welterweight champion Mickey Walker and kept his world middleweight title. He did not earn huge ring money, but he was a main constructor of his entertainment industry.

In no other competitive activity could a man make a million dollars in one minute—and this at a time when a skilled laborer made one dollar in one day. The bare financial facts were enough to make boxing the king of sports.

It turned out that the 1920s was the best era for the lighter boxers who actually had the most exposure to the public because they fought a few times a month, versus their heavier counterparts who boxed a few times a year. While large fighters, who dominated the best cards in any arena, made more money, the modern mini-gladiators put on great preliminary shows. With their seemingly endless stamina they provided entertainment for blood-hungry spectators and increased public interest in the "sweet science" of boxing.

One of the best in business was the lightest boxer of all, Jimmy Wilde of England, who proved to be an iconic fighter. He never weighed more than 102 pounds, but he could floor rivals twice his size. This tall, anemic-looking man with no apparent muscle had such punching power that he was the subject of medical investigations. But no lab tests could explain his prowess. In 1916 he celebrated his world flyweight title by going to a pub, where in four hours (with a tea break) he knocked out twenty-three large barrel-chested challengers who had foolishly underestimated the new champion. He won all the bets, and he kept winning in the ring—more than one hundred times in a row. His fame spread throughout the world, and he was a huge box office attraction. He credited his huge success to his training: running after his bicycling wife and sparring with his wife as he tried avoiding her random and wild punches.

In 1919 Wilde battered Joe Lynch in London and traveled to America, where he attracted massive crowds wanting to witness his phenomenal ring abilities. Ironically he lost in a ten-round decision to Jackie Sharkie in Wisconsin. He proved most unlucky when fighting Americans; he returned to England, and then two years later he lost by TKO to Pete Herman in London. At age thirty-one he crossed the Atlantic one more time, only to be knocked out in the seventh round by Pancho Villa in New York. A crowd of 40,000 witnessed the drama that so bruised the legendary boxer's ego that he never walked in the ring again. In his thirteen-year boxing career, Wilde fought over four hundred times, lost only a few matches, and was never knocked out. He was nicknamed "The Mighty Atom," and versions of him were swarming in all the rings of America. One of them was Jack Britton (real name William J. Breslin), known as the "Boxing Marvel," for he entered the ring 350 times during his 26-year career. He shared fame with his archrival, Ted "Kid" Lewis (the first to use a protective mouthpiece), whom he fought twenty times in six years. He won the welterweight world title three times. In 1922 at age thirty-seven, still holding the title, he made $150,000. In his entire career he grossed $400,000, which he generously split with his conniving manager, Dan Morgan.

An equal contributor to the sport of boxing was Johnny Dundee (born in Italy as Giuseppe Carrora), who went from a street fighter to an incredible 22-year professional career, during which he fought 341 bouts, making him third in ring history for the number of bouts fought. Easily able to adjust his fighting weight, Dundee fought seven world championships and had the distinction of holding the first world title in the junior lightweight category. At age thirty, he won the featherweight world title from Eugene Criqui (who held it only fifty-five days) after knocking him down four times in fifteen rounds. Dundee was double world champion between 1921 and 1924, in featherweight and lightweight divisions. He fought the lightweights Willie Jackson (eleven times) and Benny Leonard (nine times). The repeated fights for the world junior lightweight title that passed from Dundee to Jack Bernstein made both of them famous. Dundee had his own distinctive style as a clean fighter, famous for his confusing, speedy tip-toe dancing. He was a sharp hitter but not a KO puncher, scoring only some twenty victories that way. He lost only two bouts by knockout. Not a big earner, he was a huge name with an everlasting legacy.

Benny Leonard (born Benjamin Leiner) is another unforgettable Golden Age of Boxing fighter. He defended his world lightweight title fourteen times in the first year alone. In 1921 he made $200,000 and retained his crown after knocking out Richie Mitchell three times in the sixth and final round—but not before he was knocked down in the first round, causing his Jewish mother to dramatically faint. Actually Leonard bet at least $10,000 on himself that he would finish the famous brawler in the first round, and probably his mother knew this. He was a perfectionist, one of the few fighters who were analytical, and he was a master at talking down to his adversaries and thereby disarming them. His fights were carefully orchestrated by promoter Tex Rickard. In July 1922, at his Boyle's Thirty Acres, a crowd of 50,000 paid $330,000 to see "The Ghetto Wizard" defeat the Jewish southpaw (left-handed) Lew Tendler, a slugger at best. Leonard received $121,755; Tedler, $62,500; and Rickard, $90,653.

One year later the rematch was an even bigger financial success. Held this time at Yankee Stadium, tickets to see Leonard win again brought in $452,648. Out of 209 fights, Leonard never lost by KO or by decision, except once—by fouling Jack Britton, who kept his welterweight title in 1922. Leonard held the world title for seven years and seven months, and he retired undefeated at his mother's request in January 1925. He retired after some three hundred fights at the unheard-of age of forty-three, still defeating quality boxers.

However, it was the bantam category that produced boxers that the public couldn't get enough of. The small-framed fighters were relentless, always putting on a great show, especially when the world title was on the line. Beginning in 1920 the title ping-ponged from Pete Herman to Joe Lynch, back to Herman, and then again to Joe Lynch in 1922, when he defeated Johnny Buff, who in his turn defeated Herman. But in 1924, Abe Goldstein took the crown away from Lynch who had previously KO'd him. Nine months later, Eddie "Cannonball" Martin took the title from Goldstein after fifteen grueling rounds, only to pass it to Charley Phil Rosenberg, who kept it until 1927.

There was always non-stop excitement for spectators at these bantam battles. The rematch fights between Pete Herman and Joe Lynch for the world title was consummated in fifteen rounds in New York, with Herman declared the winner by decision. Herman stood only five feet two inches tall and weighed in at 116 pounds, but he twice won the world title, and in London he defeated the famous Jimmy Wilde after seventeen gruesome rounds.

But the shining star of the bantam category was Joe Lynch, the repeat reigning champion of the world, who, at five feet eight inches, seemed too handsome and frail to box. That impression lasted until he entered the ring with such confidence that he immediately garnered respect from rivals and spectators alike. In 1920 alone, he won against Abe Goldstein by KO in eleven rounds and defeated, by decision, Little Jackie Sharkey and Pete Herman in fifteen rounds. The next year Herman regained the title from Lynch, and then it was Johnny Buff's turn (he was the oldest of all of them) for the world crown. Almost blind, Herman retired from the ring in 1922. Meanwhile the title was snapped back by Lynch, who in 1924 lost the title for the second time to Abe Goldstein.

Goldstein was five feet five inches tall; he had left his career as a newspaper writer to become a hell of a fighter, winning against all the major fighters of his time. He lost the crown to Eddie "Cannonball" Martin (Italian-born Edward Vitorio Martino), who lost it to another Jewish contender, Charley Phil Rosenberg. In February 1927 Rosenberg vacated the title, because he was heavier than 118 pounds, and his rival Bushy Graham won the fifteen-round fight by disqualification. Graham (baptized Angelo Geraci) was also five feet five inches tall; he was pitted against the best fighters the bantam category could provide, from the Italian and Jewish champions to black Kid Chocolate, the versatile Irish Tommy Ryan, and the Aryan-looking Joe Lynch.

It was Bud Taylor, "the Blonde Terror of Terre Haute" (two rivals died because of his punches), who took the crown in 1927 and kept it away from underdog Tony Canzoneri. Taylor vacated the title to box in the next category, and Bushy Graham became world champion after defeating "Corporal" Izzy Schwartz at Madison Square Garden in May 1928. Clearly, the bantam division was flooded with talented and determined fighters. It's no wonder the Golden Age of Boxing was also called the Golden Era of the Bantams, starring the Italian and Jewish boxers, who often experienced Irish rioters when their conationalists failed to win.

All these highly ranked combatants would be Joe Grimm's adversaries if he wanted a crack at a title. To get near them, he had to defeat their contenders, challengers, and underdogs, some ten fighters who were already lined up in the same quest. For the moment, local wonder Joe was busy gaining experience by winning big in his corner of the world.

Chapter 11

Opportunity Knocks

Joe ended the year 1923 with five straight victories against ambitious rivals. Things looked bright for him. His name was recognized in the Fall River area, and he felt good walking on the street, being stopped with friendly handshakes, and having his shoulders patted. Everyone seemed confident that Joe was on his way to stardom, and finally his mother accepted that boxing was his ticket to a better life. Indeed, with his prize money the Hashim family moved to a better house and a better neighborhood on Bedford Street. Sister Evelyn was helping her mother with seven-year-old Catherine and five-year-old George. Joe's father found a job in a grocery store, where Mike used to work, and Mike was now a full-time barber in his brother Louis's shop. As for Joe, he was a full-time fighter and a part-time Scout leader. The Christmas and New Year holidays were the time when the Hashims' saying, "An empty hand is a dirty hand," was in a full use, and when gifts were exchanged during nonstop visits from family and friends; the dining room table was constantly full of food prepared by Rafka and her daughters.

Joe was enjoying a rare time out when in the second week of January his trainer called the barbershop and told Mike to have Joe get ready for a fight the next Friday in New Bedford. Joe went immediately to the gym and squeezed four training sessions into the week. The event promoter was matching Joe with Tony Carney of New Bedford, whom he had beaten two months before. Carney also lost the previous two fights but, to his credit, defeated the well-reputed Johnny Dias before that. What Joe knew about Carney was that he was not a heavy hitter and he could easily be intimidated.

But the ring reality was a surprise. Joe faced a rival very different from what he expected. From the opening round, Carney began scoring points with repeated jabs and engaged in close combat, showing his determination to stay on top of the fight. "Do it, Joe!" cheered the Boy Scout troop and the betting spectators. Not wanting to let them down, "Joe shot the right straight out and Carney nearly sat down on the carpet," as described the next day by the boxing reporter of the *Evening Herald*. If not for the bell, he could have finished Carney in the next few seconds.

After two nondescript rounds, Joe took the lead and changed tactics from sporadically trading punches to a solid stance with bent legs wide apart, gloves swinging from belt level, delivering side-to-side powerful punches. Carney went into a clinch and pushed Joe into the ropes with all his might. Joe "swung off in an effort to hit Carney on the way across the ring … he missed his try, and as he shot past Carney, the latter swung a well-directed punch to Joe's chin." The audience went silent. Joe lost his balance and the punch directed him straight to the canvas for "a rather peculiar knockdown" from which "he scrambled to his feet in a jiffy," the same reporter wrote. He continued, "In the fourth and fifth Joe won out by a safe margin," and Carney was bleeding severely, hardly breathing, and fighting in retreat.

It was a gruesome encounter that everyone expected to end any moment with a KO. Referee Ralph Tickle was ready to stop the fight at the slightest sign of Carney losing consciousness, but the Bedford fighter finished each round on his feet and managed to walk to his corner. "What's going on?" asked Mike, nervous about his bet on his brother's KO victory. "You outpunched yourself," explained Coach Tickle. "Steal time and rest in the next round, and then floor him!"

To the audience's delight, Joe began faking powerful punches that scared Carney into fast retreats. Contrary to previous rounds, when Joe would go for a chase, this time he waited for Carney to move toward him, and "he had Carney beaten to the punch with every start." However, at the end of the sixth round, Joe couldn't open one eye and his right ear was burning with pain. For the life of him, he could not remember how it happened; the spectators didn't know either, nor did the referee. Tickle pulled his silver dollar from the ice bucket and pressed it against the swollen eye, and Mike covered the red ear with an ice pack. "Two more rounds to go, Joe!" announced his coach. "He's finished!" stated Mike. But again, Carney survived another two brutal rounds when Joe's efficient right cross and left half hook worked over and over, only staggering the other who exceeded all survival expectations. With his last drop of energy, Joe brought the fighting to a rousing close, with spectators on their toes. Yet, Referee Tickle raised the arm of Carney as the two Portuguese judges awarded the split decision to the fighter now on the verge of collapsing. Long, protesting shouts went on until the next bout started.

The next day, the New Bedford newspaper printed with capital bold letters, "Carney Has Slight Edge on Joe Grimm." The edge was that he refused to be dropped on the canvas. The Fall River paper concluded that "the boys supplied plenty of action and despite the fact Carney won the verdict handily, Joe gave one of the best exhibitions of his career against a formidable opponent and his work was appreciated." It was clear to everyone that Joe lost by a stolen decision. That night before he fell asleep, he once again acknowledged to himself that if he'd won by a KO, no one could argue whom the winner was.

As Tickle reviewed the fight, he realized that Joe had scored his last knockout exactly one year before. Something obviously wasn't right. Moreover, since they were expecting tougher matches with better and more experienced fighters, who were therefore less vulnerable to KO punches, it was clear that Joe had to step up and improve his ring skills and punching power. No doubt about it: there was no substitute for hard training. It was time to go back to basics and polish each aspect of Joe's fighting ability and correct mistakes that had been made in the past. A two-month training period with four sessions a week was agreed upon, even by brother Mike, in spite of the fact that Joe's being out of the ring meant no bets and no money. The good news was that since the National Boxing Association set the minimum age at eighteen for a professional fighter, Joe could apply without lying about his age. He did and received his license.

Joe was eager to put in extra work to perfect his moves, including relearning to hide his chin in his left shoulder. A major focus was improving endurance. By increasing running distance and the number of repetitions, Joe steadily built more stamina. Coordination was one of his strengths; Joe polished this by practicing hitting combinations, body moves, blocking incoming blows, and slipping through punches. The speed bag never sounded faster and better. Joe practiced his hitting power with heavier gloves, aiming for increased speed and strength at the end of the last thirty seconds of each round. He perfected his best shots of right cross and left half hook against the heavy bag and sparring partners, always heavier and taller than he was. Calisthenics, shadowboxing, lifting weights, and punching by holding elastic cords completed the training. He was often described as fighting like Dempsey, but Joe's style was more like Harry Greb's swarming, minus dirty tricks to harm the rival.

Vainly Mike and Joe begged the promoters for a meet with Tony Mandela of Worchester, who had fought at the Casino before Christmas and made a favorable impression on the public. The *Evening Herald* described him as "the greatest attraction ever billed under a main bout and was given the best reception ever tendered a new comer in his first appearance by a local crowd." Joe saw him in the ring and during training, and believed he was "ready to take on Mandela at 118 pounds for any number of rounds," publicized the same paper about Joe's open challenge. Bobby Tickle was described as "Grimm's mentor" who vouched for the fighting capabilities of the "fast improving East Ender" of Fall River.

Bobby Tickle was indeed a good trainer and manager, but he had obvious limitations. So Mike offered to play the role of promoter, even though he knew no one from the elite boxing circles who could advance his brother's career. In frustration, Joe and Mike went to New Hampshire, trying to get fight dates with Joe Corelli, Johnny Harko, and Johnny Fox of Boston, or any other good bantams and featherweights. The inexperienced and confrontational Mike showed little tact and diplomacy, and by playing a big-shot negotiator, he turned everyone off with unrealistic demands and an air of superiority. For the time being, one thing was very clear: for Joe to improve his boxing record and "go places," Joe had to fight outside of Massachusetts, and not with the same local opponents with whom he was repeatedly being matched.

Many of Joe's fellow local boxers had good promoters who made that happen for them. On March 17, Chicks Suggs of New Bedford defeated the title challenger Johnny Curtin of New Jersey by a TKO in the seventh round. The black boxer duplicated Carl Tremaine, who also knocked out Irish Curtin in the sixth round at the Madison Square Garden a year before. Charlie Doessereck, who was Curtin's manager and promoter, was afraid that his aging star was washed out. Then he remembered Joe Grimm. Considering him a possible replacement, Doessereck took a trip to Fall River to witness the third "to talk about" fight between Grimm and John Dias, both eager to settle an old score. It just happened that the *Herald News* promoted the fight by showing Joe's picture in fighting stance, with black punching bag gloves and black trunks, sporting a close-cropped hairstyle, the photo captioned "Smiling Joe Grim[m]," and a boxing note announcing the fight with rising local star Dias:

> Smiling Joe Grim[m], who made a hit with all of us, will furnish us with more fireworks. Joe has heard about our new set of boxers and is very anxious to try them out, so …
> Joe is fighting Young Dias 10 rounds on the 11th at the Fall River. This will be worth seeing. Dias is licking them all.

The news about important New York and New Jersey promoter Doessereck being in the audience reached Joe in the dressing room. Since Joe was heading the card at the Casino, his fight was the last, and he diligently warmed up for it. Mike, agitated, could not stop moving around, saying, "You cannot lose again. This is the fight that will make or break you!" He lit one cigarette after another. "If you beat Dias, you're practically number two after Chick Suggs in all of Massachusetts and New England." Joe nodded while silent Tickle was wrapping his hands with gauze.

"Imagine, brother, this big man came especially for you! It was my letter that did it! Your next fight can be in Madison Square Garden!" Glancing at Tickle, Mike immediately realized the blunder he had made. He quickly added, "Of course, Mr. Tickle, you can still be his coach. No one can train Joe better than you."

But Tickle showed no hard feelings and calmly responded, "Joe should do what's best for him. Once I was in his shoes. Ready?" He slapped Joe's back, signaling him to stand up while Referee McDonald and Dias's trainer walked in the room to check the wrappings and the gloves. The door remained open, and a wave of noise and smoke from the arena entered the small room.

It was three months since Joe had been in the ring, and his appearance induced a hurricane of welcoming shouts and whistles, interrupted by "Our Joe strikes again!" shouted over and over by the noisy Scout troop. Joe stepped in the middle of the ring and lifted his arms with a large winning smile, making hundreds of cheering spectators stand up and lift their arms as well. Doessereck was impressed by the welcome, which confirmed his feeling that Joe was championship material. Dias also stepped in the ring, attracting many ovations from his New Bedford fans. After the announcer introduced the fighters, McDonald gave the instructions and the two restless boys, who could not look in a better shape, stepped to their corners and waited for the bell. "This is your ticket to Madison Square Garden. Go for it!" Mike firmly whispered as the strike of the bell opened the first round.

The ringside reporter of the Fall River *Herald* wrote the next day that "Grimm took the first round by storm, slamming Johnny to all corners of the ring, with a series of two handed attacks." Dias somehow recovered his composure and kept Joe at distance with long and sharp jabs, like he had done before so efficiently. But this time he was counterpunched brutally, and blood began trickling out of his mouth. Until the end of the round, Dias was pounded with stiff shots over and over, forcing him to move backward across the ring. Only the bell saved Dias from a KO. Joe's fans were on their feet, screaming, "Go for KO!" Looking around, Doessereck liked what he saw and smiled.

During the break Joe was sloshed with icy water by his overzealous brother, and Tickle told Joe he was doing great. Dias's cornerman tried unsuccessfully to stop the bleeding, while his couch was shouting something in his ear. Whatever instructions he received, Dias made good use of them. As Joe launched a new attack, Dias used his rapid footwork, forcing Joe to punch the air while enabling his rival to land well-placed blows. At one time Dias counterattacked in full force, and Joe had trouble escaping punishment. It looked like Dias had recovered and maybe even had taken the lead. At least that's what his fans wanted to believe.

But from the third round on, Joe relentlessly struck Dias's body and head with both fists, to the delight of the Boy Scouts and Fall River spectators. Round after round, Joe proved himself to be the master of the ring, showing an excellent command of his actions and inexhaustible stamina. Dias fought bravely, and once in a while, when he lashed with his left and right swings, his signature punches, his fans screamed with happiness. He moved a lot but could not avoid a serious battering that made him stagger; still, he remained on his feet. As for Joe, he "continued to pummel him in the close sessions."

In round eight Joe decided to finish off his traditional rival who had tainted his boxing record with two defeats. He unleashed one attack after another, forcing Dias to run around the ring and be stopped by Referee McDonald. Obviously, he was doing everything he could to escape a KO. He was not a coward and continued to counterattack, but Joe's landings came from all angles and directions and were too painful and risky to absorb. The reporter ended his coverage with "It was a snappy fight and well applauded by the fans. Dias was outpointed and outpunched by the little Syrian mittster, but both boys were deserving the credit for their showing." The sports page was headlined with the largest and thickest capital letters, "Joe Grimm Beats Dias." With his arm raised high by the referee, Joe enjoyed the crowd that could not stop its ovations as he proudly left the arena.

With a long tan coat draped over his left arm and a brown fedora in hand, Charlie Doessereck lost no time in entering the dressing room, where he congratulated Joe and Tickle, telling the coach he remembered his competitive boxing years. Mike was out to collect his bets. After small talk, Doessereck went straight to the reason for his visit.

"So, Tickle, what do you think of this hot shot kid?"

"I think he's on his way up and I may lose him!" The coach smiled.

"I think you're absolutely correct." The well-dressed man heartily laughed. He continued, "Young man, I'm going to apply for your New York and New Jersey license. As soon as I have them, you move to my stable in Bayonne and meet the rest of my boys. Bring anything you need for a long stay. By the way, Tickle, does he, or do I, owe you anything?"

"Absolutely nothing, sir."

"Then, kid, here's my card with my address, and $100 for you to come to Bayonne by boat. What's your telephone number?" He handed a fountain pen to the coach, who wrote down his home number and the number at the barbershop.

Taking the paper with the phone numbers, Doessereck waved it in front of Joe's eyes. "Do we have a deal, kid?" The young boxer looked at his coach, who nodded. With a relieved smile, Joe nodded as well. "I sure have a deal!" Doessereck shook Joe's hand. "Keep up with the good fights!" Then he turned to the coach, shook his hand, and said, "You're a good man, Tickle. If you ever want to relocate, let me know. I can sure use you!"

The promoter put on his hat. He pulled a white scarf from his coat sleeve, and Joe and Tickle helped him put on the long camel-hair coat. The folded newspaper with Joe's picture was sticking out of one large pocket. In the other pocket there was another newspaper with a prediction underneath: "Meets Johnny Dias in Semi-Final on Friday Night—Is Favored to Win." With one swing, Doessereck wrapped the silky scarf around his neck and left the room, pleased about the easiest negotiation he'd ever had.

While Joe finished dressing and Tickle went out to get the envelope money, Mike stormed into the room, all in sweat. "He come yet?"

"Mr. Doessereck already left," explained Joe.

"He left? Without talking to me?" shouted Mike. "What did he say?"

"We have a deal." Joe showed his brother the two bills of $50. "When he calls me on the phone, I'll move to his stable in Bayonne."

"Did Tickle negotiate for you?"

"No need for that."

"Where is Doessereck?" Mike ran out the door, but then he came right back. "That damned promoter got in a car and already left."

Tickle walked in with the money envelope, and Mike put it in his pocket. "Coach, do you know what's going on with my brother? Don't we need to know more about this Doessereck character? Ask him questions or put something in writing? After all, he's from New Jersey!"

Tickle smiled. "I wish he was my promoter when I needed one. Don't bother, Mike, he knows his stuff and Joe is in good hands."

"I have a problem with the entire situation," mumbled Mike as he nervously lit a cigarette.

Joe and Mike little knew what was going on in the boxing world, when the ever-volcanic bantam category erupted again into chaos on March 21, 1924. On that day title challenger Abe Goldstein defeated world champion Joe Lynch in a fifteen-round decision at Madison Square Garden. The event marked the end of Lynch's long reign and opened the path for many contenders with stellar records, such as Eddie "Cannonball" Martin, Charley Phil Rosenberg, Bushy Graham, Pete Herman, "Midget" Smith, Bud Taylor, and other challengers who were waiting next in line. Among other lower-ranked candidates to the title were the reputable Kid Chocolate, Tony Canzoneri, Battling Battalino, Frankie Genaro, Young Montreal, and Pete Zivic, to name a few. Countless others who established a good reputation in the ring, like Spencer Garden, Irving Shapiro, Johnny Vestry, and the local Massachusetts celebrity, Chick Suggs, battled their way to become top names on the endless list of bantam hopefuls who never made the history books. For Doessereck, having the promising Joe Grimm in his stable where he could groom him was a smart move that could pay big in a few years. Grimm had already proven himself to be a durable fighter; he would now be well positioned to climb the thorny ladder of challengers.

The extraordinary news about Joe leaving Fall River spread like wildfire, and suddenly Joe was the talk of the town, especially after the *Herald News*

printed the headline in bold letters: "Joe Grimm Will Box in New York." Mike explained to everyone who walked in the barbershop that for sure he would go to Bayonne to protect Joe's interests. The boys' parents were speechless: two sons who were the primary breadwinners were going to leave the house and move to a different state, so Joe could take a more severe beating? It didn't make sense, and Rafka began crying again.

If this wasn't enough turmoil for the family, more upheaval was to come. Mike and Joe's sister Emma and her husband, Louis Massery, had a shocking proposal: the entire family should move to Pittsfield, on the other side of Massachusetts, where Louis had his business and the couple lived. The reason was more money and more security, as Louis explained. It just happened that one of the largest grocery shops in Pittsfield was poorly run by another Lebanese family who owed too much money to Louis's White Star Supply Company. The street corner shop also had a spacious apartment above it that came with the commercial lease. It would make a perfect home for the Hashims, who already knew the grocery trade, Mike agreed. Business-astute Louis made a good case and convinced his in-laws that the family could not only take over the shop, but, when they paid off the old debt, they could end up owning the entire brick building that also had a narrow clapboard house attached to it. Louis took Mike and his parents to see "the real deal," and all returned in total agreement. As Mike said, it was "a once-in-a-lifetime opportunity—we can't pass it up!"

For the time being, though, the Hashims would stay in Fall River, with Mike working in his brother's barbershop. Joe kept training with Coach Tickle as he waited to the phone call from Doessereck. His future depended on Doessereck's getting him the boxing licenses.

Chapter 12

Farewell, Fall River— Hello, Bayonne

Encouraged by the prospect of fighting in New York and New Jersey, Joe felt good seeing how many people rooted for him. Meanwhile, the Fall River *Herald* used bold capital letters to announce "Joe Grimm Heads Cards at Union A.C. Show Tonight" in a news item about the "All-Star show" featuring "boxers who have proven their ability." On that Monday evening of April 28, 1924, Joe's opponent was again Tony Carney, who still believed that he could beat "the hero" in another ten-round bout. As soon as Joe paraded into the arena and into the ring as the star of the event, spectators gave him a standing ovation, screaming "Our Joe!" over and over.

Under these circumstances, Carney lost the fight before beginning it. Until the end of the eight rounds, Joe kept chasing his rival, shaking Carney's body and head with both gloves, to the delight of the spectators. Nevertheless, Carney was experienced enough not to let Joe do his fight unimpeded and took advantage of any opportunity he could find to score. Joe won by a large margin and settled the grudge score with stubborn Carney once and for all. When Mike saw that the envelope held $65, a record payment, he kissed the money and exclaimed, "Headlines pay goooood!"

In the second week of May, Joe met another opponent, believed to be a much better and stronger fighter, for a ten-round bout—Johnny Fox from Boston. In the dressing room, Tickle gave Joe advice: "The most important thing for you is not to get hurt before leaving for Bayonne. Don't take a risk. Getting a KO isn't important. Just win the fight."

Joe entered the ring with his usual confident smile and shadowboxed toward his fans, who were already screaming for a KO. Johnny Fox, who was a featherweight, looked to be in better shape because he was four pounds heavier and put up a good fight in the first round. But "Grimm nearly doubled Fox up in a knot in a second round when he shot a left hook to the Bostonian's midriff," wrote the ring reporter in the next-day's paper. That was the beginning of the end for Fox, whose liver pain lasted for the next seven rounds. In the last round, with nothing to lose, "Fox started at a slambang pace but Grimm was ready for him and the belated spurt was cut short with a series of two-handed exchanges with the Fall River boy on top in the scoring." Arms up, flexing his biceps, Joe smiled as he victoriously circled the ring to prolonged ovations. In the dressing room he received another ovation from Mike, who counted $70 in the envelope.

When another ten-rounder was scheduled at the end of May, against John O'Donnell, Joe was ready for it and dedicated to what might be his last local fight and victory to his loyal Fall River fans. After that he kept training, but Tickle refused to let him box in the ring. The coach's main concern was to deliver Joe in one piece to Doessereck. Right before the Fourth of July, he received a telephone call from Doessereck, who had obtained Joe's boxing licenses and invited him to come to Bayonne as soon as possible.

The Hashim family met to decide what to do. Mike clearly stated, "I'll go with Joe where we can make a fortune. If not, we can always come back and work in the barbershop or in the grocery store!" The lure of a fortune made a lot of sense to the money-strapped family.

The newspaper reporter who covered Joe's departure from Fall River credited his popularity "mainly to his cleanliness in the ring. He is a young gentleman and will never take unfair advantage of an opponent ... Win or lose Joe has always given action and has proven a formidable foe. His host of admirers are looking forward to hear favorably from the local youngster in the near future." A new set of leather luggage was presented to Joe by the same fans who also threw a party in his honor. The following day's Fall River *Herald* sports story was headlined, "Grimm to Join Doeserick [*sic*] Stable," with the subtitle, "Popular Local Bantam left Saturday Night for New York Where He Expects to Achieve New Fame."

Joe and Mike arrived in Bayonne by traveling first class on an overnight passenger ship. They found Doessereck's house at number 39 East, around the corner of Thirty-First Street. After walking the ten stairs to the front door of the white three-story building, Mike pressed the white button of the electric bell. They had no idea that Doessereck was also an immigrant, his family having come from Germany in 1888 when he was only one year old. He went to school and then worked as a barber and bakery salesman in Manhattan, where he also tried boxing, only to decide that managing fighters was better for him than fighting in the ring. At age seventeen he married Catherine Reihl, who was a couple years older than he was, and they immediately had two sons who eventually worked in the shipyard after the family moved to Bayonne in 1920.

A well-dressed woman answered the door. Without waiting for the boys to say anything, she turned and shouted, "Chas, is for you!" and disappeared. Seconds later, Doessereck, also dressed in his Sunday best, approached the door with a large smile and arms outstretched, greeting Joe with a glad handshake. "Hey, kid, welcome to my stable. Come in. You too, come in," he added, looking at Mike. "Let me show you around. You already met my wife, Cathy, who is going to cook for you, and here is the dining room where my boys like you eat. Next to it is the kitchen and a bathroom."

He showed one room after another and headed upstairs. "No girls and no parties in this house, and no smoking, because my wife is allergic to it! Lights are off at 10:00 p.m. because we're in training, which is at 10:00 a.m. and 5:00 p.m. I run a tight ship!" Doessereck firmly and proudly announced.

"We need another bed," said Mike, who already didn't like the nonsmoking policy.

"Who are you?"

"I'm Mike, his older brother, the one who sent you the envelope with the newspaper clippings!"

"Why are you staying?"

"Because he needs me to win. I'm his cornerman and personal manager. Where he stays, I stay!" Puzzled, Doessereck collected himself and said, "Then I needed to charge him double and deduct it from his purse." The brothers exchanged a look, and the promoter understood their thinking. Then like any tactful businessman, he asked the boys to make themselves comfortable and be downstairs in one hour, because he would take them out for lunch.

An hour later, they walked inside a Bavarian restaurant on the corner of Broadway. After small talk, Doessereck unbuttoned his coat, crossed one leg over the other, and raised his glass with water for an appropriate toast. "Here's to you, kid, and to many wins to come!" The promoter put his elbows on the table and, leaning forward toward Joe, explained what he believed to be a very important fact about professional boxing. "See, young man, you can be the best in the world, but if you're in the wrong place, then no one will ever know about you. You can be butchered in the ring and have your brains smashed for $20 or for $200,000. That's why you need me, to put you in the right ring. Not too long ago, I gave Gene Tunney his first professional start in boxing, and I was right on the money."

Retaining the key word "money," Mike crossed his legs in the same manner and, blowing a cloud of smoke, interrupted. "What about a contract?"

"Yes, we'll have one—a New Jersey contract—a handshake!" the promoter firmly stated. He did not like Mike and decided to put his airs to rest by accentuating each word. "For now, we're in a trial period. You can fire me or I can fire you for no reason!" Doessereck leaned back in his chair. His penetrating eyes slowly went from one brother to the other. Softly and slowly, he spoke his favorite motto. "There are no guarantees in life. Especially in boxing. Remember that!"

The hungry boys turned their eyes from the promoter to the food, and wolfed the meal without saying a word. When they returned to their room, two smaller beds were in place. The Hashim brothers were exhausted and fell asleep quickly. In his bedroom Doessereck looked at his wife and said with a deep sigh, "I hope I didn't make a mistake with Joe …"

In fact, Joe could not have arrived at a better time. When Doessereck had come to see his fight with Dias back in April, the promoter was facing a crisis that shook his status in the Bayonne area. On May 17, the *Bayonne Times* had published a letter from Doessereck that began, "The invasion of Staten Island pugilists, aided and abetted by 'Hen' Connolly, the great matchmaker of the local boxing club, to eliminate once and for all boxers that live and make their home in Bayonne, seems to have gone on the rocks." Allegedly, Connolly intended to bring superior boxers who were going to knock out Doessereck's fighters, like Willie Shaw and Billy Vidabeck. Connelly primarily wished "to get rid of the local boys by overmatching them … and eliminate them from getting engagements in his club."

Three days later, Connolly answered with a brief letter in the same newspaper, underlining, "Let the boxing fans who know me and those who know Doessereck's reputation, judge for themselves just how much weight they give to his letter." A tug of war between the two matchmakers and promoters was in full blow, and Doessereck was determined to win. One of his smart moves was to show that he was also open to bringing outside boxers to Bayonne, and Joe Grimm was to be a great addition to his stable. Except for one thing Doessereck hadn't anticipated: Grimm came with a personal and interfering manager.

Monday morning during a breakfast of potato pancakes and blood sausage, the brothers met four other rooming boxers, and together they walked to the nearby gym, inside the Knights of Columbus building, also located on Avenue C. Joe spotted some fifteen boxers of different categories training in the large gymnasium, which reminded him of the basketball court in the Fall River YMCA but with some differences. For one, while in the ring, each sparring partner had cushioned leather headgear, a rubbery mouthpiece, and a groin aluminum cup strapped over his trunks. Nick, the old coach, instantly liked well-mannered and dutiful Joe, who all of a sudden was in the company of challengers and contenders for the American and world titles. In turn, their eyes focused on Joe's large, heavy fists, and the coach couldn't help himself, saying, "Those are some sledgehammers you got, son!"

Joe immediately recognized featherweight Johnny Curtin, the idol of New Jersey and the pride of Doessereck's stable. Eight years older and three inches shorter than Joe, the Irish-looking Curtin was trying to recover from the five losses he had suffered since the beginning of the year 1924. These included a devastating KO in the seventh round inflicted by Chicks Suggs of New Bedford. A few years before, he had fought Abe Friedman five times and won twice. To his credit, Curtin scored a clear victory by points against Bushy Graham, the future bantamweight champion of the world. There, too, was the Slavic-looking Johnny Kochansky, three inches shorter than Joe and always dressed in black with his hair parted in the middle, who likewise coveted the bantam and featherweight division. In the entire year of 1923, he lost only once—to Harry Felix at Madison Square Garden, after having beaten him up two months before. So far this year Kochansky had many wins, four by KO, and he aimed to defeat Petey Mack of Jersey City and eventually challenge the champion title. The next best hopeful in Doessereck's stable was the good-looking light-heavyweight Billy Vidabeck (William Veydovec) who in the last two years had scored sixteen wins (six by KO) and suffered only one defeat. Not yet a contender for the title, he was featured in *Boxing Blade* magazine's April 26 issue. Two years later he would score a draw with Jimmy Braddock, the future heavyweight champion of the world.

There were other notable stablemates in the gym, as well. The bottom line was that, excepting Kochansky, who was two years older than Joe, Doessereck's fighters were either aging or not yet ready to become contenders. An infusion of new blood was desperately needed in the stable, now under attack from Hen Connolly, who obviously knew the situation. Little aware of the entire situation, Joe now landed like a wedge between rivals Curtin and Kochansky. Doessereck loved it, knowing that all three of them would work hard to stay ahead in the game.

Like in Fall River, Joe trained with full commitment. Coach Nick agreed that Joe was an inside puncher and definitely a stationary flat-foot boxer with bent knees and arched body. It was better than standing erect, which would have made him a much larger target to be hit. Joe's natural hitting ability was amazingly good, Nick agreed with Doessereck.

The brothers settled in, with Mike continuing to look for a job and Joe for a rival.

✧✦

Joe did not have to wait long. Doessereck used him as a substitute to fight Julio Abassilia, a Philippine bantam who wished to follow in the tracks of his illustrious conationalist Pancho Villa, the American and world flyweight champion. In fact, Abassilia, who now was the champion of his country, used to spar with Villa, so he was an experienced fighter. On Monday, July 21, one week after he set foot in Bayonne and four workouts later, Joe went for a weigh-in at 3:00 p.m. and met his Asian rival, a pleasant-looking taller guy, who was desperately determined to build up his winning record. They met again the next day at the Oakland Arena in Jersey City before going to the dressing rooms. Mike was strapped for money but ready to place his bets. He asked his brother about the chances of putting the Asian guy down. "I have to do it, don't I?" Joe smiled. "Say no more!" Mike sighed in relief, rushing to the bookie.

Coach Nick went with Joe to the dressing room to wrap his hands and help put the gloves on, another novelty for Joe: these black gloves were

104

more like mittens, weighing only six ounces, much smaller and lighter than the fighting gloves used in Fall River. His puzzlement was interrupted by Doessereck, who rushed in with a beautiful red package tied with a yellow bow. "This is a good luck gift from me and Mrs. Doessereck. Open it!" Joe pulled the flowery wrapping paper off and held up the most beautiful boxing robe he had ever seen. It was made of burgundy satin, with a gold-trimmed hood and sleeves, gold sash, and most importantly, large gold letters were stitched in an arch on the back, "Joe Grimm." Visibly impressed, Joe said, "Thank you, sir!" and gratefully smiled at his promoter. "Put it on, it's yours!" Doessereck took the white towel off Joe's shoulders, and Joe slipped on the shiny robe.

Mike returned with the spit bucket, a container with ice and water bottles in it, and another novelty, a large yellow sponge to wash the face. He asked Joe to turn around a few times and laughed. "Now that everyone knows your name, you better win!" Joe's fight was the opener for headliners Joey Kaufmann of Brooklyn and Joe Cole of New Jersey, both bantams and potential opponents. More than five thousand people, most of the men wearing white panama hats, overpacked the open arena to see the event, bringing in $6,500 in ticket sales, while hundreds of others were turned away. Another opener was provided by Irish Johnny Curtin and Pete Mack. Considering everything, Joe knew for sure that he was in the right place to fight.

Joe's appearance in his beautiful burgundy gown raised many eyebrows. He brushed his feet in a rectangular box filled with resin powder, another novelty for him. Joe refused to have a mouthpiece and wear the aluminum groin cup under his white trunks. He watched how the smiling Filipino guy toured the ring to collect applause and cheers, and soon the announcer walked into the ring. "Shall I take the gown off?" Joe wondered. "Keep it on. It's good publicity!" encouraged Coach Nick.

When the announcer introduced Joe as "the unbeatable New England youngster with twenty-four knockouts in a row," the public was puzzled, mostly believing it was a gimmick; yet some whistled and screamed, half amused. Referee Joe Jeanette was a large black man, another novelty, since Joe had never seen a black referee before. He checked the gloves, gave the instructions, and the boys went to their corners. This was Joe's first international fight, and he didn't quite know what to expect. Toward the end of the first round he found a large opening to the midsection, and he rapidly fired a couple of stiff punches that shook the Asian guy's body off his feet. Noticing the tough warning delivered by determined-looking

Joe Grimm, the formerly lethargic public jumped with expectation. But experienced Abassilia quickly got the message and began to move away from his assailant, now in full attack. When the round ended, he walked tall and confident to his corner. Splashed by Mike with icy water from the sponge, and massaged by Coach Nick, Joe refused to sit, which attracted another murmur of approval from the audience. In the crowd, Doessereck noticed everything, and he liked it.

The second and third rounds showed plenty of struggle as each boy tried to take the lead and impose his own way of fighting. They kept moving back and forth, as if pulled by an invisible string, throwing punches to mark their brief successful attacks. Abassilia began to wave his longer arms in front of Joe's eyes, sending annoying and confusing "kangaroo punches" that were unsanctioned by the referee. "How good is he?" asked Joe during the break, still refusing to sit down. "Why don't you try his chin?" answered Nick. "Just put him down!" mumbled Mike. In the fourth round, Joe did just that, battering holes in defense and sending sharp blows to the chin. It turned out that Abassilia was an extremely flexible fighter who went with the blow, absorbing only a fraction of its severity while continuing to wave his arms. To Joe it was like fighting an octopus.

In the same chivalrous spirit Joe carried the next round with Referee Jeanette hardly touching the boxers, each waiting for the other to show fatigue and slow down. To the delight of the spectators this didn't happen, and the sixth round had the two ambitious bantams fighting toe-to-toe just like in the first round. Fearing that the fight might go either way, Joe intensified his attacks and kept ramming Abassilia against the ropes. And there it was, that split second after the Filipino dropped his guard to protect his liver, when Joe drove a powerful left hook and a straight right to the jaw, after which he stepped back to let his rival drop onto the canvas.

A thousand loud sighs from the audience went with the fall. Joe rushed to the neutral corner, while the kneeling heavy referee began counting, hitting the floor with his right palm at each second. Abassilia slowly rolled from his back onto his fours, and holding onto the ropes, he got up when the bell rang. He never fully recovered from that punch and bravely lasted two more rounds, after which he collapsed in his corner. The audience was on its feet cheering Joe, who smiled broadly as he pumped his arms. From nowhere, Doessereck appeared in the corner and, holding the fancy gown for Joe to put it on, said, "Kid, this one is for the record!" Together they went to the dressing room.

While Joe took a shower, Mike and Doessereck rubbed their hands with visible delight and reviewed the excellent show Joe had put on in his debut. The arena promoter entered with money envelopes and handed them to Doessereck, who in turn handed one to Coach Nick. Mike hesitated for a few seconds and said, "I usually collect for my brother."

"There's nothing for him to collect. As a matter of fact, Joe still owes me $54!"

"What? How do you figure that?" Mike was stunned.

"Travel, boarding, and training expenses. No charge for the robe, though."

"So, how much money did he make tonight?"

"One hundred fifty dollars."

The brothers exchanged a knowing look. Mike lit a cigarette and looked straight into Doessereck's eyes. "Expect some changes in your math." He walked out of the room and learned that the arena owner grossed $5,500. Doessereck told Joe that his next engagement was already lined up in two weeks, shook his hand, and left with Coach Nick.

❧❦

Joe got dressed and returned to the arena to watch Irish Curtin scoring a draw against Petey Mack (who was knocked down once) after a gruesome twelve-round fight. Joe believed he could win against either of them. To his surprise, after the event was over, Referee Jeanette spotted Joe and offered to give him a ride home. A former truck driver and true car connoisseur, he owned the newest Cadillac, with four large chromed headlights framing the radiator, that made people turn their heads. Throughout the ride, he asked Joe about himself and concluded, "You, man, is blessed with a hell o' punch and talent to use it!" He handed Joe his card. "Stop by ma' gym zom'timez and le'z talk ... Okay?"

As Joe got out of the beautiful custom-made Cadillac, Doessereck pulled his vintage Ford into the driveway and froze as he saw Jeanette smiling and shaking hands with his fighter. "What does he want?" the promoter asked as he unlocked the house front door. "He asked me to stop by his gym and talk." Doessereck quietly gulped. "Where's your brother?" Joe shrugged his shoulders.

What Joe didn't know was that Mike, like the good personal manger he was, had gone to send a telegram to the Fall River *Daily Globe* to announce the excellent news. The next day, an article ran in the paper, headlined with capital bold letters: "Joe Grim[m] Wins Big Bout at N.Y." The story described how "the Fall River boy floored the little brown brother for the count … and received a big ovation from thousands of fans who packed the park." As had happened often before, the writer spelled Grimm sometimes with one "m." He continued, "Grimm's showing in his first bout in the metropolis brought him great praise … and the local boy is due to make a name for himself in his new surroundings." The reporter assumed that "Doessereck is planning to send him against some of the best boys at his weight in the Metropolitan district … because the Fall River boy has the makings of a star." In the meantime, Joe couldn't wait to tell his brother the entire incident with Jeanette and Doessereck. Mike rubbed his hands and grinned. "Didn't I tell you that we're in big demand?"

CHAPTER 13

AMONG THE BEST

Doessereck had a good reason for experiencing a near heart attack when Joe got out of the elegant Cadillac driven by Jeanette. The black referee owned a very popular boxing gym, in which many past and future world champions seemed to train. Just mentioning some of the famous names would be reason enough for Jeanette to convince the youngster and his brother to join his stable. In the small area around Bayonne there were many good managers and promoters, all star makers, such as Frankie Churchill, who managed world champion Pancho Villa, and now Mike Ballerino, the promising featherweight and junior lightweight who lived in Bayonne. The "Italian Bull of Bayonne" had the distinction of fighting Pancho Villa nine times in two years, some of the fights having fifteen or twenty rounds. There was also the overly aggressive Leo Diamond, who managed bantam world champion Johnny Buff, and the equally overly argumentative promoter Joe Gould, who would manage Jimmy Braddock, the future heavyweight world title holder. Jimmy Brienza of Newark switched from practicing law to managing good boxers, like "Spark Plug" Russell and Johnny Dixon, and bragged about his recent acquisition, Joe De Phillipo. Now there was also newly arrived Hen Connolly, full of ambition and aiming to prove that Doessereck was over the hill, even if he was still in charge of the Bayonne Athletic Association.

Of all of these, the most competitive, and second only to the legendary manager and promoter Tex Rickard, was Leo Flynn, a former unsuccessful amateur boxer turned successful professional dancer. He lived in New York City and understood show business, whose lessons he applied to boxing.

One of these was "If you don't appear in public, you disappear." Another was "No purse is too small, no opponent too tough." Flynn put his mottos to work, and he was credited with having the largest stable of boxers appearing in rings all over America, regardless of how important the event was. He was Dempsey's manager and the last manager of the aging Jack Renault, the best Canadian heavyweight and Dempsey's best sparring partner. At the present time Flynn had high hopes attached to middleweight Al McCoy and featherweight Billy Marlow. But his money was on the most promising welterweight, Dave Shade, who since 1918 kept winning in the best arenas of the country. Equally inspired was Sammy Goldman, who got a good grip on Tony Canzoneri, who soon would hold the world title in three categories. Numerous other managers and promoters were engaged in complicated competitions to establish their fighters and dominate certain weight categories.

Still, the name Doessereck carried a lot of weight in boxing circles, as he was a matchmaker for Boyle's Thirty Acres, the Jersey City site of the Dempsey–Carpentier heavyweight title bout in 1921. He had his office on Forty-Second Street in New York City, and he managed the nearby Pioneer Athletic Club that housed many boxing events. Quick to take advantage of anything good for him, Doessereck credited himself for two unforgettable matches that took place at his club. One of these was in March 1909, when the legendary ferocious world middleweight champion Stanley Ketchel, nicknamed "The Michigan Assassin," met heavy-hitting Philadelphian Jack O'Brien. The sturdy Irishman mercilessly battered the champion from rope to rope in the first seven rounds, but that soon changed into a slaughter delivered by the proud Polish fighter who knocked O'Brien unconscious for many minutes after the final bell that saved him. There were different boxing rules at the time, and Ketchel was not credited for a KO victory.

But he did get that credit on May 27, 1910, when he fought Willis Lewis, who had just come victorious from a Paris tournament. The crowd was behind Lewis, who lived in Manhattan, and, sure enough, his smashing right punch broke the nose of Ketchel, who found himself covered with blood. He could hardly finish the first round. But in the second, he returned with a killer's revenge and delivered a hurricane of cruel punches that made Lewis spit out two front teeth, and seconds later, he ended up knocked down with his head in the resin box for rubbing feet. The crowd was in shock while their favorite was carried away to the dressing room, where a doctor struggled to open his paralyzed jaws and save his life. The two glorious fights entered the history books and solidly put Doessereck's club on the map. With that, his managerial career took off.

There was no doubt that Doessereck was a true veteran in the boxing industry. He was the successful manager behind heavyweight Alfred "Soldier" Kearns, who began his career in 1909 with fourteen straight KOs. Kearns was considered the white hope of his days, a collective wish that never materialized. Four years later the New York Athletic Commission denied the former world champion Bob Fitzsimons the chance to fight Kearns, who was twenty-four years younger. Fitzsimons sued; he lost the case, but Doessereck made big news because of his trashed contract. As a promoter he made news again when in 1912 he defied the State Athletic Commission's "non-decision" rule and ordered Referee Patsy Haley to award a decision to Jim Steward in a close fight with "Gunboat" Smith at the National Sporting Club he managed. Doessereck was eight years ahead of the "non-decision" abolition, and while the referee lost his license, the shrewd promoter kept his boxing license by insisting that he had run an experiment with the public and officials, as suggested by Commissioner O'Neil.

Ever active in politics, the German-born Doessereck proved his American patriotism by promoting boxing shows as part of the money drive for the United War Work Campaign in 1918. He proved instrumental in the passing of the Walker Law in New York State and of the Hurley Act in New Jersey, advancing the boxing industry to a spectacular and profitable level. He was the matchmaker for the Oakland A.A. and Royal A.A. in Jersey City, as well as Pioneer S.C. (former National Athletic Club) and Irving Club in New York City, along with Thompson's Stadium in Staten Island. As manager and promoter, Doessereck shared the highs and lows of hundreds of boxers who reached fame and fortune or ended up in the gutter of anonymity and of poverty. It taught him to be a quick reader of character and a razor-sharp negotiator who always had something hidden up his sleeve. Reporters consulted him to predict the outcome of the next fights. A piece in the New York *Evening Telegram* on November 14, 1921, noted that "Doessereck is a mighty good judge of boxers," and indeed, he spotted the unknown Gene Tunney and booked him to fight a ten-round bout at the Pioneer Sporting Club in 1918. It had been a lucky break for the future world heavyweight champion.

Famous promoter Tex Rickard often used Doessereck as matchmaker for Madison Square Garden, and he even trusted him with the opening bouts of the Fight of the Century between Dempsey and Carpentier at Boyle's Thirty Acres. Once again, Tunney owed his first major public exposure to Doessereck, who booked him for the opening fight before that most memorable event. In fact, the grateful champion was still consulting Doessereck on boxing matters. Succinctly put, Doessereck saw and knew everything about professional boxing, and to outwit him one had to wake up very early in the morning.

Doessereck's managerial position with the Pioneer Sporting Club proved to be one of the most lasting jobs in the boxing industry. With 3,500 seats, the boxing arena, located at East Twenty-Fourth Street, was a perfect size for non-title bouts. Some of them proved famous, as that on New Year's Day 1922, when Doessereck matched the former world bantamweight champion Joe Lynch against challenger Al Walker. The event also included a match between his own boy Willie Shaw and Johnny Darcy, who eventually would become his client.

Doessereck also had the merit to discover and manage the black flyweight Panama Al Brown (born Alfonso Teofilo Brown), who turned pro in 1922. At five feet eleven inches, he was unusually tall and skinny for his category. He had a devastating punching reach of seventy-six inches that proved merciless, and he kept winning by KOs until he scored a draw with Johnny Breslin. It was more like a victory for Panama, now an established underdog who quickly moved to Manhattan. Then his career made a spectacular leap to Paris, where he became famous for his boxing wins and for a flamboyant lifestyle. His move to Europe was a big loss for Doessereck, who now hoped to find a replacement in Joe Grimm, an equally good puncher but with an infinitely better temper than the moody black homosexual. However, good-natured Joe depended on his brother's decisions, which made Doessereck nervous and less trustful of the Gentleman Boxer.

Aware of Doessereck's mixed feelings, Joe practiced hard at the gym and noticed an increased respect from his stablemates after winning against the Filipino guy. The training sessions became increasingly hard and more regimented: the morning sessions consisted of practicing "fancy moves" and new tactics repeated with Coach Nick, now helped by an assistant; the evenings were dedicated to sparring and improving physical condition. Joe's arms worked like nonstop fast pistons as he learned about hip and shoulder power. Most importantly, he proved to have amazing recovery capacity. His endurance could extend for more than ten rounds against many sparring partners, the punching bag, or rope skipping. He always ended each workout with his favorite routine—the speed bag. He made it sound like a musical instrument as he changed the rhythm, the power, and the direction of rapid punches. It was clear that Joe was no longer a raw boxer; he was ready to meet increased challenges in the ring.

On that high note, the next Sunday Joe went to weigh in before the August 4 fight and learned, to his surprise, that he would oppose another Filipino guy named Vincent Punji, who was ranked a better boxer than Abassilia. Joe took a quick look at his rival's skinny arms and neck, at his frail hands and chin, at his large oval face, and said in Arabic to his brother, "Whatever money you have, bet on a sure KO, let's say … in the third round …"

"How sure are you?"

"Rock solid!" Joe smiled, pushing aside his concern about the torrid summer weather and the fight taking place in the ballpark of Jersey City.

The next day Joe confidently entered the ring of the same unroofed Oakland arena in which he had last fought. It was filled again with five thousand overheated spectators, the men dressed in light jackets, ties, and panama hats, the women in their best dresses and large colorful hats, all now vividly remembering the burgundy gown with Joe Grimm on the back. "Looking good, Joe!" and "Go for it, Joe!" sounded from all over, and unlike the last time, Joe responded to the cheers in the same way he did in Massachusetts, flexing his arms up and down above his head and grinning. The public loved the little boxer with a pleasant attitude. Joe threw a few shadow punches, and the crowd responded with increased enthusiasm. After the short introduction that described Joe as "still undefeated" and Punji as "most versatile," Referee Jack Masterly recited final instructions and sent them to their corners. Mike helped Joe take off his shiny robe and reminded him, "Not the first, not the second, but the third. Okay?" and the brass bell rang.

The two bantams clashed in the middle of the ring. Joe charged with a terrific flurry of punches that immediately convinced Punji to step back and use body mobility and arm-waving techniques to absorb the blows with the least possible damage. It was clear to Joe that the two Filipino boys had trained together, learning how to cushion the hard blows; Joe felt once again that punching them was like hitting a jellyfish. However, his ducking-and-weaving opponent could snap unexpected and powerful punches that he threw with a slight jump forward. The jump served as a good springboard for an attack and added extra weight to a blow, but to Joe it was a liability in the ring: while up in the air, one was the most vulnerable to be hit. Over and over Joe provoked the Filipino boy to repeat the same mistake, giving him a sense of security while Joe set him up for coming disaster. The crowd was screaming as they saw how Joe never stopped throwing punches and how Punji jumped with stinging counterattacks.

The first round ended as a clean fight during which Referee Masterly circled the ring at his own pace. Back in his corner, Mike swirled the towel into Joe's face and reminded him in Arabic, "Not this round. Okay?" Coach Nick succinctly said, "Take him out when he jumps!" Joe nodded to both and took a sip of the icy water to cool off in the 100-degree heat that scorched the ring in the open arena. The bell sounded again.

When Punji approached, Joe noticed his face was covered with bruises, and bluish bumps were visible on his head. Holding nothing back, Joe engaged in his own fight, but again the battered Filipino struck back during a leap, scoring many points of his own. Waving his arms and twisting like a cat, he succeeded in putting distance between himself and aggressive Joe, who began to throw punches in the air. Punji was a smart fighter who now decided to take the initiative. But his rival was a clear inside fighter who, by bobbing and weaving, sustained nonstop attacks with torrents of hooks and uppercuts that landed hard and were painful on the body. The two bantams were fast and relentless, and they seemed to compete for which one threw more punches, delighting the spectators with the kind of fight they paid to see. Among them was Doessereck, who carefully watched each move Joe made. The bell rang, and Mike reminded Joe again about the third-round KO. Joe drank more icy water that cooled his lungs and soothed his overheated body. He hadn't realized that the hot temperature could bother him so much; he planned to end the fight soon.

The third round began with Joe in crouch position, mounting a windmill attack cherished by the audience, which witnessed how Punji was battered from one post of the ring to another. Once in a while Joe would fake a powerful punch and watched how the Filipino leaped backward, another major mistake. Seconds were flying, and Joe began implementing his KO plan. He initiated a sudden attack that prompted Punji to do his predictable counterpunch with a jump. In that split second, Joe, who anticipated the aerial move, caught him with a powerful right cross that crashed into the small jaw, doubled by a left hook that dropped Punji flat on the canvas. The public was off their seats and went wild! Joe walked to the neutral corner and watched how Referee Masterly counted ten seconds and asked Punji's cornermen to help the motionless boxer. Then he lifted Joe's right arm up in the air, circling him around for everyone to see the winner.

When he returned to his corner, Mike had already gone to collect his bets, but Doessereck was there to embrace the winner and lift his arm one more time for everyone to see both of them. "Another big one for the scorecard!" the promoter congratulated Joe and offered him an envelope with $150 in it. Mike returned, and the brothers huddled together as Mike looked in the envelope, wondering if Doessereck had taken out his $54, along with other expenses. Regardless, this was Joe's largest purse so far. With a mischievous smile, Mike pulled out a roll of money from his pocket and, waving it at Joe, declared that what was in the envelope was "small change" in comparison with what he'd won from betting.

It happened that the fight was also witnessed by Irish Johnny Curtin, who was impressed by Joe's punching power. Since Joe's arrival, Curtin walked on thin ice, because both men competed in the same bantam category, and only one could move forward after eliminating the other. When the two sparred in the gym, it was clear that in a real fight Joe could easily floor Curtin, who was smaller and not a KO puncher. No one knew what maverick Doessereck had in mind, but it certainly appeared that he kept both on their toes and played one against the other. With Joe winning so far and Curtin losing the next two fights to Frankie Genaro and Jackie Gordon, he was in an uncomfortable spot. Besides, he was older, shorter, and suffered from painful attacks of gastritis that stopped him many times from training and fighting. From sparring with Curtin, Joe learned an important fighting tip: stay centered all the time, and at all costs avoid being out of balance.

Mike and Joe with their elementary school class, ca. 1913. Mike is in the bottom row, far left; Joe is next to him.

Boy Scout Troop 14, ca. 1918. Joe is in the back row, second from the right, holding the flag.

EAST END YOUTH SHAPING UP
LIKE REAL ARTIST IN RING

Joe Grim, Clever Local Bantamweight—Insert, Joe in Uniform
As Assistant Scout Master.

Fall River *Evening Herald News,* 1923.

THREE COMING CHAMPIONS

JOHNNY WILSON
JUNIOR LIGHTWEIGHT
OF NEW BEDFORD

JOE GRIMM
HARD HITTING BANTAM
OF FALL RIVER

TONY THOMAS
122 LB. FLASH
OF NEW BEDFORD.

Fall River *Evening Herald News,* 1923.

Headlines announcing some of Joe's fights.

The Bayonne Times, 1925.

JOE GRIM
Boxer who is to meet Melrose here
Monday night

Berkshire Evening Eagle, 1927.

GRIM SCORES K. O. IN HIS FIRST N. Y. BOUT

JOE GRIM K. O.'S COLE AT HOBOKEN

Local Boy Makes Hit Wit[h] Fans In 10-Round Bout

GRIM WINS OVER WALTER BABCOCK

JOE GRIM WINS BIG BOUT AT N. Y.

JOE GRIM BEATS MICKEY WALSH

JOE GRIMM WINS BY KNOCKOUT

Former F. R. Boy Drops Johnny Mac of Hartford

GRIMM WINS BY K. O.

Joe Grimm, formerly of this city but who now makes his home at Pittsfield, Mass., knocked out Mickey Roberts of Worcester in the fourth round [...] K. O. [...] Garrin [...]

Jack Francis of this city and Young Joe Grim of Fall River were opposed to each other in the second bout. Francis showed more agility and his hit-and-get-away tactics had Grim guessing for the first half of the round. But when Grim succeeded in closing in on his opponent, the Fall River boy proved himself an able socker. He crashed both hands to Francis's jaw so powerfully that Francis was soon in groggy condition, and just a second before the bell that would have saved him, the New Bedford boy's seconds tossed a towel into the ring.

[...]ng like [...] in New [...]tory in [...]knocked [...]round. [...] York [...] in the [...]ant fu[...]

JOE GRIM STOPS W[...] IN THE EIGHTH ROUND

In the curtain raiser Eddie Lester did some fine work with his left hand, jabbing Young Joe Grimm to perfection and to the delight of the fans. Grimm was determined to take everything that Lester shot out and he waded right into Lester in the fifth round and gave him such a beating that Lester dropped from exhaustion. He regained his feet and swapped with Bobby Tickle's charge. He was again dropped and this time for the full count.

[...]rt Was
Terry
Motor

[...]s in the lead[...]
Grimm crossed[...]

quick right to his chin that floored the Morgan street fighter for the full count. Coogan had been doing well up until the time he left himself open for Grimm's wallop.

Stable Mate of Suggs

Joe Grim, who is to meet Johnny Mack in one of the feature bouts at the Winter Garden Monday, was a former stable mate of "Chick" Suggs. The local pugilist is well known in New York, New Jersey, Fall River and other New England cities where he has appeared in main bouts. He fought a draw with Harry Felix in New York and won a decision over Irish Johnny Curtin in New Jersey recently. He is better known in Fall River as Gentleman Joe where he has appeared in several of the main attractions. To date out of 13 bouts he has won 11 and figured in one draw. Joe is in the best of condition and is training hard for his bout Monday night.

Dec 23, 1921 — K O'd
Jackey Coogan in two Rds. Ref. Kid Degasse N.B. F.R.

Jan. 2, 1922 — K O'd
Jimmy Ewos of N.B. in 1st rd. F.R. Ref. Jackson N.B.

Jan 27, 1922 — K. O'd
Eddie Lester in 5 rds F.R. Referee R. Tickle F.R.

Feb 3, 1922 K. O'd
Eddie Lester 1st Rd

April 28, 1924
Won over Tony Carney 10rds at N. Bedford ref John Moore Boston

may 9 1924
Won over John Fox of Boston referee McCartly of Taunton

may 28 1924
won over John O'Donnell 10rds ref Billy Burnett
went to N.Y.

July 21, 1924 won over Julio Abicella Philippino 8rd Oakland AC. Jersey city ref Joe Jeanette

Sample pages from Joe's handwritten notebook.

Nov 28 1927 K. O'd
Georgie La Fay Albany at winter gardens 8rd Pittsfild Ref Morey

Dec 16, 1927 K. O'd
Mickey Roberts Worcester in 4 rds at winter gardens Pittsfild ref Decker of Springfield

Feb 27, 1928 won over Jules Simbotti of Bridgeport at i, winter garden Pittsfl

Aug 4, 1924 K. O'd Vincent Runji Philippino 3rd Oakland A.C. Ball Park - Jersey city

Aug 29, 1924 K O'd Mickey walch 3rd in west N.Y. N.g. referee Joe Jeanette

Sept 3 1924 Won good draw with Harry Felix at Long Branch N.J. weight his 130 - Joe 122
3 months after he won the worlds junior Lightweight title from Vincente of Cal

Joe Grimm, ca. 1925.

Mike Hashim, ca. 1926.

Back row, from left: Mike, David (father), Elias, and Joe.
Bottom row: Catherine, Evelyn, Rafka (mother), Adele with
Florence, and George. 1927.

The grocery store owned by Joe and Mike, in Pittsfield,
Massachusetts, ca. 1927.

Elizabeth "Betty" Simon and Joseph Hashim on their wedding day,
April 28, 1938.

Joe and two of his children, Marion and Joe Jr., on his 95th
birthday, with his favorite dessert (strawberry shortcake),
February 6, 2000.

Had 24 knockouts in a row

Joseph Hashim, 78, a successful Pittsfield entrepreneur, is a man with a dual identity.

The former Fall Riverite also goes by the name of Joe Grimm, an unseemly name for a Lebanese immigrant. But Grimm it is.

That's what he answered to in the 20s, when he was establishing himself as one of New England's top bantamweight and featherweight boxers. Grimm was the last name of of an outstanding pre-World War I Italian fighter.

Hashim had 70 professional fights. He won 61 of them and had one draw. His record includes a string of 24 consecutive knockout victories. The streak was broken by Red Larrabee. Hashim won the fight on points.

Most former boxers have the characteristic trademark of a mashed nose. Not Hashim. He attributes it to "knowing when to duck."

He did get his nose broken once. It happened late in a fight. That was after being advised by his corner not to mix it up.

"I thought the guy was a creampuff, until he proved otherwise with a right flush on my nose. It blinded me. But I was able to clinch and waltz the guy around until my head cleared. The referee kept trying to cut in but I outmaneuvered him. I hung on and won the fight on a decision," said Hashim.

He began boxing at 18 in the Fall River area. His manager was Bob Tickle, who had two sons who were policemen. Ralph was a detective on the Fall River police force and Herb served in the State Police.

Some of Hashim's Fall River stablemates at Tower A.C. on Haffards Street were, Jabber Smith, a welterweight and Slip Higgins. As a youngster, the late Police Chief Charles A. McDonal

(Continued on Page 6

Joseph Hashim

Article in the *Berkshire Eagle*, 1983.

Joe Jr. (Joseph Hashim) and the author, holding Joe Grimm's green
boxing trunks, in 2011.

The author and Mike Jr. (Michael Hashim), looking through his
father's memorabilia in 2011.

Chapter 14
A Taste of the Good Life

The next day after Joe's training session, the two Hashim brothers entered a tailor shop on Broadway, where Mike asked for the owner. An older Italian with little gray hair but a black pencil-sharp mustache came from the back room, and Mike thundered a confident "Mario sent me here!" The owner smiled. "*Si, si, si,* my cousin!" and shook the hands of the boys, who ordered two "wool suits of English quality." Without hesitation, Mike chose a three-piece navy-blue suit, and Joe, after carefully looking around at the many dressed mannequins, decided to have a double-breasted taupe-brown suit. Mike wanted the jackets to have "functional buttonholes in lapels" and pants with cuffs. He took out the roll of money and asked how much down payment was needed, but the owner blushed and dramatically stated that "no friends of Don Mario need to do that!" The brothers spent some time with the measurements, and both were pleased with the plush treatment they received in the tailor shop.

But that occurrence paled in comparison with what happened next, when Mike stopped in front of a barbershop with a large entrance glass door etched with white lily flowers and red roses. At the side of the door was a revolving pole with red, blue, and white spirals, confirming a fine tonsure establishment. When the boys walked in, the barbers and clients warmly greeted them, all having watched Joe's fights and recognizing him. Puffing his chest and biting his mustache, Mike felt it was his duty to announce in a most convincing voice, "My kid-brother-to-be-world-champion!" Mario, the owner, held Joe's hands while explaining that he also had tried boxing but settled for the mandolin. As proof, the delicate mandolin was triumphantly displayed between two large mirrors on the side wall with many colorful posters of Amalfi and Sorrento. Above it, there were two small American and Italian flags, their poles crossed.

The men from the barbershop looked just like Mike and Mario, with round bellies, the same pencil mustache, dark wavy hair saturated with lotion, large eyes, and broad smiles, all of them chain-smokers. Their conversation revolved around new jokes, sports, women, food, and politics, mainly following Mussolini's exploits. The boisterous, laughter-filled, and argumentative chatter from all visitors to the barbershop rose above the jazz music pouring out of a beautiful Radiola Grand radio situated on a marble tabletop. The strokes of straight razors as they were sharpened by barbers on the leather straps attached to the back of the chairs sounded to Joe just like the speedy punching ball.

As for the spacious shop, it was state-of-the-art: everything was new, beginning with the five impressive red cushioned Paidar reclining chairs framed with chrome, sitting on conic bases with hydraulic pumps to adjust the height. Large imported crystal mirrors with floral designs in each corner rested on green marble counters covered with scissors, perfumed jars of different colors, straight razors with ivory handles, hair clippers, and combs of all sizes. In the middle of each counter was a white sink in the shape of a basinet with cold- and hot-water brass pipes and blue marble faucets. The barbers were dressed in white jackets, white shirts, and green ties that matched the color of the walls. The floor was covered by well-polished vinyl, reflecting lightbulbs all around the mirrors, as well as the large electric fans dropping from the high ceiling cast in gray putter. Comfortable red leather sofas were lined up along the walls, facing white coffee tables covered with large green marble ashtrays, backgammon sets, sports magazines, and daily newspapers. One wall was just a large window framed with green velvety drapes that allowed a full view of the busy commercial street. The rest of the walls were covered with posters of movie stars above wooden partitions with hangers for coats and hats.

The shop proved to be a hit with the customers, especially when local girls learned that Mario specialized in bobbing hair, Manhattan style. In fact, Mike was hired just because he knew how to do the new "hair arts." One day when Mike asked Joe to come to the shop and hang out with him, a young female customer brought her girlfriend in for a flapper's haircut. With all the other barbers busy, Mike washed his hands, put on the white jacket, and invited her to his empty chair. He attentively engaged in small talk and began cutting the long reddish hair at ear level. To Joe it was an amusing scene to see a young woman with deep-red lipstick among five bold men with white foam or hot towels on their faces.

The waiting girl was skinny, blonde, dressed in white, and sat next to Joe on a sofa. She thumbed through a magazine and once in a while looked at him. Finally she smiled. "Aren't you Joe Grimm?" The noisy shop became silent at once, and Joe found the strength to say, "Yes, ma'am!" and smiled back. "You don't look that tough, like in the ring!" Mike almost dropped the scissors, and Joe answered in a soft voice, "I'm not a tough guy, I'm a boxer." Everyone burst out laughing.

"I'm Gina!" She extended her arm, and her delicate hand vanished in his grip.

"And I'm Mike, his brother and personal manager!"

"I'm Tina!" said the girl from the chair.

"I'm Mario, the owner!" They all looked at each other and laughed.

"They should put your poster on the wall." Gina pointed to the other pictures with movie stars, among them Rudolph Valentino. Joe didn't say anything, but he was impressed and touched by the unusual encounter. No woman had ever approached him before. Mike finished his tonsorial job that brought him a ten-cent tip; a regular man's haircut was fifteen cents, and a shave five cents. The brothers rushed to open the door for the delicate girls, who giggled and left a trail of strong perfume of violets behind them. Gina and Tina stopped in front of the shop's large window, admired each other's hair, and waved to the boys with dropped jaws.

"Well, that was nice, but I've got something much better to show you. Wait until you see this!" Mike stepped back from the front doorway of the shop and took a key chain from his pocket. Joe followed as he went out another door that led to a side hallway and connected the front door with a narrow stairway. He took Joe upstairs into a smaller corridor with only one window at the end. As he unlocked one door after another, he described each room. "Here's the bathroom with the shower, here's the kitchen with an electric stove and electric refrigerator, here's the pantry and the storage room, and here, are you ready my brother? Here is our extra-large bedroom with two extra-large beds, built-in closets, and windows, all clean and extra convenient!"

An electric bulb with a green shade was hanging in the middle between the beds that were separated by a night table with an alarm clock on it. The walls were off-white, and the bed covers were green. The linoleum that covered the entire apartment was also green. After he allowed Joe to register all the new scenery, Mike continued. "The beauty of all this is that I work downstairs and you're closer to the gym. What we have to do is to clean the shop and the rest of the facilities each evening after closing. We also pay the monthly utilities for the entire house. Not a bad deal, huh?"

Mike took a step back to enjoy the stunned face of his brother. Then he said in the same firm voice, "You stay right here, take a nap, or talk to the men downstairs, while I go talk to Doessereck!"

Pressed by Joe's big winnings and the threat of losing him to another stable, Doessereck agreed to let the brothers move out, but Joe's training schedule had to remain the same. In a gentlemanly manner he also waived the outstanding balance and basically agreed to all the conditions raised by Mike. One of these was that Mike be present in his brother's corner during any fight and that he be introduced to anyone in the boxing business as "Joe's personal manager." Both demands proved to be enormously costly mistakes in the long run, but for the time being Mike had taken a stand and was happy about it. When he returned with their luggage to the new upstairs apartment and described the "business meeting," Joe was stunned. How smart his brother was!

"I forgot to tell you the best part," Mike proudly stated. "Are you ready for this? We also have a phone to use, free of charge! It's the one in the barbershop, but only during off hours. Now we can talk to Emma and Louis in Pittsfield all night long!"

Joe shook his head, astonished. From that moment on, he would never second-guess Mike's decisions.

The boys celebrated with Lebanese food cooked in their new kitchen. Eating the familiar meals was a treat for Joe and a shot in the arm for his fighting shape. The spicy aromas of the baked lamb, *baba ghannuj, kibbi mishwiyyi,* and *mihshi malfuf biz-zayt* (eggplant appetizer, ground lamb meatballs, and stuffed cabbage leaves), with other delicacies, drifted to the shop below. The gourmand, Mario, offered to finance the brothers so they could open a small Mediterranean diner next door. Mike was tempted to use the ready money, but having a restaurant was a twenty-four–hour operation that clashed in every way with the unpredictability of the boxing business.

Indeed, the boys were very good. Mike worked overtime to make more money and pay their bills, and Joe continued his training, as before, even though no other fight was scheduled for him. In comparison, the other guys from Doessereck's stable were busy competing each week, and Joe went to all their matches to provide friendly support. It definitely was a huge step forward and upward for Joe to be in the middle of so much pugilistic activity and to have the opportunity to meet many fighters with championship records and learn from them. What he had to do was to "patiently wait his turn like everyone else," Doessereck assured him.

The best possible news for the brothers reached the stable on August 10, when Johnny Dundee, the world featherweight champion now at age thirty-one, announced that he would vacate the title because he wanted to fight as a lightweight. In Mike's opinion, Joe could successfully fight one category heavier and aim for the featherweight title. The problem was that other boxers from Doessereck's stable, like Curtin and Kochansky, already fought in that category and planned to challenge the same title as well. The tension in the gym could be cut with a knife, but no one said a word. All waited to see what Doessereck would decide.

For the next two weeks Joe kept training. Mike, who "smelled a rat," had no problem confronting Doessereck in his home, where they disagreed about everything they discussed. While Mike insisted that his brother was a hot prospect who deserved to be tested against better boxers, the experienced promoter believed that a foolish risk could end Joe's career after one disastrous bout. Regarding the featherweight title, Doessereck reminded Mike that the boxers who had been with him for a long time and paid bitter dues to stay in the game deserved that priority. Under no circumstances would Joe, who came a month ago from nowhere, beat them out in eliminations. Besides, no promoter in his right mind would match obscure Joe with any of their high-ranking featherweights. The reason was simple: Joe was not a main-attraction fighter, nor a box office sensation. Moreover, he was going to face increasingly faster and better opponents.

"Be reasonable and understand that boxing is a business like any other. You have to have a proven product before mass-marketing it," Doessereck patiently explained.

"What happened to the American dream? Everyone loves to root for the underdog!" argued Mike.

"Joe is far from being an underdog. First, he needs to be a topnotcher, a challenger, then a contender," responded the promoter, who had aged in the boxing business. But the hot-tempered brother stood up and interrupted with a blunt "Maybe not!" The promoter shook his head in disbelief.

Before leaving the house, Mike asked what was going to happen with Joe in the near future. Doessereck answered that it was too early to talk about it. Then he gently pushed Mike toward the door, repeating his favorite motto, "There are no guarantees in life, let alone boxing!"

Joe paid no attention to the dispute and trained as usual. All his other stablemates were booked for fights, but not Joe. Unhappy and strategizing, Mike played a tricky card and told Doessereck that they needed to go back to Fall River to attend a family reunion.

"What about Joe's training?" Doessereck shook his head, annoyed.

"We have a gym and a coach there, don't you worry!"

"When are you coming back?"

Mike cut him short. "When Joe has a good fight waiting for him!"

The boys picked up their new suits, for which Mike paid a "bundle," and after buying gifts for the family, they left the next evening for Fall River on the same luxury liner that had brought them to New Jersey. Just like before, they saluted the Statue of Liberty as the ship passed by.

Back home, Joe tasted what it was like to be a real hero: relatives and friends came to see him, he went to visit the Boy Scout camp, and he worked out at the gym with Bobby Tickle, where the rest of the boys treated him like he was already a champion. But most important was his visit to the *Daily Globe*, where he and Mike, smartly dressed, gave interviews and described in detail how great their new lives were in New Jersey. Beautiful write-ups about Joe's future in the ring made him feel important and a man with a mission. One of the articles stated, "Our Joe Grim [*sic*] is training faithfully with a lot of stars in Bayonne, N.J., and his condition is perfect. Doesserick [*sic*] being much impressed with the Fall River boy, is sure he has the makings of a star. A legion of fight fans in this city is rooting hard for his success." The beautiful words touched a proud nerve, and Joe was eager to go back and continue his quest, especially after Mike put on the kitchen table $300 in bills of ten, as proof of Joe's success.

Joe's dolce vita ended when Doessereck called Bobby Tickle with the news that Joe had a fight set for the next Friday. With four days left, the boys rushed back to Bayonne, happily saluting Lady Liberty once again.

✄✄

One evening Doessereck came to the gym, talked to everyone as he assigned the next bouts and their locations, and finally came to Joe, telling him about the weigh-in.

"How are you doing, kid?" asked the promoter.

"Great, sir!" Joe stopped pummeling the heavy bag. "If I felt any better, I'd need a twin brother," joked the youngster.

"You'd be better here with no brother at all," Doessereck muttered.

Joe didn't answer and continued to punch the bag. Obviously, something was not right, but for now, he cared only about the upcoming fight with Mickey Walsh of nearby North Bergen. After the weigh-in, Joe took another look at Walsh, his sturdy body covered with white, round muscle that looked like lard. Then he told Mike in Arabic, "You can bet on a first-round knockout!" Mike did exactly that the next day.

Joe's bout was one of the openers that night, scheduled as a ten-rounder before the main event to warm up the public. Only the presence of Joe Jeanette in the ring as a referee gave it more weight and importance. Now that they knew each other, the black celebrity lingered in the dressing room when he came to check the gloves and joked with Joe. "Man, you pack a mighty punch in tzat glove. Are you zure ain't a horze zhoe in tzere?"

"Is more like an anvil." Coach Nick laughed.

"Then put it to a good uze!" Jeanette shook Joe's hand and left, crossing through the doorway with Mike, who had just finished placing his bets. Shortly after, the small group walked to the ring; confident Walsh was already there. He looked amused at Joe's burgundy robe and probably cracked a joke, because his corner burst into laughter.

"Did you see that?" Mike was steamed.

"The laugh will be on them," said Joe as the announcer walked in the ring and presented him as "a nonstop victorious puncher." Turning to Walsh, who had a smirk on his face, the announcer described him as "one of the best in his division." They waited for Referee Jeanette to climb in the ring and deliver a short instruction about "a clean fight." The boys touched gloves and went back to their corners. The sound of the bell brought the excitement of the public to a noisier level.

Determined to end the fight and quickly leave the ring, which was stifling hot with no breeze to alleviate the tropical temperature, Joe launched a total attack, hitting Walsh with everything he could swing. Walsh was a slow starter and not ready for such lightning punishment, and he tried to

132

fight back as best he could. After a minute of a nonstop shower of punches that ripped large holes into the other's defense, Joe reached his ideal close-quarter fighting distance. Walsh's corner screamed instructions that were drowned out by the noisy public, and against the ropes he became a fixed target for Joe. In a crouching position that allowed him to charge each blow with leg power, "Grimm drove a terrific straight right to the jaw and Walsh was out for some time after the regular 10 seconds," reported a newspaper. Joe's coup de grâce proved that hundreds of hours of practice in the gym paid off big time. Now trusting its effect, he stepped back, watching how the robust Walsh melted like a soft white candle on the canvas. Walsh was considered "by New York writers as one of the best boys in the East at his weight, and a brilliant future was predicted for him," mentioned the same newspaper.

Joe walked to a neutral corner, where right there, next to the ring, the frail-looking Gina was screaming wildly, punching the air with her little fists. Their eyes met, and Gina tried to approach the ring. It was not exactly the moment to socialize, as Referee Jeanette took Joe's right hand and held it high. They toured the ring, walking around the busy men who tried to revive Walsh. The announcer climbed in the ring and shouted, "The winner by a knoooockout in the first round iiiisss Gentlemaaannn Joooeee!" The public immediately picked up the name and chanted "Gentleman Joe! Gentleman Joe! Gentleman Joe!" Doessereck appeared from nowhere at ringside and led Joe to the dressing room, patting him on the back and repeating that this winning "was another good one for the scorecards." When the envelopes came, Mike counted $200, a record payment. Doessereck offered the brothers a lift to the barbershop after the boxing event was over.

Surprisingly, Mike did not say a word about his brother competing for the title. He felt that the facts spoke for themselves, especially because Johnny Curtin, the darling of New Jersey and the great hope of Doessereck, had been defeated a few times in the same month that Joe scored one rolling KO after another. As his self-esteem reached unexpected heights, Joe felt good about himself. With his usual monkish dedication, he immersed himself in longer workouts.

With champion Dundee leaving the featherweight crown up for grabs, everyone in the barbershop agreed that Joe should be pushed forward. After Mike reproduced his discussion with Doessereck, all accused the promoter of sabotaging Joe's career, and word spread quickly around about the entire matter. Soon the gossip reached Doessereck's ears.

Chapter 15
The Making of a Champion

The common belief was that boxing is about two rivals who want to slaughter each other for supremacy in the ring and a bigger purse; a boxing champion is the best of the best at knocking down others in the ring. The public pays to see gladiatorial fights, and less aggressive boxers are disqualified by the referee for "not trying." Teeth, jaws, eyebrows, ribs, arms, and hands broken in the ring are marks of valor and the source of wild pleasure for spectators, who at that moment seemed deprived of any compassionate feelings or intellectual abilities. But aggressiveness, fighting skills, brute strength, lightning speed, and a deadly punch are not enough to elevate an excellent boxer to the star level. Behind each boxing champion are hero makers and myth creators—the boxer's manager and his promoter.

A good manager has always been vital for a boxer, regardless of how talented and undefeated he may be. In the 1920s, the manager provided not only training and medical care but often room and board for the wannabe champion who otherwise might be penniless and basically homeless as he sought to change his life and seek fame and fortune. As a rule, the earnings from any fight were equally split between the boxer and his manager, who deducted his expenses before splitting the purse. Usually, an oral agreement sealed by a handshake was good enough as a contract, another honor system inherited from the cowboy era. Equally important was the promoter, hired with the approval of the manager, who was an image maker with the public relations connections to transform a brawler into a star.

✦✦

Many years were needed for a prospect to become a challenger and then a contender for a title, time when he earned little money but spent a lot to excel in the "science of boxing." Jack Dempsey (born William Harrison Dempsey) had been a winning fighter since 1914; he earned $20 a fight until he became a household name. In 1916, Dempsey and his manager, Jack Price, went to New York City, aiming to get Dempsey better fights. Instead, they ended up penniless and slept on benches in Central Park. Both returned by train to Salt Lake City. He hooked up with the well-groomed fight manager Jack Kearns, whom Dempsey nicknamed "Doc" because he was able to doctor any situation. Always broke, both struggled to stay in the game while Dempsey, now renamed the "Man Killer" by Doc, kept winning by knockouts even as he seemed to invent the "expense account" and continued to accumulate debt.

When in 1919 Jack Dempsey became the heavyweight champion of the world in Toledo, he received nothing out of the $27,500 that was his share, since the win money was hardly enough to cover his previous living and training expenses. In order to increase his income, Dempsey did publicity stunts, touring the country, appearing in circuses, and fighting in staged exhibitions. Kearns believed in his boxer so much that he ordered a tailor to make six suits for himself and six for the future world champion at no cost; in exchange he offered the craftsman the distinction of being known as Dempsey's tailor. Kearns wanted to show how prosperous he and his client were, and they acted accordingly. "Fake it till you make it" was the way to move forward. They both lived in expensive hotels on borrowed money with a huge interest. But only in this way could they rub elbows with the makers and breakers, befriend newspapermen and radio reporters, and eventually find a rich investor. Their handshake agreement still entitled Kearns to handle Dempsey's business for a one-third interest and an equal split of any boxing earnings. So far, there was nothing, but that would change the next year, when Dempsey would defeat Bill "KO" Brennan of Louisville, Kentucky. Manager Kearns would pocket $100,000 guaranteed out of the entire $150,000 paid by ticket holders. Dempsey's newly hired promoter, George L. "Tex" Rickard, received only $15,000. A cowboy from Texas, he was responsible for the success of the famous black fighter Jack Johnson and Jess Willard, both heavyweight world champions.

Rickard knew a winner when he saw one, and two years later, he went one step further to gamble on Dempsey's money punches. He decided to host an international contest between his client and the European champion and the world light heavyweight holder, Georges Carpentier. With that in mind, the unabated promoter went ahead and built a huge arena in Jersey City. After spending $325,000 for hiring 500 carpenters with 400 helpers who used 2.3 million feet of lumber, he built an octagonal stadium of 300,000 square feet, with the ring platform in the center, ready for the Fight of the Century. The impressive construction, named Boyle's Thirty Acres, was finished in two months and was a publicity stunt in itself. But Rickard's inborn instinct for gambling went further and guaranteed the two fighters the unheard-of total of $500,000. Moreover, he placed the "secret" training camp for the French boxer in a well-guarded Long Island estate, increasing the curiosity of commoners and the rich alike. On the other hand, he charged a one dollar entrance fee to the public who wanted to watch Dempsey train at the dog track in Atlantic City. The stunts worked like a charm and attracted the curious public to see what all the hype was about. Hype or not, Rickard, the ultimate myth maker, turned out to be right on the money.

The greatly heralded fight took place in the afternoon of July 2, 1921, with more than 90,000 in the audience, which, due to Rickard's ceaseless promotional stunts, included personalities ranging from Jersey City Mayor Frank Hague (who received $80,000 off the books for approving the construction of the arena) to the state governor Edward I. Edwards, and from tycoons Vincent Astor, Henry Ford, John D. Rockefeller, and William H. Vanderbilt to movie stars like Al Johnson. Because of that elite participation, the event also broke the record in women's participation when two thousand of them, all dressed up and eager to share the excitement, were seated near the ring by some of the six hundred ushers, another publicity stunt. But nothing compared to Rickard's success in gathering around the ring the top reporters and journalists from France, Canada, England, Spain, Japan, and South America, along with, of course, the New York and New Jersey papers, including the local *Bayonne Times*. Yet, the impressive press attendance was topped by an even bigger media stunt—the match was covered by the first live national radio broadcast of RCA over the entire American East Coast. The event paid off handsomely and made Dempsey and Rickard very rich.

An inveterate gambler, Rickard had already proved that Americans loved anything bigger than life and that big investments could generate equally big money. It was that grand idea he took to the small town of Shelby, Montana, firmly believing that Dempsey fighting on the Fourth of

July, 1923, would attract tens of thousands of viewers. The challenger was Tommy Gibbons, a smart and strong fighter with some forty KO wins, well-known by his Minnesota fans but not in Montana.

Every demand of Rickard's was met by the thrilled Shelbians, so one day before the fight, all arrangements went mathematically right and according to the written plan. A million-dollar gate was already counted as ready cash by the involved banks. All was good until reality struck—only 7,700 spectators trickled into the stands, instead of the more than 50,000 expected. Only a few of the $50 ringside tickets were sold, and some 13,000 who could not afford the tickets were admitted for free to look good for the cameras and buy food and drinks. The string of bad luck continued when the incredibly hot day melted the ice cream, boiled the other refreshments, and spoiled the food. The afternoon fight could not start under a more adversarial circumstance for any profit. On top of Rickard's many other problems, Gibbons turned out to be a very good challenger, giving a hard time to Dempsey, who won by decision in fifteen rounds. Dempsey lost a lot of prestige, and Shelby lost everything. Four banks went bankrupt, paying Dempsey's guaranteed $300,000. Gibson received traveling expenses. Eventually the stadium lumber was taken apart and sold board by board to bring some money to the filamentary investors.

Two months later, money-hungry promoter Rickard brought Luis Angel Firpo of Argentine to fight in New York City. Rickard presented Firpo as "The Wild Bull of the Pampas." He was, in fact, a huge, badly trained lad with a devastating punch, set to go against "Jack the Giant Killer," a circuslike publicity event escalated by a frenzy of wild expectations. Once again, Dempsey's training camp in Saranac Lake sold tickets to some 3,000 curious viewers, including Hollywood stars Mary Pickford and Douglas Fairbanks, along with "Scarface" Al Capone, always a heavy bettor on the champion. On the memorable evening of September 14, 1923, the Polo Arena turned out to hold only 80,000 fans; another 35,000 could not get tickets and were turned away. Even so, $1,188,882 was collected at the gate. No promoter's dream could match that financial success.

The lucky crowd breathlessly witnessed how Dempsey was knocked down seconds after the fight began, only to lash right back at Firpo and put him down three times in a row. "The Wilde Bull" not only got up, but his slaughtering assault of five paralyzing punches sent Dempsey through the ropes to land on the ring judge and reporters' table amidst their paperwork. They pushed him back in the ring before the ninth count and in time to safely end the first round. At the next bell, Dempsey went for a kill and finished up his dangerous rival. It all happened with eleven knockdowns in two rounds, the best ever pugilistic contest in the history of boxing. Dempsey's and his promoter's pay was $500,000 for a three-minute fifty-seven–second fight, and Firpo received $156,250. It was Jack Dempsey with his glorious rags-to-riches saga that brought respectability to boxing, and legions of new fighters rushed into the ring.

Ugly implications took place when the relations between boxer and manager went sour, and trust was broken. Greed was followed by revenge when Kearns was fired, and he sued Dempsey for $700,000 for breach of contract. It ended up in a "draw."

Rickard understood the importance of media and encouraged the press to accept a new publicity stunt designed to help restore Dempsey's patriotic credentials. Rushing to produce a convincing "vintage" photograph, Dempsey was dressed in brand-new working overalls with ironed creases that drew attention to his expensive designer shoes, probably worth a few months' salary of any worker seen in the background, none of whom was dressed in the same outfit. The champion smiled, holding a compressed-air riveting machine, as he did during the war in a shipyard. But clearly he was not "Dempsey the Riveter," and none of his many detractors were won over by the photo. It took going to court for Dempsey to officially have a jury clear his name.

Rickard prematurely died in 1929 of a ruptured appendix, without fulfilling his last dream—to build a second Monte Carlo in Miami. His $15,000 bronze casket was put on display in the middle of Madison Square Garden. Some 20,000 mourners paid deserved respect. Standing next to the casket, Jack Dempsey could not stop crying. Always timing everything to the smallest detail, Rickard died just before the Wall Street crash, dragging the nation and the rest of the world into the depths of the Great Depression. It was the end of the Roaring Twenties and the end of the $50 ringside ticket. But on that January mourning day, Rickard's last show was free of charge.

From the beginning, boxing and money were a very powerful mix. Organized crime's big role in boxing was well-known, and many fighters "took a dive" to satisfy the bets against them. Penniless ex-boxers with a pug nose were in great demand to serve as bodyguards for important gangsters. Hollywood made sure to immortalize that iconic image of the failing boxer with a scary face who became the underworld enforcer. Tragically, in real life, heavyweight contender Bill "KO" Brennan (Al Capone was his backer) was assassinated at age thirty by mobsters when a bootlegging deal went bad. The good relationship among Al Capone and Jack Dempsey and Jack Sharkey was in full public display. Al Capone personally mixed gin in the water at ringside for the ever-thirsty Mickey Walker, to make sure his bets were well secured and his favorite took the belt from world champion Tiger Flowers. In 1926, when Billy Wells was ready to take the belt from Walker, Al Capone had a private talk with the challenger—who didn't show up for the fight. Many fighting deals were sealed in glitzy saloons filled with expensive cigar smoke, the tempting smell of alcohol, and the ever-present sinful feminine perfume. Securing up-front payments of hundreds of thousands of dollars for the title bout was a profession in itself for promoters, who cultivated private sources, Prohibition mobsters, and the gambling industry.

Initially, the image of the boxing champion was expected to match the Wild West hero, the blond and handsome blue-eyed sharpshooter with an obvious muscular body and tough character. But soon the increasingly darker-skin pugilists imposed their fighting domination. These nonwhite contenders kept winning. They built a large loyal audience, demonstrating that in the ring, only the best could win, regardless of race. This did not go well with John "Jack" Arthur Johnson, a black challenger (son of a slave), who in 1908 defeated the white champion Tommy Burns in Australia and then defended his reign until 1915. Due to his addiction to white women (he married and divorced three of them), the flamboyant rebel made white folks angry. They looked for a white hope to avenge their pride, but he never materialized. Johnson lived the life of an international jet-setter, recklessly spending the $1 million he had made in his career, only to end up penniless and homeless.

Things were different with world champion Harry Greb, who was his own best promoter, as he loved to go out (he was an excellent dancer), show off his fine clothes, and knock out men twice his size. After winning in 1925 against Walker, the two accidentally met inside Billy LaHiff's Tavern near Broadway in Manhattan, where they patched each other's wounds with fine illegal drinks. From there they took a taxi to a better saloon. Before entering the Slipper, Walker said he was badly thumbed by Greb and that's why he won the fifteen-round fight. Greb's German pride boiled, and he shouted back that he could beat the "Irish son of a bitch" anytime, even right now, and a street fight erupted. As fists started to fly, clients from the busy saloon stepped out, and the neighbors, the cars, and pedestrians stopped to watch; everyone placed bets on the savage fighters who tried to murder each other. A policeman broke up the fight, and the two split to approach some female admirers. After all, what was a drinking contest without being trashed in a brawl in front of the fans?

This out-of-the-ring fight had a more substantial reason behind it than pure vanity. It happened after Greb played a cruel joke on the gamblers who mostly bet on his victory. The night before the fight, he dropped drunk out of a taxicab in front of a nightclub full of bookies, and two of his beautiful female companions pulled him back in the car that then sped away. The upset bettors rushed to change wagers against their favorite. Actually, Greb was never more sober and in better shape during the fight, and betting a lot of money on himself, he won huge. The sad part of the story is that during the fight, Walker's thumb made Greb completely blind in one eye. On the gentler flip of the coin, Greb fought the left-handed Theo "Tiger" Flowers, the black religious fighter who brought his Bible to the ring. It seemed to work miracles, because the "Georgian Deacon" stripped Greb of the title twice in 1926.

However, it was the gutsy Greb who defeated the heavier Tommy Gibbons and Gene Tunney and was ready to strip the heavyweight Jack Dempsey of his world title. Greb was immensely confident in his winning abilities, as indicated by his declaration, "I am positive I can defeat Dempsey in a twelve or fifteen-round decision bout. My biggest thought would be to keep from getting knocked out. That is all I would have to do in order to win a decision bout with Dempsey, who is no harder to hit than he may be knocked out ..." But Dempsey's manager turned down the fight, good publicity for both fighters.

Meanwhile, the talk of the town was the stub-nosed brawler Mickey Walker, with his irresistible Irish charm and legendary deadly left hook, matching his drinking bouts and love for women—he married seven times, one woman three times. He really did not need a promoter. When in the ring he was a dynamite fighter who held back nothing to win, mostly in a bloodbath greatly cheered by the spectators who paid to see just that. Nicknamed "Toy Bulldog" for his nose shape, he could take an incredible amount of punishment and returned it twofold. In 1919 he was fighting in New Jersey for $10 a win, after a string of some thirty hard-won victories. By November 1922 he had conquered the world welterweight title by defeating champion Jack Briton in a controversial ten-round decision. Doc Kearns, Dempsey's former manager, took over Mickey's career, challenging him to win world titles in three categories, score ninety-three victories, more than fifty by knockouts; he lost only 14 fights out of 163. He made $4 million in his career and paid everyone around him, mostly the money-hungry Kearns.

Due to rocky lives and adventures that defy reality, many champions created their own legends. The talented and hard-hitting Jimmy McLarnin had numerous nicknames, beginning with the suggestive "Belfast Spider." He was also known as the "Irish Lullaby" (for putting his opponents to sleep in the ring), and the menacing "Beltin' Celt," as well as the fearsome "Dublin Destroyer" and "Dublin Dynamiter." Additionally, he achieved a reputation as "Murderous Mick," and due to his numerous KO victories against Jewish fighters, he was labeled as the "Jew Beater," "Hebrew Scourge," and the "Jewish Killer." He ended up with the name "Baby Face Assassin," relating to the contradiction between his gentle young-looking face and his deadly punching power.

Another case in point is the dashing welterweight, middleweight, and light heavyweight champion Kid McCoy (real name Norman Selby), who became "the real McCoy." With a split personality, he had a pathological need to lie, steal, and do tricks in the ring, where he displayed an unusual ferocity and savagery. He invented his own "corkscrew punch" by copying his cat's "paw jab," and he defeated men who were up to one hundred pounds heavier than he was. He fought before World War I and made his mark in the ring when he floored the light heavyweight Joe Choynski sixteen times while he himself went down twelve times, only to win after three rounds, during their fourth contest. Tall, skinny, and pale, he looked nerdy, not nearly a prizefighter. However, his countless brawls in bars and saloons were legendary; dressed in the latest fashion and looking like a dandy, he put down anyone who did not believe he was the real McCoy. Yet he was at the same time well groomed, polite, and extremely charming. His own publicity stunts were larger than life, attracting the friendship of Charles Chaplin and director David W. Griffith. His personal life was riddled nonstop with amazing amorous and swindling adventures endorsed by nine wives; he killed one rich lover because she refused to marry him.

Fighters and their handlers lived colorful lives that were the talk of the town. In no other sport would young Charles "Bud" Taylor, who in one year alone was expelled from school thirteen times for fighting, grow to be admiringly called the "Blonde Terror of Terre Haute" (two rivals died because of his punches in the ring) and the "idol of idols in Los Angeles." Taylor was the ultimate fighter, who in his first victorious contest was paid $3, and $5 in the next. In spite his twenty-one straight victories, the puny, skinny teenager was refused by each manager or promoter, only to be named the world champion in 1926. He defended his crown until 1928, when he was recognized as "the outstanding bantam of the land." His title was taken away by the same National Boxing Association that gave it, because most of his fights had been in heavier categories.

Not too different was the story of James Braddock, who never took a boxing lesson before he won his first fight by knockout. He was paid $35, only to make $4,000 after nine victorious bouts and almost double that amount five fights later. Breaking his right hand, he was considered over the hill, and no manager would touch him for years. He decided to break his hand again fighting in the ring, where he had fractured it in the first place, instead of paying a doctor to do so in order to reset the badly healed bones. It took him four fights to refracture his hand in the first round when he hit Paul Swiderski's head, and he still won by decision seven rounds later, fighting with one arm. The ever-doubted Braddock made a spectacular comeback, and years later he would defeat world champion Max Baer. Named the "Cinderella Man," he became the symbol of triumph against all odds and inspired millions not to give up a dream.

Legends about boxers grew even after they retired. Pete Herman, the bantam world champion, was hit by premature blindness. After winning four out of his last five fights on instinct alone, he returned to New Orleans. Completely blind, he became a popular bar owner, specializing in predicting the future of prizefighters by touching and feeling them. When Primo Carnera, the heavyweight world champion, went under his scrutiny, Herman said, "You are nothing but a big muscle-bound oaf!" He was right, since the Italian giant could not really punch hard and lost the title after the New York mobsters disposed of him.

A different legend was created by handsome Gene Tunney, "The Fighting Marine," who worked as a lumberjack to improve his stamina, even though he was the only fighter to read the classics and carry on philosophical conversations. It was the time when college boys played savage football games or engaged in brutal wrestling matches, yet none of them would step in the ring. This smart Irish marine was credited with "triumph of mind over matter," as he was his own best mentor and teacher. The aristocratic-looking Tunney was brilliantly managed and promoted by Billy Gibbons, and he became an absolute champion, defeated only once by Harry Greb. Otherwise he crushed each boxer he ever faced in the ring, including Dempsey twice, for which the crowds never forgave him. The first time he and Dempsey fought, in Philadelphia in 1926, their sensational bout brought a record of 120,757 ticket holders, who paid $2 million. One year later the rematch in Chicago set another legendary record of $2.6 million.

Besides toppling Dempsey from the pedestal, Tunney was blamed for dropping quotes from Shakespeare, about whom he lectured at Yale University. His friends were George Bernard Shaw, William Faulkner, and Ernest Hemingway. Unlike other champions, Tunney retired at the peak of his prize career as a multimillionaire and became director of two banks and eight industries. Indeed great fighters always came with colorful crews and handlers—each a character that could inspire Hollywood movie scripts. And the pubic loved them to death!

Boxing thus became part of Americana at many levels and remained a most profitable entertainment business, parading men with muscles and brains whose biographies grew by mythical proportions. The featherweight Johnny Kilbane was the world title holder for an incredible eleven years (1912–1923), and his last name became the verb "to Kilbane," which meant "to beat" someone. His immense popularity helped him advance in politics, and he became a state senator from Ohio. To be seen in the presence of a famous boxer was a treat for everyone, including Teddy Roosevelt who was proud to name world champions Sullivan and Fitzsimmons his good friends. The makers and breakers of the time—tycoons, politicians, and presidents of the United States with their "bare knuckle" politics—came and went, "rolling with the punches," "saved by the bell," or "throwing in the towel." Other boxing expressions that became part of everyday language included: "go the distance," "keep gloves up," "hit below the belt," "time out," "cornered," "mock punch," and "top-notch." Men's underwear that looked like boxing trunks became known as "boxers." The supreme compliment of "she knocked me out" remains to this day, and one can find a "real McCoy" in any walk of life.

So far, Joe had proven himself to be marketable, with his winning smile, his inborn gameness, and a genetic gift of strength, speed, and endurance, amplified by determination and pugilistic skill. That was good enough for Doessereck, who could smell a future champion. The only thing Joe didn't have was the time to wait in line for his turn to challenge a title.

Chapter 16
Keep on Winning

There were no guarantees in life (no argument there), especially in prizefighting, and nobody knew it better than middle-aged Doessereck, whose existence could be easily described in one word: boxing. As mentioned before, he had long experience in managing and promoting excellent professional boxers, but not much luck turning them into champions. At the present, his best client, Irish Johnny Curtin, had certainly deserved a shot at the title for a long time, but instead he was endlessly battling Petey Mack, Willie Shugrue, Spencer Gardner, and other topnotch featherweights, also going nowhere with their remarkable wins. In the same category of frustrated challengers was Mickey Brown, whom Tex Rickard called the "greatest crowd pleaser in the world." He was almost a regular at Madison Square Garden, where he knocked out Willie Davis and Australian champion Tibby Watson, and fought sensational rounds against Mike Ballerino, Carl Duane, and Tony Vaccarelli.

At the present time Joe Grimm belonged to the latter struggling group, and he was scheduled as a last-minute substitute against Harry Felix of Brooklyn, a promising welterweight undefeated in his last fifteen fights. His record said it all: some of his wins were against Johnny Kochansky at Madison Square Garden, besides defeating Joe Kestner in Brooklyn. Felix was an excellent six-rounder, now ready to be tested in an eight-round exhibition fight against a believed nonrisky opponent. Four days after the last fight, at the weigh-in, Felix was eight pounds heavier than Joe, who took a good look at the highly ranked boxer before accepting the uneven fight. The slick Jewish guy was two years older, two inches taller, and had a body frame that was too large for his skinny legs, arms, and neck. Still, he was so handsome that he could pass as a ballroom dancer or a stylish waiter in a very expensive restaurant, and his friendly face had confidence written all over it.

Because this particular boxing exhibition was part of a benefit event for the New Jersey Policemen's Association and big donors were expected, the fights took place in Long Branch, a luxury resort community by the ocean, also called the "Hollywood of the East." There Joe realized how well some people lived and entertained, and for the first time he saw a massage table in the dressing room that was also equipped with lavish couches and beautiful mirrors and sinks, just like in Mario's barbershop.

"This is what I call a good life, my brother. Now, how about that win?" Mike rubbed his hands.

"I'll try my best!" answered Joe, doing a little warm-up before he sampled food from the table. Coach Nick was already sitting at a table and enjoying dinner. "Easy, son. It's not good to fight with a full stomach," he pointed out.

"It beats hunger, I'll tell you that much," mumbled underweight Joe. He felt like he was in a dream as he walked in the huge ballroom with Greek columns, Venetian chandeliers and sconces, large mirrors and paintings, and a big band playing next to the ring. Joe, Mike, and Coach Nick paraded into the ring as the band played a lively military march.

After announcements and the introduction of numerous benefactors and patrons, to Joe's surprise the announcer described him as "Gentleman Joe with the most KOs in a row!" That not only sounded good, but it rhymed! Felix was introduced as "the next title contender." Finally, the referee called the boys into the center of the ring, where they politely bumped gloves and the band played again. After receiving instructions from the referee, Joe and Felix returned to their corner to the same lively march.

For the first time Joe was meeting a boxer who was not eager to score big or throw a final wallop. To the contrary, Felix took his time to study the fight, and the first round passed without too much commotion from either scrapper. Basically, they feinted and circled each other as each managed to slip in a few fast gloves. What Joe quickly and gladly realized was that Felix had all the qualities needed in the ring, except a powerful punch. Back in his corner, sitting on the round chair with his arms on the ropes, Joe looked straight at Felix, trying to ignore Gina giggling and saying, "Come on, Joe!" and "Get him, Joe!"

At the gong the two boxers met in the middle of the square red canvas. Everything around them was so civilized—even the spectators were busier talking among themselves than watching the fight—that neither boxer seemed inclined to launch into a bloody fight. Observing this, Mike realized that betting was out of the question. For the next three rounds, Joe indulged in sparring with Felix with enough brutality to be called a fight, but so entertaining that it could be called a show. In the fifth round, Joe quit dancing around, and soon enough he caught Felix with a few powerful punches that shook his body. At the end of round seven, Coach Nick said, "Felix wore himself out." And Mike ordered, "Flatten the Hebrew!"

Frustrated in his efforts, Joe tried new ways to take Felix down. One of them almost worked, when repeated left hooks to the liver made the other boxer gasp for air. The audience gasped as well. Joe doubled and tripled his sharp left hook, chasing his retreating opponent, who somehow stubbornly ended the round by walking tall to his corner. "What else can I do?" asked Joe. "Don't let him rest," said Nick. "Go for the kill!" Mike urged. The final round was by far the best, when both boxers wanted to prove their ability to dominate and, if possible, to terminate the fight before the gong sounded. Joe kept pressing harder and harder, but Felix used amazing footwork to avoid being a steady target and punched back with fast hands. The ambitious boys fought to the finish with nothing held back. Joe clearly dominated the fight, but it was declared a draw since it was a "No Decision" fight.

In fact, Felix proved to be an excellent boxer who continued his record with another twenty-nine undefeated fights. In 1925, *The Ring* magazine ranked Felix one of the best ten lightweights in the world. What Mike understood was that his brother practically beat Felix, who had defeated Doessereck's featherweight, Kochansky. Clearly, Joe was above them, excepting one important fact—the fight with Felix was not official. Still, the *Bayonne Evening News* did point out that Grimm's performance was a "good showing" and said it "was a big boost for Charley Doessereck's new boxer."

Joe quickly took a shower, and after Mike showed him an envelope with $225, another record payment, he rushed to meet Gina and see his stablemate Kochansky battling Willie Davis in another "No Decision" eight-rounder. Afterward, Gina took Joe to a private party. Joe was so impressed, he asked, "How come you're here in Long Branch?" She giggled, wrapped her delicate hand around Joe's bicep, and answered, "Because I live here, silly!" The "champ" was out of words.

Around midnight, a shiny Chrysler stopped in front of the barbershop, where worried Mike was waiting in his slippers, wrinkled boxers, and sweaty tank top, smoking one cigarette after another. Gina said something and her friends laughed in good humor. She kissed Joe, who, by stepping out the car, returned to his own reality. Mike was speechless—especially the next day, when Gina came again to the barbershop, bringing another girlfriend for a bob cut.

When later on Joe returned from the gym, Mike scratched his head. "Gina is too rich for you. Nothing but trouble!" Joe replied, "But she's also very beautiful and smart." His brother reinforced his comment, "As I said, nothing but trouble! Remember, you're from Fall River and live in Bayonne. Besides, you are in training, not like me."

There were some striking similarities between the two distant cities of Fall River and Bayonne, a former colony of 1,700 settlers that was an extension of the Dutch community from Manhattan. It had become a large city of 77,000 residents who mostly worked in the many shipyards of the area and seventy-five major factories, among them Electric Dynamic, Gulf Refinery, and Standard Oil Works, which had operated since 1877. The Texas Company alone employed 5,000 people. Framed by a large body of water just like Fall River, both cities had glorious churches and monumental libraries, and impressive buildings that housed banks, public schools, the city hall, and the YMCA. The library in Bayonne had been a $50,000 gift from Andrew Carnegie in 1904; he then donated another $30,000 to enlarge it.

Unlike most cities in the United States in the 1920s, Bayonne had gas lamps and then electric lights on all the streets. The center of the city between Thirtieth and Fortieth Streets had hundreds of boarding houses with good furniture and services, including the use of a telephone in the hallway and a common full bathroom. The busiest avenue of all was Broadway, with its happy combination of expensive shops and cheap but very good places to eat owned by immigrants.

Bayonne was a cosmopolitan city with five newspapers. If someone wanted to report news to the paper, they needed only to call the main desk of the *Bayonne Evening News* by asking the operator to dial 947 or, if that line was busy, 948. The *Bayonne Times* had ample space dedicated to sports, including a well-informed "Gossip of the Ring" column that was popular with readers.

The peninsular city was thriving with cultural activity. Its majestic Opera House opened one day before the Joe Grimm–Harry Felix contest, with the lovely musical comedy *Irene*, which turned out to be a major hit. The city had ten theaters, used for a variety of social and cultural activities, including boxing. Most of them were located along Broadway Avenue and had names like the Bayonne Theater, the Bijou, the Embassy, the Plaza, the Lyceum, and the Victorian-built park, which over the years had attracted famous entertainers, including Jim Corbett, the world heavyweight champion.

The newly built De Witt Theater, with 2,700 seats and a $35,000 Wurlitzer organ, was the place for big indoor boxing events and for showing boxing movies, while the recently renovated Strand Theater hosted engagements for the Broadway Boxing Club. A new addition was the Casino on First Street, like the Casino in Fall River, which staged frequent boxing tournaments; local fans paid one dollar for the cheapest seats.

Entertainment was a huge industry in the Bayonne area, and people rooted for their local performers on the stage and local boys in the ring, whether they were challenging rookies, favorite contenders, or beloved champions. Bayonne, the "City of Churches," was also the home of highly rated boxers like Mike Ballerino, Jimmy Becker, Young Cicarelli, Mickey Donahue, Mickey Dunn, Young Freno, Johnny Kochansky, Freddie Krebs, Pete McGloughlin, Gordon Munce, Pete Scarano, Georgie Scott, Willie "Tiger" Shaw, Jeff Smith, Billy Vidabeck, and the latest addition, Joe Grimm.

Because of the "No Decision" ruling in New Jersey, more and more top-notch boxers came to the Bayonne area to enrich their ring experience without jeopardizing it. Unless one was knocked out, no boxing record would mention if he won or lost. When securing a decision by a knockout, a winner would make headlines around the country. In one week alone, remarkable professional fighters were scheduled to meet at the Oakland Club. According to the *Bayonne Times* of September 8, 1924, among the top billed was Doessereck's light heavyweight Billy Vidabeck, who was going to meet Lew Chester.

But the biggest attraction on September 8 was the much-anticipated contest between bantams Billy Kennedy and Jimmy Mendo, the highest-ranked challengers entitled to dethrone Abe Goldstein, the world king of this much-disputed bantam weight category, who would win against Tony Ryan that day. Billy Kennedy had a fearsome reputation reflected in his nickname, the "New Orleans Demon." He defeated Steve Smith and Mickey Walters, and he was scheduled to meet Petey Mack at the famous Boyle's Thirty Acres arena in the fall. Mendo was the "speedy bantam" champion of Philadelphia, well liked by local spectators, for he had never lost a fight in New Jersey. He also had the distinction of defeating legendary Joe Lynch. Mendo quickly advanced to top billing because he was knocked out only once. It looked like many boxers were given a chance to prove their value in the ring at a September event, and Mike wondered why his brother Joe Grimm was not included in this highly publicized competition.

Mike confronted Doessereck, who argued that he was not the matchmaker for the affair. Besides, Joe was not nearly as good as the bantam category names mentioned by the Bayonne newspaper; to throw Joe in the ring against any of them would terminate his career. From Doessereck's stable only Vidabeck was scheduled to fight. Granted, Joe was a local star from some place in New England, but here in New Jersey or New York, the name Grimm meant nothing to the audience and promoters.

Mike didn't like the explanation and left, furious. Wanting to prove his point, Doessereck decided to teach the brothers a lesson in respect. He matched Joe for the next fight with Tommy Teague of Indiana, who was visiting New York to fight his way to become a title challenger and make money to cover his expenses. He was in a bitter rivalry with Bud Taylor, so his manager was looking for someone worthy, but not too worthy, to fight his man. The readily available Joe Grimm seemed to be the right opponent. At the weigh-in on September 18, the well-rested Teague showed a good muscled body, a face marked by his past fights, and a confident disposition. The odds were against Joe, who was shorter, younger, and less experienced. Mike understood he was not to place a bet on his brother.

An eight-round bout was scheduled before the main fight, and the imposing announcer introduced Teague as the "Next Terror of Terra Haute" and Joe as the "Jack Dempsey of the Bantams." Referee Joe Jeanette summoned the boys to the center of the square, and after a brief instruction "to have a clean fight," he asked them to shake hands. After the bell sounded, Joe realized that he faced not a club fighter, but a versatile veteran who was not likely to tolerate much of Joe's aggressiveness. Teague kept feinting with his left to test Joe's reaction, setting himself up to deliver a real blow that could do harm. It was a beautiful sneaky move that old-timers used a lot, and the public loved it, but Joe was unaffected by it.

Since real professionals don't rush, rounds two and three were very similar to the previous action, but Joe pressed a few times and unloaded combinations of stiff punches that attracted noisy interest from the spectators. So far, the public indulgently treated the opening fight as a routine part of the top billing. But in round four, their interest was aroused when Joe relentlessly began to chase his opponent from ring post to ring post with power shots that landed heavily on Teague. Teague, in turn, counterpunched with repeated fast jabs that held Joe back. Rounds five and six found Joe in a firm crouching stance, throwing short taps to the body, while Teague kept counterpunching to neutralize the rest of the attack. Unwilling to step back, soon the two were banging away at each other, to the delight of the aroused audience.

At the break, Coach Nick asked Joe, "Where are your left hooks and right crosses?" Leaning against the ropes, Referee Jeanette smiled at him and nodded his head. That was enough to revive Joe, who darted into action for the seventh round. Rejuvenated by a second wind, Joe increased his assaults and bent, ducked, rolled, and weaved around Teague's long punches. Suddenly Joe saw the much-awaited opening and placed his left hook to the liver and right cross to the jaw. The two master punches stunned Teague, and his knees wobbled.

"Take him down!" screamed Mike. The public, who always craved such moments when the best hits of the fight came with injuries and blood, let loose with wild cheers and threw punches in the air. Determined to end the fight right there, Joe went for the final blow, only to be stopped by the bell. He turned around, and, refusing any care from his corner, he watched how the punch-drunk Teague, holding the ropes, dragged himself on rubbery legs to his corner, where the stool was pushed under him. His face was puffy with red and purple swells. At this point, the spectators remembered that Joe was from Bayonne, and hundreds, then thousands, chanted, "Joe the winner!" and "Joe KO!" Once again, Doessereck appeared in the ring corner and shook his fist in triumph.

The last round found the two boxers fighting tooth and nail for more than a minute, giving and receiving generous punches, until Joe's right cross found the target and almost shattered Teague's jaw. The shock nearly paralyzed Teague, who somehow managed to remain standing on shaky legs, his eyes blank. Unwilling to play "Gentleman Joe," the Bayonne guy moved forward to end the fight, only to find himself in the muscular arms of the huge black referee, who sent Joe to a neutral corner.

When the bell rang for the last time, the public released tumultuous ovations of "Gentleman Joe!" and "Little Dempsey!" that resounded over and over. Tommy Teague, face covered in blood, collapsed in his corner. By underestimating Joe, Teague had blown his chance for a comeback. Or at least that was the immediate public perception.

Doessereck was already at the ring corner to hug Joe and repeat, "Kid, these are championship rounds!" An envelope with $250 confirmed his enthusiasm. Mike was ecstatic. It was the fight one would pay any money to see, described by one present reporter as a "sizzling eight-round affair" and "a brilliant fight." Because of it, Joe made a lasting mark in the spectators' memory. What they wouldn't learn until the next day—Joe found out at the barbershop, where everyone gathered around to read the newspaper—was that the *Bayonne Times* reported, "Joe Grim Loses Tough Bout To Tommy Teague At Oakland Club." Everyone who had seen the fight was stunned. Doessereck shook his head when he saw Joe later. "You can't count on a newspaper decision unless there's a knockout," he said and sighed. What Joe learned again was that there are no guarantees in the ring.

Meanwhile, after the fight Joe got dressed and went back to the arena to see his stablemate and sparring partner Curtin, the headliner, fight Willie Shugrue, both billed as "New Jersey idols." Curtin proved a superior fighter and knocked down his opponent in the eleventh round, when Referee Jeanette stopped the fight to save Shugrue from unnecessary punishment. Again, Doessereck went crazy with happiness—by winning the fight his Johnny Curtin became the New Jersey featherweight champion. Making the win even sweeter, Shugrue's promoter Hen Connolly had bragged in all the newspapers that his man would terminate Curtin and his manager.

Later that night in Doessereck's car, Mike just could not help himself and talked again about the title shot. The promoter replied that to be a contender, one had to be a top-ranked boxer and belong to the small, elite group of the best five or six fighters qualified to challenge the title holder.

"Isn't Joe good enough?"

Doessereck responded, "Yes, Joe is a local star, but he still has to confront the real stars with real stellar records known all over the world."

Nevertheless, Joe was in the right place at the right time, and something spectacular might happen.

"So, what does he have to do?" asked Mike.

"Wait for his turn. Fame has its own price!" said Doessereck in a dry voice as he stopped in front of the closed barbershop with the lit red-and-white pole endlessly twisting.

"How about Joe fighting in the featherweight division? People in the barbershop read in the *Bayonne Times* that Dundee's reached the end of his career because Jack Bernstein beat him. Joe can floor Bernstein!"

The unwanted suggestion hit a nerve, and the promoter choked with astonishment. After clearing his throat, he gave an indirect answer. "Look at my poor Johnny Curtin, who is eight years older than you," he said, pointing a finger at Joe. "For years he packed each arena in the country, including Madison Square Garden, but still he couldn't fight Joe Lynch then, and he can't fight Abe Goldstein now for the title, even though last month we guaranteed the Jewish champ $7,500 and the right to bring his own referee! Go figure," lamented the promoter.

What Doessereck knew well was that even if Joe proved to be better than Curtin, he was not in any position to start his featherweight boxing record from scratch and defeat middle-level boys like Joe Celmars, Boddy "Knockout" Dawson, Young Eddie, Spencer Gardner, Jackie Gordon, Jack Housner, Rocky Kansas, Danny Kramer, Petey Mack, Billy Marlow, Sammy Mandell, Charlie Rosen, Willie Shugrue, Chick Suggs, and Mickey Taylor, never mind meeting the top contenders and champions, such as Benny Bass, Johnny Kilbane, Little Jack Sharkey, Bud Taylor, Jack Bernstein, Louis Kaplan, and Johnny Dundee. So far, another contender, Mike Ballerino, had in the last few months defeated Joe Foley, Joe Nelson, Billy Fitzsimons, Bobby Wolgast, and K. O. Joe O'Donnell. There were others who were just as good, including Cuddy Marco, Joe Souza, Joe Colmera, Joe Ryder, Mickey Brown, and Steve "Kid" Sullivan. On top of all this, there was challenger Johnny Kochansky, who was also in Doessereck's stable. He had just won over Bill Henry of Chicago, but still, as noted by a Bayonne reporter, he "faced such formidable foes as Sammy Mandell, Mike Dunee, Joe Burman, Ernie Gooseman, Harry Kabakoff, Sid Terris, Willie Kobler, Babe Herman and Harvey Bright." It would take Joe years just to make a name for himself in Doessereck's stable alone, much less fight in a heavier weight division.

Meanwhile, in his bantam category, Joe still had to meet the approachable Frankie Conway, Georgie Mack, Willie Spencer, Tommy Ryan, Joey "Spark

Plug," Herbie Schaeffer, Jackie Snyder, Harold Smith, Steve Smith, Johnny "Kid" Troy, Mickey Walters, and then the distant Bushy Graham of Utica, "Memphis" Pal More, Billy Kennedy, Jimmy Mendo and Benny Schwartz of Philadelphia, Johnny Vacca of Boston, Pete Zivic of Pittsburgh, and Jack "Kid" Wolfe of Cleveland, plus at least three best bantams of Chicago— Frankie Henke, Jimmy Kelly, and Ollie O'Neil. Never mind the bantams of New York City, like Frankie Albano, Willie Darcey, Harry London, Augie Pisano, Johnny Vestri, and finally, contenders Eddie "Cannonball" Martin, Charley "Phil" Rosenberg, "Midget" Smith, and Phil Verdi. Only by defeating most of them could he be called a challenger. It was a long and difficult road to the title disputed by Johnny Buff, Joe Lynch and Abe Goldstein.

Unaware of the intricate politics of prizefighting, Mike did know one thing for sure: his brother was a KO puncher who kept winning and the crowd loved Joe. To Mike, that was the undeniable main thing in boxing, and Joe would be a champion sooner or later, with or without Doessereck. In turn, Doessereck believed Joe was a durable fighter, but with Mike around he was a very unreliable client. However, the day after, Doessereck came to the barbershop to tell Joe, who was resting on a coach, that the next day, September 20, he would be fighting Joe Malone of the Bronx at the Ridgewood Grove in Brooklyn. The weigh-in was two hours before the fight. In the beginning, when Joe was called in as the last-minute substitute, it felt like he was filling in during an emergency. Now, three months later, it had become a pattern. As always, he readily agreed.

"Not so fast, brother!" Mike, who was shaving a client, intervened. Holding an open straight razor in his hand, he stepped between Doessereck and Joe. "Isn't Malone a featherweight?" Doessereck nodded. "Then we want $300 guaranteed!"

The promoter frowned, thinking that Joe would be making more money than Johnny Curtin, and realized once again how much he disliked Mike. But Joe's personal manager brother was so firm in his commanding voice and had such a nonnegotiable attitude that Doessereck agreed. That night Mike slept happily, knowing that he could bet on his brother's victory, since in New York judges rendered a decision after the fight was over.

The Ridgewood Grove Sports Club was situated near the Queens border on Saint Nicholas Avenue, and it could house up to 5,000 spectators. There seemed to be a full house on the evening Joe entered the ring. Obviously most were rooting for Malone, who was an up-and-coming fighter undefeated in the last year, and his appearance in the ring was welcomed with loud cheers. A local referee, dressed all in white, called the boys for instructions, and soon the bell marked the beginning of the first of eight rounds. Mike returned to the ring corner from placing bets on his brother, disregarding the fact that Joe had had an exhausting bout only two days before.

From the beginning Malone was bad news for Joe. He was a typical club fighter who wanted to show off in front of his fans and began the round in full force. But Joe could not be baited into a brawl, and for the next three rounds, he changed the tempo of the fight, taking the lead by outmaneuvering the furious boxer who made tracks of smoke in the air with his missing gloves. Between breaks, Coach Nick advised Joe against any clinch that would result in head butts and other unwanted injuries.

In the fifth round, Malone charged Joe with all his heavy artillery, mainly windmill punches pulled from the floor. It was a tactic he soon regretted when Joe planted one single right cross on the jaw that set the confused Malone back on his heels until he rested against and between the ropes. It could not be a better setup for Joe to hammer his rival to the canvas, but he waited for the referee to allow Malone back in the ring. The public liked that and applauded Gentleman Joe. The bell rang, and the boys went to their corners. Coach Nick and Mike could not believe their eyes. "You just missed a knockout!" both yelled. "Pick your moment and finish him off!" added the coach.

In rounds six and seven Malone turned into a cautious fighter who avoided exchanging blows and did everything to stay away from Joe's hard punches. Arms up all the time to cover his face and almost running around the ring, he seemed relieved each time the bell signaled the end of the round. As expected, round eight was entirely dominated by Joe, who caught up with the running Malone and delivered sharp hooks to his midsection and right crosses to the face. One right punch landed flash on his nose, which began to bleed heavily, and both fighters were covered in the blood. It was Malone's blood. The officials, reporters, and expensive ticket holders, including many ladies at ringside, covered their clothes with newspapers, loving each second of the slaughter. When the bell marked the end of the fight, even the referee's outfit had changed from white to red, and everyone in the ring sighed with relief.

It was an unusually hellish fight for Joe, who collected the well-deserved $300 and entered "won decision over Joe Malone" in his personal notebook.

However, the $300 was Joe's largest pay ever. Mike was ecstatic about his negotiation.

The next day Gina entered the barbershop, where everyone was discussing Joe's last victory. "My brother is waiting outside in the car. Let's go for a ride!" Joe was happy to do something besides boxing or talking to the clients in the barbershop, and agreed. Giggling, both rushed inside the car, leaving Mike mute and angry. "Where to, champ?" asked William, smoothing his driving gloves over his fingers. Knowing nothing but boxing, Joe decided they should go and visit Joe Jeanette's gym.

Chapter 17

Puzzling Events

Within a ten-mile radius of Bayonne were the sister cities of Elisabeth, home of rising boxing star Mickey Walker; Jersey City, home of Johnny Curtin; Newark, with Giovani Salerno; and West Hoboken, where Little Jack Sharkey (Giovanni Julio Cervati) lived and where Referee Jeanette conducted his boxing business. West Hoboken, famous for making lace and other embroidery, was unlikely to be identified as the home of the former heavyweight black contender. Yet Jeanette (birth name: Joseph Jeanettei) was a remarkable presence among the heavily white Dutch, English, German, Irish, and Italian population. His fifteen-year fighting career was filled with hundreds of victories, showing fifteen fights against Sam Langford and ten against future heavy champion Jack Johnson, both blacks. Because of his skin color, Jeanette was never put in a position to challenge any white champion of his time. However, he held a distinctive and unchallenged record, when in Paris in 1909 he battled Sam McVey for three and a half hours and won by TKO after forty-nine gruesome rounds with forty-nine knockdowns between both stubborn black combatants. Jeanette retired practically undefeated at the age of forty.

Now, the forty-five-year-old Jeanette, the ever-handsome "Iron Man," still looked like a statue of a boxer, and he still climbed in the ring not only as a referee and sometime judge, but also as a fighter in exhibition bouts. Nevertheless, his main connection with the boxing world was his gym, which was famous for its lowest membership fee and friendly atmosphere. Notable patrons included featherweight "Little" Jack Sharkey, Joe Celmars (the Polish lad who went toe-to-toe with Johnny Kochiansky), and Mike Ballerino, who won against Joe Souza at Madison Square Garden. Among other regulars was light heavyweight Jimmy Francis, the archrival rival of Billy Vidabeck.

Gina decided to go shopping with her brother and pick up Joe later. Approaching the gym, he heard lively jazz music played on phonograph records, creating a Harlem-type atmosphere. He was taken aback by what he saw around him. Dry and fresh spit with a phlegm and blood mixture formed a muddy layer that covered the floor; peeling walls with patches of missing plaster were clumsily covered with old boxing posters hanging crookedly; a dirty, wobbling fan dropped from the ceiling held by a wire; and flycatcher ribbons were waving all over. Inside and around the ring, furious shadowboxers threw punches at imaginary foes. A few heavy punching bags, all patched, were mercilessly beaten by ambitious boys with little power in their fists. Joe would have left the gym if he hadn't spotted Joe Jeanette, smiling at him from a dark corner.

"Hey, man, at lazt you came!" Jeanette said as he approached Joe, and they shook hands. The gym owner whistled and then shouted in his deep baritone voice, "Men, lizen up: thiz iiizzz Gentleman Joe, the real thzing I told you about!" The boys paused to wave their hands and gloves, and went back to their training business. One of them, looking anemic, too tall for his weight to be a serious fighter, was the Irish Jimmy Braddock, another regular client of the low-maintenance gym.

When asked how everything was going with Doessereck's stable, Joe didn't hesitate to tell him everything, including what Mike was thinking. The former great underdog listened carefully. It was obvious that the legendary boxer understood the system, and he tried to explain to Joe how managers and promoters made money by rotating their challengers. In fact, the champion might trade places with a few underdogs, because the more fights there were, the more money the public would pay to see them disputing a crown. "Man, tell you, I could floor an'one in my time. I wuz real gooood! ... But I ain't fit the zyztem, un'stand? No, even Jack Johnson ain't give me a shot to the dam' title ... Nev' mind the white boyz, Jezzs Willard and Dempzey ... Hey, man ... I'm telling you ... iz all about money ..."

Grimm and Jeanette were quiet for a while, looking at some twenty boxers working out with the belief that one day they would become rich and famous champions. Then Jeanette said with a large grin, "Fortunately," and he pointed to different posters faded by dust and marked by flies, "I was in mighty fine comp'ny with Sam McVey, Harry Wills, and the 'Greatest

Fighter Nobody Knows,' Sam Langford. None of uz ever got near the damn title. Any ti'le ... I'tel'u man, it happen' to the bezt of uz ... Make zum money and run for yo' life from thi' shitty biznez that can kill you ..."

Later that evening, Joe told Mike all about his conversation with Jeanette. Mike's reaction was brief. "Who wants to do business with him in the first place?"

Three days after Joe's fight with Malone, Doessereck rushed to the gym to tell Joe that he had qualified for a semifinal against Johnny "Kid" Troy of Jersey City, a promising starter with no defeats yet in his professional career. "What kind of final?" wondered Mike and the guys from the barbershop, but Joe didn't know. Two days later at the weigh-in Troy was 125 pounds, forcing Joe to fight in the next division, in which his stablemates Irish Johnny Curtin and Johnny Kochansky disputed their priority. The six-round preliminary fight took place at the Oakland arena, where Joe's appearance in the ring was greeted with applause and some ovations. Local boy Troy was received with even more encouraging whistles and even louder screams, showing who was the favorite in the ring.

Round one began briskly with an expected exchange of blows. Joe threw a few solid left hooks to the body, fully felt by Troy, who counterpunched with some success. At the bell, Joe was ahead by points, as he had proven himself to be a more skillful puncher. Rounds two and three were a repetition of the first, but the fourth round was a dramatic change when Joe decided to floor Troy, carrying out an unstoppable close-range attack that almost made the referee stop the fight. At the bell, Troy staggered badly until he dropped onto his corner stool. "He's finished!" proclaimed Mike, regretting the lack of betting. But Coach Nick advised caution, since Troy seemed to be the type to lose with honor, by inflicting all damages he could. Just by looking at the angry and sour rival, Joe could guess how rough the next rounds would be. There was nothing like a desperate fighter who wanted to save face.

Well instructed by his corner, in round five Troy readjusted his tactics to keep Joe at a distance, and he scored with a few fast jabs. Encouraged by the happy reaction of the audience, he initiated a two-fisted attack, only to walk straight into Joe's trap that came with a rain of counterpunches. The well-aimed blows landed loudly all over Troy's body, and again the referee stood by, ready to stop an unnecessary punishment. So far, "it was all Grim in every round, but Troy, when he looked to be almost on the verge of a knock out, provided plenty of excitement by pulling wild, death-dealing punches from the floor," wrote a reporter. As anticipated, Troy decided to go for "all-or-nothing" and put all his hopes on sheer punching power. With an amazing vigor triggered by frustration, he became violent and dangerous, swinging wild punches that would sink Joe to the floor if they landed on him. But Joe was too agile. "It was just a breeze for Grim. His clean punches had Troy playing the role of a sandbag," concluded the same reporter. After the final bell and accumulation of too many punches, dizzy and bitter Troy refused to come to the side of the referee, and Joe was the undeniable winner. Gina was beside herself with joy, and spectators waving panama hats all over, with choirs of cheers, saluted the victory. Unlike the past fights, Doessereck didn't come to the ring corner to congratulate Joe, who collected $250 given by the event's matchmaker.

With three brutal fights in one week, Joe was tired and didn't go to the gym the next day. Instead he hung around the barbershop and listened to the fiery discussions among the clients and Mike, all against Doessereck. They all agreed that Joe was ready to excel even in Madison Square Garden, the ultimate arena for any boxer and promoter. After all, many of Doessereck's boys, like Irish Curtin, Johnny Kochansky, and Billy Vidabeck, performed in the Garden, so why not Joe, with a similar, if not even better, boxing record? They believed Doessereck was up to no good, since he did not even book Joe in his own Pioneer Sporting Club, which he'd managed for some twenty-five years. It was a renowned boxing arena where many important people came to see the fights and spot the potential contenders.

As for Doessereck, business could not be better. His bitter rival "Hen" Connolly had vanished since the Broadway Sporting Club now had different owners, and a new boxing arena with four thousand seats was going to be built on West First Street. Named the Bayonne Casino, the sports facility would also accommodate basketball, handball, and roller-skating. William Hermenau, the head of the enterprise, declared to the press that he was looking for a matchmaker for the arena, and Doessereck considered himself a front-row candidate for the job. In that capacity he would practically rule boxing affairs within and beyond New Jersey's borders.

Almost a month passed without any fights for Joe, who continued his training. By sparring with Curtin and Kochansky, he again realized that he was at least as good as they were. And he told that to Mike, who, boiling with fury, decided to have another talk with Doessereck. The promoter listened very calmly to the frustrated brother and explained to him that Joe was a very good fighter who did not yet rank near the top. Therefore, he was not ready to appear in Madison Square Garden, nor in his Pioneer Club. Mike rejected this and insisted that Doessereck should give Joe a chance because he would surprise everyone with how well he'd do.

"I'll consider him for the Pioneer, but not for the Garden," the promoter relented, trying to get rid of the personal manager.

"Why not the Garden?" Mike would not let go.

"There's no Garden for Joe to box in!" Doessereck shook his head, weary of being pushed. "The old Garden is going to be demolished, and the new one will go under construction."

Mike, for a change, was speechless and looked at the floor, considering his next move. Doessereck took a moment to enjoy his one-upmanship and then gently pushed him out the door.

The next afternoon when Joe was washing his boxing outfits in the bathtub upstairs, Gina paid a visit and asked him to come for a ride. She was beautifully dressed in a light-green two-piece outfit with elegant shoes to match, white gloves, and white bowl hat. Her violet-scent perfume made Joe dizzy. He happily agreed, saying, "Wait in the car and I'll be there in a few minutes." It took more than that to put on his best shirt, tie, and new suit. He pulled out the bottom chest drawer and took five bills of $10, tied the laces to his new white-and-brown "spectator" shoes, and ran to the car, avoiding the barbershop filled with noisy clients. Mike was busy with a customer but saw him and went outside after him, only to see Joe waving through the car window. "I'm going to check on the Garden!"

Gina looked at Joe and could not believe he was the same person she knew. Even William, who had the same shoes and was wearing a tweed golf suit, admired Joe's well-tailored brown suit and asked, "Champ, what garden are you talking about?" Joe knotted his tie and responded, "The only Madison Square Garden where the best of the best fight!" The brother and the sister looked at each other and burst into laughter.

"Champ, that's in New York City, and gas is fifteen cents a gallon!" With a casual gesture, Joe pulled out the banknotes and waved them while returning the laughter. "Gasoline is not a problem, nor is a good restaurant meal!"

William pushed the gas pedal and the car started down the street. "Okay, okay, you twisted my arm enough. To the Garden!"

Joe had never been in Manhattan before. William slowly drove downtown on Broadway and uptown on Fifth Avenue so he could admire the tall buildings, the monumental churches, the large windows of department stores, and parts of Central Park. There were a lot of automobiles, tramcars, police cars, trucks, and regular horse wagons, all rushing and miraculously missing the well-dressed people hurriedly crossing the streets.

As the car left Madison Avenue, they faced a majestic Spanish-style building with a thirty-two–story tower adorned with a lot of square windows; columned openings dominated everything else around. On top of the tower a graceful gold statue of the Greek goddess Diana slowly turned in the mild wind of the beautiful October afternoon. This was the place where, in March 1916, heavyweight Jess Willard defended his title against Frank Moran, and four years later Jack Dempsey knocked out Bill "KO" Brennan of Kentucky in the twelfth round. Hundreds of the highest-ranked boxers fought in the same ring, making the building the most famous arena in the world, now a moribund landmark destined for the wrecking ball. It was to be replaced with a new Madison Square Garden at Fiftieth Street and Eighth Avenue by the genius promoter Tex Rickard, who had raised almost $6 million for that purpose.

Driving around between Seventh and Eighth Avenues, the hungry travelers smelled the irresistible aroma of fried fish, and William stopped the car in front of Paddy's Clam House. They had just gotten out of the automobile and stretched their legs when they heard a familiar voice. "Joe, is that you, kid? Oh my, my, my, don't tell me this beautiful lady is with you!" It was none other than Charley Doessereck, well dressed in a three-piece striped suit and fedora hat, walking with an extended arm toward the small group. Joe introduced Gina and her brother and appreciated what a gentleman Doessereck was when he kissed Gina's perfumed hand and then invited all three of them for "a late lunch or an early dinner, on me."

They stepped inside a rather small restaurant, decorated with a lot of woodwork designed to resemble a fisherman's joint, the perfect theme for the menu that was based on fish and shellfish. Small tables made of rough planks touched by a layer of wax were close to each other, and a waiter pushed two together. Before sitting down, Doessereck addressed the thirty-some men in striped summer suits and white jackets seated in the restaurant that catered to sports clientele, especially boxing.

"Hey, everybody, this is my golden boy, Joe, the Little Dempsey!" He raised Joe's arm. The men clapped and whistled. A few came to the table to shake Joe's hand and approvingly pat Doessereck on the shoulders. There were many old-timers, few ex-fighters, Joe saw, and some of the men looked like they might be business managers, all dressed in double-breasted pinstriped jackets or ivory linen suits, sporting panama hats or straw boater hats and colorful bow ties. The entire place seemed to be a boxing shrine, with walls covered by framed pictures of winners in the ring or posing in full regalia, champion belts included.

The owner, "Paddy" White, who claimed that he sold a few million clams and oysters a year, was a fanatical boxing fan. He was known for traveling thousands of miles to see a good boxing match, and everyone in the business knew him. His restaurant was a hangout for fans and professionals, partly because of its decor and food, but also because it was conveniently located in the heart of Manhattan, only blocks away from the future Pennsylvania Station.

Paddy himself, dressed in white, face and neck red from perspiration, came from the hot kitchen to take their orders. "I know you. You're the Gentleman Boxer with the burgundy robe. I saw you flooring the Filipino guys! Right?" He heartily shook Joe's hand. He tried to squeeze it harder but gave up. "That's a million-dollar grip you got. Does Charlie take good care of you?" Joe and Doessereck looked at each other with different things in mind, and both nodded. Satisfied, Paddy vanished into the steamy kitchen.

When they finished the meal, Paddy pulled a chair up to the table and talked to Doessereck about some people they hadn't seen in a long time. Suddenly he turned to Joe. "So, young man, when do I hang your picture next to Jack Dempsey?" He pointed to the wall of fame with autographed pictures of tens of well-known fighters. Joe smiled and nodded toward his promoter.

"Ask him!"

Paddy then looked at Doessereck, who said, "When the time is right and ripe!"

The lunch was over. As everyone stood up to leave, Doessereck put his hand on Joe's arm and said, "By the way, kid, I know you probably think the grass is greener with the neighbor, so why don't you check out the best boxing gym in New York City? Some believe it's top in the entire country. It's good to be educated before making a fool of yourself." He wrote an address on a piece of paper from his little notebook and handed it to William. "It was good to see you all!" Doessereck tipped his hat and left.

"He's really something," Gina said as she watched Doessereck go out the door.

"Quite a gentleman," added William. Joe nodded. He was not only very impressed by his promoter, but liked him a lot.

William drove on Eighth Avenue and stopped in front of a row of standard brick buildings with fire escape railings hanging all over. On the wall of one was a large sign reading, "Stillman's Gym—Training Here Daily." William double-parked in front of it. After walking up a dark stairway to a landing, Joe entered the largest gymnasium he'd ever seen. To him, it was as big as a soccer field, and certainly it was the filthiest and most unsanitary place one could imagine. Indeed, since it opened in 1921, the gym never had a window ajar, floors cleaned, or toilets and showers washed. Sunlight didn't stand a chance of getting into the room through the filthy windows, and the place was badly lit by a few electric bulbs. The vinegary odor of wet leather, boxing gear, and grubby canvas stung the eyes and left a foul taste in the mouth.

There were two rings next to each other, always busy with sparring rounds. Numerous smoking spectators paid fifteen cents to watch the past, present, or future champions at work. The heavy and speed punching bags were busy all the time, and pairs of boxers threw medicinal balls to each other. Many patches of floor were covered by rope skippers; trainers with flat gloves called punches to be delivered by their sweaty pupils who furiously spit and blew their noses. Others practiced their shadowboxing in front of a mirrored wall covered by a film of spit and dirt. Muscular boxers with adrenaline burning seemed to walk like ghosts in and out of the fog of dust and smoke.

It was a hell of a place that made Jeanette's gym look like a pharmacy. "Are you trying to sneak in without pay?" Joe heard and saw a man in his forties with a hawkish face and revolver in his belt that a tweed vest could not cover.

"I just got here, and I'm leaving," mumbled Joe.

"Then get out, you damned bum!" yelled the gym owner, and Joe ran back to the car.

"Let's go!" he told William, who quickly eased the car into the traffic. Joe couldn't wait to share his experience with Mike.

Mike listened to the entire story and agreed that Joe trained in good conditions, but his response to Doessereck's generosity was "He's scared stiff to lose you." He decided to have another talk with the promoter about advancing Joe's career faster.

CHAPTER 18

TOUGH DEMANDS

At the present time Doessereck was happy with Joe's ring performance, because he could easily fit into three fighting divisions between 112 and 130 pounds—flyweight, bantam, and featherweight, and any subcategory between. This meant Joe had an important place in Doessereck's stable as a last-minute replacement ready to enter the ring the moment he was called and then walk out of it undefeated. As a substitute boxer, or in his own right, Joe would fight anybody, anytime, anywhere, and still win. Doessereck understood the shifting moods of immigrants and their feverish desire to make a lot of money right now. But Mike's constant interference was a liability to Joe's career, when once again he confronted the promoter with "No one has defeated Joe. He keeps winning, but he makes no progress!"

Doessereck raised his eyebrows and then his voice. "What kind of progress do you have in mind?"

Mike matched the same tone of voice. "He's too far from a title shot."

Doessereck took a moment to compose himself. "Look here and pay attention. Johnny Curtin is eight years older than Joe. Curtin packs any arena—he's one of the best in the business, but we still have to beg Joe Lynch and Abe Goldstein for a shot at the title and it doesn't happen. Do you have any idea how hard it is to challenge a champion?"

Mike's eyes narrowed as he understood that his brother's success could endanger Curtin's career. He also understood how well Doessereck used "we." So he responded in a similar fashion. "We are waiting to be rewarded with a better booking card and more money."

Doessereck sighed heavily. He'd had enough of the self-important barber; it was time to end this discussion, once and for all. "*We?* Who do you think you are? A big shot? You're just the spit-bucket carrier and the towel-spinning guy in the ring corner. If you don't appreciate what I'm doing for your brother, then I've got no more time to waste on you. We're finished talking. Go, I'm busy." Doessereck pushed Mike out the door.

Mike was fuming when he returned to the barbershop. "The nerve of that crook!" He went upstairs and found Joe ready to leave for his evening gym practice. "I've had it! We're going home. I know enough about this crappy business now, and I can handle things myself. We'll be a whole lot better off in Massachusetts, where at least at the end of the fight there's a sure winner." Taking a breath and calming himself, he proceeded to tell Joe about the conversation with Doessereck. Joe listened with his head lowered; he didn't want to leave Doessereck. But he trusted Mike more than anyone. That evening Mike called his brother-in-law, Louis Massery, the only family member to have his own telephone.

From Louis, Mike learned that his parents and younger siblings were getting ready to pack their belongings and soon would be leaving Fall River for Pittsfield. Everything had been arranged for them to take over the grocery business and live in the apartment above the store. So, Louis advised, the boys should wait a bit longer until their family had moved in and then go directly to Pittsfield, where they would be a huge help in the store. In the meantime, their parents could use some money. Mike agreed to send $500 through Western Union. When he hung up, he filled Joe in. Both sat quietly, thinking.

The next morning Joe was at the gym, training as usual. Mike was back working in the barbershop. Three uneventful weeks passed very slowly until one Thursday night, when Doessereck came to the gym and told Joe to get ready for a weigh-in. He'd be fighting the next day in Hoboken at the Palace Garden. Joe was thrilled. When he told Mike the good news, he also added, "Bet on a sure KO, let's say in the third round!"

Mike grinned. "Who're you fighting?"

Joe shrugged his shoulders and threw some slow punches to underline his smile. As he dodged them, Mike asked, "How come you're so sure of taking this guy down when you don't even know who he is?"

Joe crossed his arms and smiled. "I'm going to show Doessereck what I'm made of, and besides, I'm completely rested for a change!" Relieved and happy to be back in the money business again, Mike rubbed his hands.

◆⊱◆

The arena was packed with local people, and to Joe's pleasant surprise, old Jeanette was the referee. "How're ya doing, ma' man?" he asked Joe while checking the wrappings and gloves.

"To do better, I'd need a twin brother!" exclaimed Joe.

The referee, remembering what he'd overheard from Doessereck about Mike, mumbled, "Better wizout him. Make sure do good today, huh?" Joe was fighting another opening bout. The main twelve-rounder was between Curtin and Willie Spencer. As for Joe, his opponent was Joe Cole, "one of the best in Jersey City, having been showing in 10-rounders for the last two years," as noted by a reporter. Obviously Cole had a lot of experience in fighting a ten-round fight, one more reason Joe decided to end the fistic affair quickly. Wearing his beautiful burgundy robe, Joe slipped through the cords into the ring, and the public generously acknowledged his presence. Joe looked for Gina in the audience, but she wasn't among the spectators.

From that strong start when both landed hard blows, the fight gradually turned gloomy for Cole as Joe began to chase him all over the ring. In doing so, he used almost elegant moves, as he constantly wove his body to the left and right with rhythmic punches. Cole was good in blocking many of them, but he was too slow when throwing his own, making him often end up on the receiving end. He left many holes in his defense, but Joe pretended not to notice as he orchestrated his way toward a KO. Now and then when Joe was dancing around, Cole got some good points and good moments, making Joe well aware that this wasn't a routine to continue.

After the first round was over, the spectators shouted their encouragement for the fighters to be more aggressive. "Brother, you remember the third round, don't you?" whispered Mike, but Joe was late again meeting Cole, who bent him over with sharp uppercuts to the stomach. The spectators jumped up, expecting a KO, but Joe maneuvered to the side, recovered his firm stance, and swung back with a whopping left hook, flashed into Cole's liver. The impact was so painful that he crouched with both arms around his middle, his face turning blue. "Hit him in the pucker!" screamed Mike, but Referee Jeanette stepped between, cutting Joe's access. He asked Cole if he was all right; the boxer took a deep breath, lifted and then lowered his arms, and exhaled a choked "Yes!"

Joe waited in the center of the ring, but Cole wanted to avoid stepping into the same hook and began to steal time, dancing around. Jeanette called the boys and ordered, "Box!" Back-and-forth jabs followed in rapid succession, looking good and tough but doing no harm. Their staccato breathing of *whoosh whoosh whoosh* seemed to lead the exchange, and for a while the boys fought head-to-head. "Drop him, Joe!" Gina kept screaming, but the round ended with no drama. "Are you going to deck him?" asked Mike worriedly, and Joe nodded while taking a long sip of the icy water. "Easy, Joe." Coach Nick grabbed the bottle. Joe stood up and threw a few punches toward his fans and cheering Gina. "Joe, the bell!" shouted Mike.

The third round started in a bad way for Cole as Joe launched an unstoppable attack, hitting the almost-defenseless opponent with everything he could throw. He lit the ring with sparks as he jabbed, swung, and threw left hooks combined with right crosses, later described as "soporific" punches intended to "put Cole to sleep." The public was delirious as Joe's sharp left hook settled the fight. Cole collapsed on the canvas, like he'd been shot. Referee Jeanette counted to ten, signaled the cornermen to take care of Cole, and raised Joe's right arm high. They walked around the fallen opponent to salute the public.

This little triumphal ring tour made Joe feel really good. Mike was beside himself because of winning "a very fat bet," and Doessereck rushed to the ring. The public was generous with ovations for the winner, showing again how little human nature had changed since the Roman times of gladiatorial arenas. The main event fight was next, and it did not disappoint. His fans and the rest of the spectators cheered the hard-won victory of their idol Johnny Curtin after twelve rounds against Willie Spencer. Little did they know that their idol was heading for a surprising string of six straight defeats. But Joe was definitely on his way up, and a newspaper wrote that "Grimm made a big hit with the fans" and he "came out of the fight without a mark."

Joe had only a vague memory later as to how he ended up with Gina, William, and Doessereck in the Bavarian restaurant for a late supper. The promoter ordered stuffed cabbage for himself and Wiener schnitzel for his guest. Waiting for the food, the promoter wasted no time in speaking to Joe. "Listen, kid, because you are the boxer and my client, not your brother, I want to explain, in front of your friends, a few things you've got to understand. Okay?" After looking around the table, making sure everyone was paying attention, he continued. "I know you're anxious to rank higher, but believe me, I'm building the reputation you need for that. Terrible things happen in this business when kids like you are pushed beyond their strength and rushed into unfixable disasters. Right now …"

Joe surprised Doessereck with an interruption. "Sir, I don't want to fight local guys like I did in Fall River. I think I earned the right to fight in New York, where at least it'd be clear if I won or lost!"

Doessereck regrouped and continued in the same fatherly tone. "Kid, you are not ready to defeat a world-class fighter who could kill you in the ring. That's why I don't want to overmatch you. I'm telling it like it is. They're my witnesses." He pointed to Gina and William and continued. "What you need right now is to gain experience and notoriety on your own turf!"

Gina was the next to interrupt. "He keeps winning by a KO and provides victorious blazing finishes. He's good!"

Doessereck looked at Gina and shook his head in frustration. Then he pointed at Joe. "At least ten guys outclass you right now. No offense, kid, but you've got to face reality."

A waiter brought large dishes overflowing with food. Before touching his schnitzel, Joe asked, "Okay, so what do I need to do?"

Doessereck pointed his finger again and this time shook it at the ceiling. "Train and wait. It takes time and patience to be a champion. There's no other way to get there. By the way, here's your envelope." He handed $250 to Joe.

"Thanks, sir! So, how long do I have to wait for a shot at the title?"

Doessereck almost dropped his knife and fork and, leaning forward with his elbows on the table, began counting on his fingers. "Let's see. The real challengers and contenders, like Abe Goldstein, the champion in your category, turned pro in 1916. It took eight years after that for him to get a shot at the title held by Joe Lynch, who's seven years older than you. Eddie 'Cannonball' Martin never lost in his last fifty fights; he knocks out everyone, but he's not near the title yet. How about Steve 'Kid' Sullivan, who is fighting victoriously since 1907 and only a few months ago got a shot at the title. And the other 'Kid' Kaplan? He's been winning big since 1919 and only now, in 1924, is near the title. Do you think you're ready to battle his stumbling blocks—Bobby Garcia, Danny Kramer, Babe Herman, and Joe Lombardo? Let's not forget some others who are waiting in line for the title—Mike Ballerino, Young Corbett, Tony Vaccarelli, and Tommy Freeman. Tommy has won thirty-nine bouts in a row since 1921. Oh, yeah, and there's also Harry Willis, who at age thirty-five is still waiting to dethrone Jack Dempsey, who in his turn demolished everyone in the ring for five years before becoming the world champion."

Doessereck took a noisy breath, leaned back in his chair, and, after taking another sip of water, continued. "So, here you are. You've been in Bayonne for three months. You've had a few good fights and think you're at the level of all these other guys! Maybe you want to face Johnny Kilbane, the world featherweight champion since 1912? You're nineteen years old, kid, and you're asking me, 'When do I get to be a champion?' Wait your chance, like everyone else. You want fame, pay the price!" Joe, Gina, and William were quiet, all looking at the table and picking at their food. An accordion player began a happy polka. For the rest of the evening, there was no more talk about boxing until the group left the restaurant. Then Doessereck, realizing he had been very blunt, pulled Joe aside. "Kid, your next fight will be in New York. Get ready for it, because it will be a hell of lot different from what you know."

Joe was dropped off in front of the barbershop by William, and Gina gave him a kiss in front of Doessereck and in full view of Mike, who was smoking in the entryway and clearly nervously waiting for his brother. After listening to what Doessereck had said at the restaurant, Mike pursed his lips. "That Doessereck is a two-faced dealer and can't be trusted. We'll show him the boxing business, don't you worry!" Joe took a good look at his brother to see if he was joking or not.

Joe felt better the next day, when Doessereck stopped by the gym and told him to get ready to fight Mike Esposito in Brooklyn in ten days. On October 29, Joe was in the ring at the familiar Ridgewood Grove Sporting Club. He was ready to fight an opening bout for his stablemate Johnny Kochansky, who was facing Billy Henry of Chicago, described as "one of the real top notchers" in the featherweight division. The same reporter believed that Kochansky was "advancing rapidly to the list of championship contenders," which was not the case for Joe, who battled an unknown bantam from Connecticut. Esposito was a solid six-rounder who had done well in the past year until he lost to Willie Suess (who was good enough to have fought in Madison Square Garden, where he lost against Jackie Snyder). In bout-by-bout records, Joe was a superior fighter to all of them. Knowing this and determined to prove it again with a big win, he determinedly climbed into the ring and wiped the soles of his shoes in the resin box. Mike placed a "hefty bet" on his brother. To his surprise, Joe was introduced by the announcer as "the undefeated Jimmy Haskins of Brooklyn." This was because his New York boxing license had been procured by Doessereck under another identity. It was a common procedure to give a fighter different names in different states, and protect him from an eventual bad record of lost fights.

The first round was a stormy one, because the burly Esposito was a solid stand-up boxer who bothered very little with defense since only the KO punch counted for him. With both opponents wanting to establish dominance, they offered a spectacular fight to the happy crowd. The second round seemed to be all war, as the boys offered bell-to-bell nonstop action, fully appreciated by the spectators. At this point they had no loyalty to either fighter, loudly cheering whichever one was doling out the more punishing blows. Joe, with his flat feet, had difficulty maintaining leg speed and keeping up with his opponent's footwork. However, it was clear to everyone that Joe could hit better and harder, as red lacerations appeared on Esposito's face. Totally impervious to Joe's boxing qualities, he continued to launch one wild attack after another, with at least ten punches in a row, a lot of them just off the mark, as if trying to score a victory by a knockout slam. Still, there were no clinches and no faulty moves.

The third round wrapped up in true bantam style, with both fighters giving their all and holding nothing back. And the public loved it. During the fourth round, Joe realized his best strategy was to maneuver Esposito. Joe planted his left hook with all his swinging power into the assailant's liver. A loud cry exploded out of Esposito. The audience was shocked to see him hanging on the higher rope. "Finish him!" Mike screamed. Joe sprang to do just that when the referee sent him to the neutral corner and began counting the staggered Esposito. The sound of the bell interrupted the referee, and the limping boy hardly reached his corner. Joe asked Coach Nick what else he could he do to win by a KO. "Do the same thing again!" was the advice, and Mike added, "Lick him for good this time!"

By the fifth round, it was again clear that a better boxer can outgun and outpower a better fighter, and Joe was the perfect example as he was ripping harmful shots to the ribs and stomach. Yet, regardless of how many excruciating punches he received, Esposito had recovered from the pounding and kept on fighting. Because he managed to keep moving around, Joe wasn't able to place his best KO punches, but he nevertheless succeeded in outslugging Esposito, who was stuck in corners with no room to sidestep or back up. By now, red lumps and swellings covered his face. At the break, Mike asked again for a KO, and Joe, breathing hard, nodded his head.

Amazingly, there was a lot of fight left in Esposito, who began the last round as he did in the beginning, with a storm of wild punches that forced Joe to keep his distance. However, at the first sign of Esposito slowing down, Joe eased into closer range and showered him with many well-driven powerful blows to the body and face. The dangerous punches forced Esposito to run for cover behind the referee. It was almost comical to see how Esposito seemed to trail behind the referee, who tried to step away from the fight. The public was clearly enjoying the scene, laughing and shouting loud encouragements to the referee, who had punches flying all around his face. Joe ended up in complete charge of the fight and finished the last round with a demonstration of masterful boxing. Shakily, Esposito dragged himself to his corner, while Mike lifted Joe's arm and the public stood up for long ovations and applause.

While Joe was taking his gloves off and putting on his burgundy robe, the announcer collected the scoring cards, looked at them, and went back to the judges to ask something. Puzzled, he walked to the center of the ring, where Joe and Esposito flanked the exhausted referee. "We have a split decision, so I give you the winner by points." The announcer looked at the two sweaty and hard-breathing boxers. "Mike Esposito from Stamford, Connecticut!" sounded his thunderous voice. The public was stunned by the scandalizing decision, and loud protests reverberated throughout the arena. A reporter from Bayonne wrote, "The decision was roundly booed by the customers who thought that Grim had won." Mike went berserk, and Coach Nick held him back from charging the judges, who were talking to Doessereck.

It was a terrible moment that continued in the locker room when Joe received an envelope with $100. Obviously Mike lost his bet, and as much as he hated to see Kochansky win, he placed the rest of his money on him. Fortunately, Doessereck's other boy had a hard-earned victorious fight, and Mike felt better. The same reporter wrote that "Kochansky looks like the best featherweight prospect in the country today and barring accidents Bayonne seems almost certain to produce the next featherweight champion."

Back in the apartment Joe wrote in his record book, "Won over Mike Esposito," because another newspaper headlined their story, "Joe Grim of This City Beats Esposito But Judges Award Bout to Latter." Nevertheless, he found it difficult the next day to hear the entire barbershop talking about his defeat and about Kochansky's tenth win in a row since May. As consolation, Joe's barbershop fans reminded him that Johnny Curtin was not doing that great either, losing in October to Charley "Phil" Rosenberg at Madison Square Garden and to Hilly Levine, also in New York City. Yet, no one could deny the popularity of Curtin and his huge drawing power for the public. Later that night Joe realized that he had dropped into third place in Doessereck's featherweight stable. Mike saw things differently and tried to console his sad brother. "At least I made good money with Kochansky. Don't worry, you'll win big in the next fight!"

Joe nodded, but his head was lowered and his collapsed body spoke of depression. "What's the use? Doessereck is right about the championship stuff."

Mike exploded. "That crook arranged with the judges to show you that you're not good enough to fight in New York!" But Joe knew better: he was not a boy wonder any longer, delivering one knockout after another. Only time would tell what his future would be. As Doessereck always put it, "There are no guarantees in life—especially in boxing!"

CHAPTER 19
THE FIGHTS GO ON

The first week of November found Joe in the gym, practicing harder than ever. He noticed that a young boxer he'd seen in Jeanette's gym was showing up almost each day to do some sparring with Billy Vidabeck (who had won seventeen of his last twenty matches, eight by KO, and lost only three). The newcomer, nicknamed "Bulldog of Bergen" after the place in which he lived, was a skinny fighter, but with good technique and a lightning right hand that Billy tried to avoid. Like Joe, the new guy was always in a good mood and displayed respectful manners. His Irishness was written all over his face and actions. The quiet teenager would come only to the evening sessions, because during the day he was working. Learning from others that Joe had twenty-four KO wins in a row, he looked at his own frail hands next to Joe's beefy ones, smiled, and said, "You're very good indeed!" Joe little knew that the future world heavyweight champion Jimmy Braddock was admiring him.

Doessereck, in spite of his amazing ability to smell fighting talent, paid no attention to Jimmy. When he realized that Doessereck was not interested in managing him, Braddock stopped coming and returned to Joe Jeanette's stable. Years later, Doessereck still could not believe he had passed up such a golden opportunity. For the time being, Joe was much more important to him than the future Cinderella Man.

Still, fights were hard to come by for Joe, who was training in good faith when he learned that Johnny Curtin was losing weight by diet and sauna to get ready for a very important fight against Eddie "Cannonball" Martin, the number-one contender in the bantam class. The winner would challenge the title holder Abe Attell Goldstein. However, the mutual agreement with Doessereck was that Joe was the main bantam fighter of the stable, not Curtin.

When hearing about "the plot," Mike went through the roof. "You, my brother, and not Curtin, are supposed to fight Martin. This is the fight we waited for, and now we're out of the real competition!" In this angry mood he went to Doessereck to plead the case, but the promoter brushed him off, saying he was "too busy and there's nothing to talk about." The Curtin–Martin fight was scheduled for November 6 at the Rink Sporting Club in Brooklyn.

The next evening, Doessereck interrupted Joe's workout and asked him if he wanted to fight at the same time in the same arena against a heavier guy, and Joe answered "yes" without hesitation. He was grateful to fight in New York and smiled with confidence. But at the weigh-in, his smile vanished when he saw his opponent Irving Shapiro, ten pounds heavier. By all other measurements, he looked to be a lightweight, three categories above Joe's.

The arena was packed to its full capacity with four thousand spectators (many others turned away for lack of seats), anxious to see the main event between Irish Curtin and Martin, the Italian who had been born and raised in Brooklyn. When Joe entered the arena, wearing his burgundy robe that muffled his shadowboxing moves, he had to wait with Coach Nick and Mike near the ring stair until the announcer introduced Abe Attell Goldstein to the thrilled audience, immensely proud of their New York boy who was now the king of the bantams. Joe saw how the handsome, dark-skinned Goldstein, who was smartly dressed, including a white carnation in his lapel, climbed in the ring amidst a hurricane of ovations that lasted almost a full minute before the announcer could speak again. The world champion gracefully bowed to each side of the ring, clasping his hands above his head. His Hollywood smile ignited more cheers.

When the noise calmed down, the announcer told the public that Tex Rickard was promoting the present fight and that the winner would meet the champion for a title bout in Madison Square Garden in December. The charismatic Goldstein kept waving back to the audience and, after he shook hands with the announcer, stepped down from the ring apron in front of Joe. The beautiful burgundy robe surprised him as he automatically shook Joe's glove with both hands, wishing a loud "Good luck, man!" Joe nodded politely and noticed that the champ was shorter, with small hands and a skinny neck. Suddenly his opponent's glamorous ring image was reduced to that of a very beatable guy.

So far Shapiro, who bravely battled thirteen times in less than a year, had won in front of nondescriptive fighters and lost five times to Johnny Vestri, Jackie Gordon, and other medium-ranked boxers. Nevertheless, he was a heavier guy, and Mike believed that Doessereck was setting Joe up for failure, to show him once and for all that he, the promoter, was right in saying that Joe wasn't ready yet for the big time.

At the bell, the opponents met with a fast and crisp exchange of punches, circling each other and trying to impose domination. The taller Shapiro threw long shots from a distance, while Joe kept bobbing to bring himself into a close-quarters fighting zone. He succeeded a few times and shook up Shapiro with hard left hooks and right straights, continuously booed by the audience. Shapiro recovered each time and kept setting a safer distance with strong counterpunches. By the end of the first round, Joe was ahead by points and had proven himself to be the better boxer, which did not go well with the hostile audience. "Take the Hebrew down as soon as possible!" ordered Mike. "Be careful of his left hook, his best punch!" advised Coach Nick.

The sound of the bell found both men in the middle of the ring, fully charged for a tough encounter. Suddenly, Joe rocked Shapiro with a powerful right cross to the chin that made the crowd groan. Astounded, Shapiro locked Joe in his arms and, breathing heavily, tried to alleviate his headache and confusion. As the two kept jumping in a tight embrace, Joe was looking at the referee to break it. He did not. Back in the corner, Coach Nick told Joe to fight from the inside only. Mike added, "This Jew is a problem."

He was indeed, when in third round, Shapiro changed his style and began stinging with repeated fast jabs. Joe kept weaving his body and trying to get closer, but Shapiro seemed comfortable in conducting his fight at the pace of a mosquito. In the fourth round, Shapiro repeatedly scored at long range, and Joe realized that his larger opponent needed punching room, so he kept trying to engage him in a close fight. Soon enough he had successfully pumped many strong shots to Shapiro's body when he himself was momentary paralyzed by a tremendous left hook to the liver—the same harmful blow he'd done so many times to others. His breathing was interrupted, his movements were frozen, and with all he had in him, Joe jumped into a clinch, waiting for the bell. Luckily, Shapiro was so carried away that he didn't sense the damage he'd done and indulged the familiar clinch until the end of the round.

It took all he had for Joe to reach his corner. Never before had he been so badly hit in the liver, nor had he ever experienced such excruciating pain. He was pale, sweating profusely and foaming around his mouth. Coach Nick tried to massage his abdomen, but that only made the pain worse. Mike used one hand to swirl the towel for more air and with the other pulled at the elastic band of Joe's shorts, so his brother could breathe more easily. Quickly the coach opened a small green bottle full of strong smelling salts, and Joe took one deep breath after another, hoping to regain his normal functions. The bell rang again.

The fifth round began, and the fight turned nastier for Joe when Shapiro, who still didn't know how badly Joe was hurt, took the lead with a blur of fast and stiff gloves. Joe, still in pain, ducked and waltzed around. "Don't step back!" yelled Mike, and Joe went for the kill—but as always, the bell sounded. Forced to go to his corner, Joe decided to end the next round before the bell.

He put everything he had into the sixth section. The close-fighting Joe glided in and out, pummeling Shapiro, who tried to avoid the painful rain of dangerous blows with fast footwork. Even though they had wanted and expected Shapiro to win, the spectators were admiring the smaller fighter, who showed great guts, stamina, and skill. It was clearly a fight to the finish, dominated by Joe, who raised everyone to their feet as they breathlessly waited to see a KO.

It didn't happen. When the last bell sounded and the furious bout was over, Joe, confident in victory, walked to his corner. But the local judges declared Shapiro the winner! One newspaper described Joe as "receiving a fearful lambasting when the bout ended." Another paper commented that "Irving Shapiro was awarded the decision over Jimmy Haskin in the first six rounder, much to the displeasure of the spectators, who booed loud and long. Haskin out boxed his opponent by a wide margin, but the officials thought otherwise." Joe had suffered one more official defeat. Mike's disappointment was tempered by his winning bet that Joe would last six full rounds. Later that night, Joe would feel justified in defiantly writing in his notebook "won over Irving Shapiro at Rink S.C. Brooklyn." To him, as well as most of those who witnessed the fight, he had clearly defeated Shapiro. He now shared his brother's anger toward Doessereck for setting him up in a fight that he seemed predetermined to lose.

After cleaning up following his fight, Joe returned to the arena to see the main card bout. Like Abe Attell Goldstein, he was curious about whom the next title contender would be. From its start, the twelve-round event was a grueling battle between Martin of New York and Curtin of New Jersey. It turned out to be a hectic fight with continuous unpredictable twists. After the first round it looked like the more skilled Curtin had the upper hand, but a well-placed blow by Martin in the second round opened a bloody cut above Curtin's left eye. Visibly affected by the streaming blood and pain, Curtin was chased around the ring by Martin, who was looking for a final delivery. That almost happened in the ninth round, when a series of punches staggered Curtin and only his willpower helped him reach the corner after the bell sound.

Curtin proved to be an amazing fighter to the end. He lost a barbarous battle. Joe closely watched the entire ordeal and saw exactly why Curtin, despite his biggest efforts, didn't have a chance: he had been food-deprived for too long. On the other hand, Joe clearly and with cool analysis saw that he could have won against Martin. He realized that because of Doessereck's sneaky strategy, he had lost the only shot to the title he might ever have. Indeed, this was the fight Joe would have needed to bring him to the zenith of his career. Not only Joe and Mike, but also Coach Nick, were firmly convinced that he could defeat "Cannonball" Martin. Furthermore, Martin defeated Curtin for the second time eight months later, by a TKO in the seventh round at Queensboro Stadium.

That night of November 6, Joe Grimm had missed the most needed stepping stone to qualify as a top challenger and meet Goldstein for the championship fight. He would never come so close to reaching his ardent dream of attacking the supreme title. As a consolation prize, he received $250 and was told that Goldstein was impressed by his ring performance. Losing not one more minute, Mike used the barbershop phone, and as usual after each of Joe's fight, he called the sports editors in Fall River and New Bedford, announcing another victory for his brother.

Joe was physically hurt and very upset, and it took him the entire weekend to heal his wounds and his pride. He went downstairs to the barbershop, where all customers, incited by Mike, were on his side and believed that Doessereck wanted to teach his overambitious boy a lesson in humiliation. On top of that, Gina came on Saturday afternoon to say good-bye, because her family was moving south, where her father had invested in the oil business. "Where shall I write to you?" she asked. Joe shrugged his shoulders and said he didn't know where he was going to be living. "My Gentleman

Boxer." She sniffled and wiped her eyes. "I'll look in the newspaper for your name!" It was an emotional moment, and Mario, with watering eyes, said, "Miss Gina, you can send your letters to the champ using my shop address, and I'll make sure he gets them," he said. Gina nodded and then kissed Joe. As he kissed her back, he embraced her with a long hug. She left, waving to Joe until her car vanished.

During Joe's Monday workout, Doessereck came with surprising news about the coming Thursday. Joe was going to fight Walter Babcock, a rising star of Jersey City. Since Babcock was a featherweight—one category heavier than Joe's bantam weight—there was an obvious problem, but Joe accepted the fight. At the weigh-in Babcock didn't look at Joe and even pushed him out of the way like he was a piece of furniture.

The Grimm–Babcock boxing encounter took place in Columbia Hall in Jersey City. The Bayonnites received Joe with encouraging cheers. Babcock, with "W.B." beautifully stitched on his white boxers, entered the ring and was greeted with tumultuous ovations by the people of his city. Joe was introduced as "Little Dempsey of Bayonne" versus "the New Jersey Gamecock." After the referee's instructions, Babcock turned around and walked to his corner without touching gloves with Joe, who was left with his arms outstretched in the air. The Jersey City fans laughed and shouted jokes at humiliated Joe, whose anger had ratcheted upward. Little did he know that Babcock had strategized exactly this, for he had seen many of Joe's fights and had studied his opponent's calm composure in the ring. His plan was to win by upsetting Grimm's state of mind. This mind game transformed Babcock's usual image. A well-liked easygoing guy, he was known as "the fighting choir boy of Greenville." But as a fighter he would do whatever it took to score a victory.

The opening bell confirmed this. An aggressive man by nature, the blond fighter stepped straight into the action with a few short flurries that raised choirs of encouragement from his adoring fans. Joe realized the foolishness of going toe-to-toe, and he began circling away to bring his fight to close quarters. So far, it looked like only Babcock was in the ring. Joe started a counterattack that resulted in a fast exchange of powerful blows that was abruptly stopped when Joe dropped on the canvas. The arena erupted in roars, Referee Masterly began to count, and Mike and Coach Nick froze with their mouths open. It was unreal to see Joe lying motionless on the floor. He slowly stood up, and his eyes followed the referee's hands waving in front of him. Satisfied that Joe was aware and ready to fight, Masterly ordered "Box!" and stepped away.

This left Babcock free to rain punches on Joe, who tried to move away and duck at random. He even tried to counterpunch, but he kept being severely hit. A clinch stopped the brutal beating, and the referee separated the rivals. In the next second, Joe was down again! The ring of the bell made the referee dash between the two entangled scrappers.

Joe walked punch-drunk to his corner. He dropped on the stool and closed his eyes, while Coach Nick again opened the green bottle of smelling salts and placed it under Joe's nose to revive him. The next bell sound woke him up, and shaking his head he saw Babcock coming toward him, ready to score the final KO. Joe avoided many wallops with his continuous side-to-side movements while delivering his own fast blows to Babcock's head and body. The new tactics threw off his rival's plan. Joe began to take charge of the fight, chasing his rival all over the ring. Soon, Babcock's beautifully chiseled face was bruised and bleeding. After a few fake moves, Joe opened a two-fisted attack "and belted his opponent around for the rest of the fight to win the decision by a wide margin," wrote a reporter. The next day the same newspaper declared Joe a winner. It was an astonishing ring experience that lived a long time in the memory of those in attendance.

From his corner, Mike made sure Joe went straight to the dressing room, where he collected $250. Mike proudly "made a fortune," because he was one of the few who had predicted his brother would finish standing up. He also believed this fight put Joe solidly on the right track in the boxing cards, and it was a step forward into the big-money league. That night he unloaded all this via telephone to the Fall River and New Bedford boxing columnists. The next day he told everyone in the barbershop that Joe had been ready to win the same way if he'd been given a chance to battle "Cannonball" Martin a week ago.

Once again, his bragging reached Doessereck's ears, and he was not happy about it. Furthermore, his best welterweight, Johnny Kochansky, had lost in a six-round decision in front of Harry Felix at Madison Square Garden. This was the same Harry Felix whom Joe clearly defeated months ago in a "non-contest" bout that was declared a draw. Once more Joe Grimm had proven himself to be a classy, superior fighter "who was not allowed to show his real potential," declared Mike to anyone who would listen to him. Most importantly for Joe, he learned again that anger and furious fighting in the ring can blind judgment and impair performance.

For the next three weeks Joe went through another lull and wondered if Doessereck was going to arrange a fight for him. When Mike went "to have a talk to the no-good match-breaker," the promoter dismissed him with a simple "Not now, I'm extremely busy!" To Mike, that was the ultimate personal insult that also showed disrespect toward Joe. Shortly thereafter, though, the promoter announced that Joe would meet up with Clyde Jones of Jersey City on Thursday, December 11, at the Strand arena. Jones was a solid ten-rounder featherweight known to supply plenty of action; he was credited for a "fight heart" and for punches with "plenty of vim and vigor," a newspaper reporter wrote. He was a promising local warrior, who had just knocked out Kayo Norton of Paterson, and he was confident of repeating the same type of victory in the fight with Grimm.

The way a boxer slides between the ropes into the ring tells a lot about his eagerness to win; Jones clearly showed that intention. And so did Joe. Referee Joe Jeanette called them into the middle of the ring for instructions and wished "Good luck to botz o' you."

At the bell, Joe dashed forward to meet a furious fighter, who, after exchanging a few punches, looked like he would walk all over him. Jones's arms worked like two pistons that could not be turned off. He was a fighter who believed that to win was to overwhelm the other with floods of blows. Joe, like any accomplished fighter, refused to brawl and knew how to deal with that by rolling, ducking and weaving, and then throwing well-aimed punches that hit the target with great effect. The spectators reacted with an instant roar of approval. As Joe the boxer dealt with Jones the slugger, they created a type of fight that always ignited firecrackers in the ring. Jones showed good style for a bully, and in the first two rounds he did a solid job scoring and forcing Joe to cautiously fight in retreat.

But in the third round, the skirmish developed into a full unavoidable battle: gloves were flying fast and hard, hitting and missing in torrents from both sides. It was exactly what the crowd loved the most about boxing—nonstop bloody action with no predictable end. But this back-and-forth frenzy didn't continue for too long. In the fourth round, Joe set up his best blows when his right cross landed point-blank on the jaw and floored Jones for a noncount KO. He jumped right back on his feet, and Mike screamed, "Get him!" Joe went for the kill by clubbing and ramming Jones in his own corner until the bell stopped the fight. Jones was helplessly clinging to the ropes and collapsed on a stool quickly handed to him by his seconds.

In the fifth round, Joe carried the fight to a climactic end. The bell found Jones clinching the ropes. Obviously Joe had won. A *Bayonne Times* reporter described the encounter: "For six rounds the youngsters pleased the fans with clever boxing and hard hitting." The fight was a clear show of the triumph of a skillful boxer over a pure puncher. Doessereck, who watched the fight, was very impressed with Joe's performance and rewarded him with $200. Mike lost his bet because he had wagered on a KO by his brother. Once again, he promptly called the boxing editors in Fall River and New Bedford with more good news.

Doessereck was, in fact, so impressed with the fight that he booked Joe to fight two days later in Brooklyn, obviously as a last-minute substitute. His rival was Bobby Burns of Jersey City, himself a substitute, and in full rebound from losing by KO in the first round with Emil Paluso of Salt Lake City. Burns was a decent fighter who in May had scored a draw with Harry Felix, with whom Joe shortly thereafter also scored a draw. Bobby Burns and Joe Grimm belonged to the same category of "sacrificial fighters," both being fillers for boxers who didn't show up in the ring. They were evenly matched, down to the same age and build.

Highly temperamental Burns had a reputation for starting strong and finishing weak. His tactic was "all or nothing," which Joe fully felt in the first round. Believing he was dominating the fight, Burns continued his stormy charges in the second round as well. He was fully backed by the roars of four thousand spectators when Joe let fly his right cross and left hook that instantly collapsed the careless Burns. But the floored guy bounced back on his feet, and the public gave him a generous reward in applause and cheers. It turned out that those few seconds changed the course of the fight, now settled in Joe's favor.

At the bell, Joe walked calmly to his corner, ignoring the booing of the crowd. He received a large splash of icy water from Mike, who was sorry he hadn't bet, but that was for a good reason: the odds were four to one against his brother. Rounds three and four proved only one thing in favor of Burns: the guy could take a lot of beating. However, Joe was already tired, and his punches failed to produce a KO, even though Burns staggered to his corner at the end of each round. When the final bell rang, Burns was groggy and Joe had an indisputable lead on points that brought him $225. Later that night he wrote in his record book the same news Mike telephoned to Fall River and New Bedford: "Won 6 rounds over Bobby Burns at Ridgewood Grove, Brooklyn."

Mike was sick to hear that Joe's main role was to be a sparring partner of Johnny Curtin, who on December 16 took a severe beating from Frankie Fasano of Brooklyn. The next day, the *Bayonne Times* headline announced, "Johnny Curtin Loses to Fasano." The subhead noted that he was "on Short End of 12-Round Slugging Match" at the Pioneer, New York, which was managed by Doessereck. Suffering one KO in a second round, Curtin fought with all his might to win the fight, but the reporter believed that he was "nearing the end of his pugilistic career …" Too many yo-yo diets had begun to affect Curtin, and that was probably the reason he suffered from acute gastritis and was unable to take a tough punch to the abdomen.

Five days later, the *Bayonne Times* headlined, "Abe Goldstein Loses His Title," and the subtitle explained, "'Cannonball' Martin Wins 15-Round Bout and Bantam Crown" in Madison Square Garden. A brief biography mentioned that Edward V. Martino was twenty-one years old, and certainly his boxing record, his build, and his skill in the ring were not better than those of Joe Grimm. What "Cannonball" did have that was better was a manager and promoter who did not waste Martin's talent and energy on meaningless fights. With his victory, "Cannonball" ended Johnny Curtin's chances of becoming a contender.

It turned out that Mike was right when blaming Doessereck for having bad judgment when mismatching his brother and Curtin against stronger rivals. In fact, the *Bayonne Times* was keen to report back in October that "meeting boxers out of his division has always been part of the game with Curtin, but he realizes now that to try to build up to an opponent's weight is a big mistake." Losing to Phil Rosenberg, Martin, and other bantams was a case in point. Joe Grimm lost because he was overmatched beginning with the weigh-in and overtired from fighting two days apart.

Doessereck kept mapping out matches and scheduled them far in advance for all his fighters—except for Joe. Mike had had enough and decided to take his brother back to Fall River to celebrate the holidays with family and think things out more. Doessereck was also stunned when Joe told him about their decision to head back to Fall River for the holidays, and he asked, "When are you coming back?" Joe said what Mike told him to say, "When we hear that I'm meeting Curtin in the ring for a real fight." The promoter was speechless and kept shaking and holding his head with both hands.

The next morning, Mike took Joe on a shopping spree and bought presents for their parents, sisters, and other Hashims. He also paid Mario two months' advance rent so he would hold the apartment above the barbershop for the brothers' return. With all this taken care of, on December 20 the brothers, loaded with presents and money, left Bayonne for Fall River. Once again they traveled on the luxury line in a first-class cabin. Through a restaurant's panoramic window they saw the Statue of Liberty and, holding their glasses like torches, toasted it with a heartfelt "To America! God bless her!"

CHAPTER 20

THE LAST STRAW

Indeed, this return to Fall River proved to be a better life than Joe could have envisioned. Relatives, acquaintances, and even people he had never met before were happy to see "the champion," hugging him or warmly shaking his hand. The brothers were expensively dressed, looked prosperous, and seemed to come from another world, a better world. Once again Joe and his family, never empty-handed, visited friends and neighbors, among them longtime friends, the Simons. After church, they enjoyed an abundant Lebanese lunch, followed by a long talk about Joe's successful career in New Jersey. Among their amazed audience from the Simon family were fourteen-year-old Alice and eight-year-old Elisabeth, called Betty, sisters who years later would become Mike and Joe's brides.

The meeting between equally well dressed Louis and Emma with the rest of the Hashims took place after exchanging Christmas gifts. Joe admired the beautiful gold ring Louis was wearing. Around the large dining room table with all the sweets and drinks in the middle, the family members discussed the possibility of moving to Pittsfield and starting a new life. This time they would be working for themselves in a family-owned store. The idea had been raised before, but now they saw it could really happen.

The bottom line, explained Massery as he adjusted his spectacles, was that the Hashims would have to pay off the debt of the present owners before taking ownership of the store. At this crucial juncture, Mike went to his bedroom and returned with bundles of cash, all in $10 bills. He ceremoniously stacked the bills on the stitched tablecloth. All eyes moved back and forth from the money to Mike. Radiating happiness, his chest swelling, he announced, "Father, you have a choice. You can buy four of the best cars with this $2,000, or you can be the owner of Hashim's grocery store." The stunned silence was broken with laughter and hand clapping. Mike nodded his head and, chest puffed, clasped his hands behind his back. "We can do this all because of Joe, who never lost a fight in the ring!" Everyone looked at Joe now as they cheered and clapped. Mike sat back down at the table while everyone excitedly talked. His eyes met Joe's, and they knowingly smiled at each other.

Louis leaned back in his chair and grinned as the family members chattered. As soon as everyone began to quiet, he cleared his throat and tapped the stack of money. To cover the debt, $1,300 was needed. But the store needed to be renovated, and the upstairs apartment had been long neglected and needed work for an extension as well. The $2,000 on the table should be enough for all of this, he judged. The discussion, in Arabic, became heated as it continued with little resolution, punctuated by key English words: "business," "dollars," "pay bills," and "manage." When they reached the ownership point, all agreed at once that Father and Mother Hashim must be the only proprietors. Once again, Joe made it clear that if Doessereck called him back, he would go. He'd make more money boxing than doing anything else. Everyone agreed. The new year of 1925 would bring big changes to the family, everyone agreed as they left the table. Right now, good plans were in place, and the whole family was looking forward to a better future.

Realizing that he was getting heavier and lazier, Joe went to Bob Tickle's gym, where he enjoyed a welcome he never expected. Each boxer was asking for his advice. He demonstrated new techniques and described, by doing, how different stars he had seen conducted themselves in the ring. Former fans and new fans came to see him working out and sparring. He was being treated like a celebrity! Mike stopped by one night and entertained them with many stories about the great boxing events he was part of in New Jersey and New York.

Mike happened to be at the barbershop when Doessereck called for Joe. "I'll take it!" he said. Lighting a cigarette from the one he had been smoking, he winked at the shop's customers, who were frozen in expectation. He then answered the phone with "It's Mike. Give me some bang-up news I can't refuse!" His pencil mustache spread in a wide grin, and he kept nodding and winking at his motionless audience.

By this time Doessereck had hung up, but Mike kept "listening" and summarized by saying, "So, what you're saying is, you're ready to match your 'Irish' Johnny Curtin with my Joe Grimm for a headline fight in New Jersey? And this will be around January the fifteenth, with other top-notch boys doing the opening rounds." He nodded, looked at his shoes, and then looked at the ceiling. "We'll talk more about that. I'm sure we can come to an agreement. My brother and I will see you after Christmas." He hung up the phone and smiled at the wide-eyed crowd as he lit another cigarette, blowing the smoke in large floating rolls.

The news about Joe battling Johnny Curtin, who was well-known in the Fall River area, spread like wildfire. Joe intensified his workout to get ready. Even though Mike had bluffed about the length of the call, indeed Doessereck had told him about the fight with Curtin and the date it would happen. Until then, the two brothers, feeling like celebrities, would enjoy their best Christmas ever.

Back in Bayonne two days before the fight, the brothers quickly returned to their known daily routine. Joe learned at the gym that he and Curtin were headliners in an exhibition bout taking place in the very same gym for a local fund-raising event. The fight began with friendly punch exchanges that gradually escalated into an ambitious contest dominated by Joe. The whole affair was politely described by a local paper:

> Joe Grimm, with a build like a second Dempsey, was the battler facing Irish Johnny Curtin in the main bout. Curtin's craving for the bantamweight crown was not a bit lessened by his exhibition last night and Grimm mixed up in lively fashion with him to the satisfaction of the crowd.

The match did nothing to stop Mike from fuming. Doessereck had played a dirty trick on them, he complained in the barbershop; the fight was staged so if Curtin lost, it wouldn't jeopardize his status. In other words, Joe got nothing out of it except a humiliating $25. As for Doessereck, clearly he never dreamed of upsetting Curtin, whom he believed to be real championship material. The promoter had no intention of moving Joe up in his stable, placing him above Curtin—never mind dealing with the brother who kept Joe anchored to his Lebanese family.

In the meantime, Gina wrote to Joe each week, sending her letters to the barbershop, where Mike picked them up and tossed them in the garbage.

"What Joe doesn't know can't hurt him," Mike confided to Mario, then asking if he could work overtime to make more money, needed by the family. With no fights assigned to him, Joe was discouraged and depressed. Still, aware that if he was ever to battle his way to the top of the cards, he had to play it Doessereck's way, he wanted to be in good fighting shape in case of a "stand by" call. He intensified "active training," as Doessereck called the workouts, trying not to dwell on the distressing fact that he was the only one in the entire stable without a fight schedule.

Luckily, proud Babcock asked for a rematch, and the fight was scheduled for the end of January, as part of an all-star show. Thanks to their last heated fight, the local newspapers played their part building expectations for the fight that would determine the best upcoming bantam in the region. A cartoon of the two boxers appeared in the *Bayonne Times* under the title, "Scrappers on Strand Card," showing Joe with dark hair and black trunks facing Babcock with blond hair and white trunks with a W.B. monogram on his left leg, exchanging furious punches. Underneath was the caption in capital letters, "Joe Grimm and Walter Babcock Will Mix It Up in the First of the Eights. This Mix-Up Will Be Worth Going Miles to See."

Finally, Mike was happy. His brother was booked as a headliner for a major boxing event! The *Bayonne Evening News* announced it:

Return Go for Grimm and Babcock

> Joe Grimm, the popular little gamecock of the Doessereck stable, will oppose the "Fighting Choir Boy," Walter Babcock, of Greenville, in the first eight-round number, and if this affair is anything like their initial meeting, the fans will be well repaid for their visit to the Broadway playhouse.

Because of Mike's memorable phone conversation in the Fall River barbershop, Doessereck was now known by the entire boxing population of Fall River; the local newspaper picked up the interest in the distant fight:

> Joe Grimm, popular little East End fighter who for a time gave the fans of this city several real thrillers in his matches in the local ring, is now going great guns in the metropolitan district. Joe has been a member of the same stable as Irish Johnny Curtin, under Charles Doessereck for many months and during that time Grimm has acquired

a number of scalps both by the knockout method and by showing his superior knowledge of the game.

All in all, the return affair between Joe Grimm and Walter Babcock at the end of January generated much interest in Hudson County, and fans from both camps filled the arena beyond its capacity. When Joe walked in the ring and shrugged off his burgundy robe, a roar reverberated through the arena. He was only 118 pounds, but he fit the image of a winning fighter to the last detail: a robust appearance, calm and reassuring moves, the engaging smile, and an attitude that called for respect and admiration. Not to be outdone, the heavier Babcock was a fine-looking young man and equally impressive fighter. His packed muscle, tough look, and obvious confidence gave him that air of invincibility. It was hard not to like both little gladiators.

Moments after the opening bell, gloves smashed with speed and power, but neither boxer stepped back while the cheers around them grew louder and louder. It was obvious that both boys had the same fighting plan in mind, attacking each other with punching combinations for a while. At the end of the first round Joe had landed more scoring blows, which infuriated his overaggressive opponent. In his corner on the stool, splashed with cold water from the yellow sponge by Mike, Joe listened to Coach Nick advise him "to get inside and carry your own fight as usual."

At the bell, Babcock launched a "bulldog attack," forcing Joe to step back and cover himself the best he could, while fans from both camps competed to scream the loudest. Joe counterpunched his way out of the trouble spot, sending Babcock to the side with a few strong blows to the body. The end of the three minutes found Joe maintaining a comfortable lead on points; yet, Babcock was dominating the fight. "Can you floor him?" shouted Mike, who was fanning the towel in front of his brother for cooler air. Joe took a sip of icy water and nodded a few times.

In the third round, overconfident Babcock, carried away by the apparent success of his much-applauded assault, let his judgment slip, allowing Joe to move in closer. Joe machine-gunned a few deceptive blows to Babcock's body, followed by a right cross to the jaw that toppled Babcock to the canvas with a thump. With the floored guy staring unmoved at the lights above him, the spectators turned momentarily mute, only to explode with deafening roars when the black referee began counting. Babcock struggled to stand up and then bravely took a fighting stance, convincing the referee to order "Box!" Joe went to end the fight with precise blows to the body and head, setting his opponent on the verge of another KO, but the bell saved him. From his corner, Joe saw that panic on Babcock's face. "Take him out!" he heard Mike yell over the hubbub of excited spectators.

For the next three rounds, the grueling fight continued to escalate as the roars of the public demanding a knockout from either fighter shook the arena. The stubborn boys relentlessly hammered at each other almost equally. Sweat, grunts, and squeals came out of the ring. Babcock began to bleed from a large bruise beneath his left eye, but he refused to quit. The seventh round found Joe at close quarters, doing all the attacking. His left hook pierced Babcock's liver, followed by a right cross that landed flush on his jaw. As the hurt boxer moved like a drunken sailor trying to avoid the devastating punches, Joe shadowed him in pursuit of a KO. Referee Jeanette was only feet away from them both, ready to stop the fight. During the break, Joe tried to figure out what else he could do to score a knockout, but Coach Nick assured him he'd already won the fight and urged him to "take the time to build the finishing blow." Mike firmly whispered, "Go for the kill!" as Joe leaped forward with the bell.

During the last round, Babcock fought with one eye closed and did what all losing opponents tend to do—he shot wild punches from the floor and hoped for one to land deadly so he'd win the fight. When the final bell sounded, both fighters were smeared with blood and stunned: Joe because he couldn't win by a clear knockout, and punch-drunk Babcock who couldn't believe he'd lost again and dropped into the corner chair.

Joe was a promising fighter, and at almost twenty years of age, he was in the best shape ever and ready to meet any bantam in the world. That champion quality radiated in full blast out of him, shining under the spotlights as the referee toured him around the ring. No doubt he won again, and Joe enjoyed each second of that triumphant feeling. With a lump in his throat he took a final bow, flexing his biceps with his gloves tapping above his head. He left the ring to roaring chants of "Our Joe!" and "Gentleman Joe!" knowing deep inside that those glorious images and adoring roars would stay with him for the rest of his life.

The sum of $300 rewarded his victory, and the fight became the talk of the town. Doessereck himself delivered the check, saying, "Kid, this was your best fight ever! True championship rounds!" Mike quickly jumped at the opportunity to ask for "a serious talk." Doessereck agreed, and a meeting at the Bavarian restaurant was arranged for lunchtime the next day. That night Joe confidently wrote in his notebook that he had "won over Walter Babcock at Strand—Bayonne on January 31, 1925."

The *Bayonne Evening News* headlined its coverage with large, bold letters: "Arthurs (of Yonkers) and Grimm Win Fights." In the event description was a subhead, "Grimm and Babcock Fight Hard." The reporter wrote,

> Joe Grimm and Walter Babcock, a pair of fighting featherweights, were the participants in the first eight rounder, and they certainly worked hard to please the fans. For two youngsters who were boxing their first eight round engagement, these lads certainly fought every inch of the way with Grimm's experience offsetting the hitting ability of Babcock who shot in quite a few long rights with plenty of steam behind them.

It was clear that Grimm had won because he focused on not only skill, but also strategy, outgunning and outsmarting Babcock. Using Mike's description of the fight over the phone, back in Fall River the local paper described the event using large type: "Joe Grimm Wins Sterling Bout at Bayonne, N.J." Among the admiring comments was this:

> In an all-star show with Grimm and Babcock as the headline bout, Grimm outpointed Babcock nicely and scored a clean-cut knockdown in the third round of the bout. Grimm came through without a scratch and was ready for another battle at the conclusion of his 10 [8] rounds of boxing. Babcock was quite badly smashed up as a result of Grimm's tattoo punching … Grimm is described as having the hardest punch and his wallops had a telling effect on his Jersey opponent.

In conclusion, Grimm was credited that he has acquired all the laurels formerly held by Babcock.

Armed with the glorious newspaper headlines about his brother, Mike came alone to the lunch with Doessereck, who acknowledged Mike with immediate compliments of Joe's performance in the ring. Mike listened politely while eating his Wiener schnitzel with mashed potatoes and then thanked Doessereck for the nice words. Then he shifted gears, clearing his throat as he leaned back in his chair and stared into Doessereck's eyes. "My brother is an underdog ready to battle any bantam champion. It's time for Joe to step up. That's not a debatable point, and you know it." Doessereck flashed a patronizing smile and responded, "Well, Mike, as you may know, in boxing it's a big thing to be an underdog, and frankly, that's not what Joe is. No one in their right mind would rate Joe ahead of others as a contender for Eddie 'Cannonball' Martin's title. Your brother would lose by a mile!" Mike's face showed restraint as he leaned forward and softly but firmly said, "So what if he loses once? One bad showing cannot destroy a career. Besides, he could win. Ask anyone—they'd agree with me!"

Doessereck, already exasperated, put his elbows on the table and, with his head in his hands, repeated what he had told Joe before. "Look, what's the rush? Joe's not even twenty yet. He's got to pay his dues just like everyone else. Patience is the virtue of champions!" Then Doessereck reminded Mike that it had taken the great Johnny Dundee eleven years to become the multichampion of the world, and only at age thirty had he conquered the world's featherweight title.

But Mike would have none of it. He interrupted the lecture with a proposition that shocked Doessereck. He declared that Joe had already successfully thundered through many challengers and was ready to attack the title in a different way. Conforming to the new boxing law that had just been issued, he demanded that Doessereck put up a bond of $2,500 with the Athletic Commission. According to the new rules, any champion must accept a challenge every six months, and that meant "Cannonball" Martin would be forced to fight Joe. The promoter shook his head and took a deep breath.

"If I do that, many of my boxers will ask me for the same thing, especially Curtin and Kochansky. Where do I come up with ten thousand bucks? Besides, last summer I guaranteed $7,500 to champion Abe Goldstein if he'd meet Curtin in New Jersey, where he wouldn't even risk losing his title to points. I told him he could bring his own referee! But Tex Rickard decided to let Charles Ledoux challenge Goldstein at the Velodrome in New York. Mind you, Curtin defeated the Frenchman a few weeks before. Well, the Velodrome was almost empty in the middle of July, and the bout was a total flop for both fighters and a financial disaster for Rickard. If Goldstein fought Curtin, who's always filled Madison Square Garden to capacity, my boy would be the champion today and all of us, including Rickard, would have more money in the bank. But see, my good young man, in boxing, just like in life, there are no guarantees!"

Mike understood Doessereck's delicate position regarding his faithful longtime clients but believed his brother could step up in weight for the next category and that he was more than ready to challenge Louis Kid Kaplan, who held the featherweight world title. Kaplan was older and shorter than

Joe, and not a better puncher or boxer. Besides, he had just scored a draw with Babe Herman after fifteen painful rounds. There was no doubt that Joe was confident he could put down the Jewish "Little Napoleon," Mike pointed out. Again, Doessereck tried to explain about the "unfixable risk in the ring," to which Joe should not be exposed. "Is he a good boxer or not?" snapped Mike. Doessereck sipped some water before replying that of course Joe was very good in the ring, but despite his obvious pugilistic talents, he was still too young and inexperienced to "set his sights so high."

This being said, the veteran promoter was on the verge of running out of patience with the conversation when Mike made a statement that ended any further discussion. "You're treating my brother like trash just to help your other boys get ahead!" Stunned, Doessereck stared as Mike's fist hit the table and he spit out a further accusation that Doessereck intended to use Joe only as a convenient sparring partner and a last-minute substitute, and never planned to promote him as a main eventer. "You are depriving my brother of becoming a great fighter, and he will never be a leading contender!" shouted Mike. At this point, the promoter stood up and said in a choked voice, "I've had it! I'm not talking anymore to you!" As no reconciliation was possible, he left $3 on the table and departed, shakily placing his hat on his head. His fear that Joe was a durable fighter but an unreliable client had been solidly confirmed, once and for all.

❧❦

That very night, Louis Massery called Mike with an urgent request that he and Joe come home and help move the family from Fall River to Pittsfield and then take over the store. There really was no option, he pointed out, if the boys wanted their family to have a better life. Mike and Joe discussed it before turning in for the night. The next day Mike went to the barbershop for work and told Mario, the other barbers, and the patrons that he and his brother would be leaving Bayonne for good. They began packing.

The brothers, remembering that "an empty hand is a dirty hand," rushed to buy big presents for their family and small ones for the guys from Mario's shop. Lastly, they walked into Wigdor's Jewelry Store on Broadway, and Mike bought a beautiful pocket watch he had always admired in a large display window. Joe looked for a gold ring for himself, but none fit.

They went back to the barbershop carrying beautifully wrapped packages. The gifts of ties, pins, lighters, and cigarette cases were appreciated by the barbers and a few boxing fan clients. Joe presented Mario with a framed picture showing himself in a powerful stance, with a signed dedication. The proud Mario nailed the autographed picture under his mandolin. To everyone's surprise, Doessereck walked through the door and asked why Joe had missed the workout the day before. Mike stalked out and went upstairs.

Everyone else in the shop stopped talking and working, and focused on Joe as he said, "I'm going home, Mr. Doessereck." Doessereck just looked at him, and then his eyes shifted to the others standing around. The shop was completely quiet until Mario broke the silence.

"You never gave Joe a chance, sir. You never put him in the limelight. He always fought undercard fights!"

"He's not ready to appear in Madison Square Garden, if that's what you mean!" Doessereck shook his head, wondering if anyone understood anything about the intricacy of boxing business.

"He was good enough to appear in your Pioneer Club, wasn't he?" another Italian barber spoke up, this one bald-headed, with a pencil mustache and long sideburns.

"Of course, but he needs some more local fights to prove himself before the big time."

"He proved enough to be a winning substitute so many times and be a sure bet in the ring!" interjected a robust client, wanting to get in on the action.

"He's too young, but believe me, he's heading in the right direction," Doessereck started to say, but Joe shot him a stern look and interrupted.

"Mr. Doessereck, just once I wish I could fight in Manhattan …"

"We can do that," said the promoter, pursing his lips. "I can make that happen."

"But not for me, it looks like," Joe sadly responded. "It's too late for me."

"So, kid, you're really going to throw in the towel? Even if I get you the Garden?"

"My family needs me, Mr. Doessereck. I know I'm good and I'd get better, but time's up. I can't hang around and wait for nothing when I'm needed at home. As much as I love it, there's more to life than boxing."

Doessereck couldn't believe it. The kid was really quitting? He kept shaking his head and said, "Good things take time and faith to become reality. It often takes the low road to get to the high road in the game of boxing, just like in life …" His words fell on a silent shop, and the promoter understood it for the rejection it was. Sadly he walked out the door, mumbling, "What a waste, what a mistake." A few minutes later, everyone in the shop gathered around Joe, patting him on the back and hugging him. "You gotta do what you gotta do," said one. "Family comes first," agreed Mario. "Family first," echoed the others. "But hey, Joe, you could have gone farrrrrrr!" "We'll miss you!"

The next day, the brothers brought their luggage to the barbershop, which was packed with clients and Joe's fans. During a small but emotional farewell ceremony, Mario handed a silver watch chain to Mike and a beautiful golden ring to Joe. The ring fit perfectly on his oversize finger. The brothers were impressed to tears, and after many hugs and friendly handshakes, they left the shop in a car driven by a fan to the ferryboat terminal. It was a foggy, cold day. Later, when comfortably installed in the first-class cabin, holding the complimentary glass of champagne, the brothers looked for the Statue of Liberty. They couldn't see it but toasted her anyway, knowing she was there, still holding the torch to welcome poor immigrants with daring dreams. Mike offered a toast. "To a new life and many more KOs, my brother!"

Joe had fought fifteen times in the six months he was with Doessereck in New Jersey. He won three bouts by knockouts, six by newspaper decision, scored two draws, and lost four fights on points because of unfair judges' decisions, each of which was highly contested by the spectators. Joe was now twenty years old and still the only professional boxer with twenty-four knockouts in a row.

CHAPTER 21

A DIFFERENT REALITY

Joe and Mike were once again back home in Fall River. As usual, they were the big topic in town and guests of honor everywhere, but after a couple of weeks life settled into a new routine. Mike and Joe, and the rest of the family, felt unsettled and unsure of their futures. In fact, for almost three months Joe acted as if he had retired from boxing. He did have offers to fight at the Casino and other arenas in the area, but Mike, who was acting as his manager, turned them down. Mike demanded more money from the promoters and matchmakers than they wanted to pay, and when they stood firm, Mike told them to forget it. However, there's a show-business saying, "If you're not appearing in public, you're disappearing," and by not being visible in the ring, Joe was losing followers and popularity with the local fans. Many questioned whether he was at the end of his fistic career at age twenty, when others were just beginning it.

The puzzling situation continued until Bobby Tickle came to the Hashim family house and offered Joe a fight at the end of April. Joe agreed on the spot.

"Wait a second," interjected Mike as he stepped between the two. "What kind of money are we talking about?"

"Well, I'm not really sure," Tickle responded, shrugging his shoulders and looking Mike straight in the eyes. "But this will put Joe back in the game."

"Okay," Mike acknowledged. "We agree that's something to consider. It's not a done deal, though. We'll talk more about this." To their surprise and disappointment, however, when the April fight was officially announced, the arena was at the New Winter Garden Theater in Pittsfield, hours away from Fall River, on the other side of the Bay State. Mike, on the other hand, was pleased.

"This is great!" Mike rubbed his hands and grinned. "A whole new crowd is going to see how great Joe Grimm is! Then, we move there, everybody will already know your reputation. Show them a spectacular KO!"

Happy to be getting back in the ring and with his brother's goal in mind, Joe returned to training in Tickle's gym. In a short period of time he needed to shed the weight he'd gained so he'd make the bantam weight of 118 pounds. His near-starvation diet combined with training threatened to affect his stamina and strength, but Joe was feeling great about fighting again.

This was Joe's first visit to Pittsfield, located in the Berkshire Hills of western Massachusetts. It was a smaller city than Fall River but appeared prosperous, judging by the activity on its main street, called North Street, the architecture of the buildings, many expensive cars, and the way people dressed. He and Mike were guests of their sister Emma and her husband, Louis, whose large house looked rich from the outside and inside. Their business, named the White Star, was located on Summer Street in a large building, which happened to be in the vicinity of the Winter Garden Theater, where the boxing event was taking place. The brothers visited the warehouse that provided wholesale candy and tobacco to some 140 small stores in Pittsfield alone and numerous others in nearby towns.

Louis drove them to West Housatonic Street, where the delinquent grocery store was located. It was poorly managed by two Lebanese brothers who had run up bills with the White Star that they could not possibly pay; now they waited for the court eviction order. The corner store, which faced two streets, was inside a large red-brick building with a small apartment on top of the flat roof and a narrow clapboard house attached to the left. With his mercantile spirit, Mike saw the huge potential of the dark and neglected store. He had ideas for a major renovation that would turn business around, he told Joe, but before that could happen, "We need to win a few more good fights!"

That Friday afternoon at the weigh-in, Joe tipped the scale at 123 pounds. The only match he could get was with Frankie Renzie from a place in upstate New York that no one could pronounce. Renzie was also pushed upward from his featherweight class, because he was 132 pounds. Many were concerned about the nine-pound difference, but not Joe, who

197

was willing to climb in the ring and ready to battle anyone. That evening Joe ate two steaks to make up for days of ascetic food and enjoyed a good night's sleep.

The next evening he entered a boxing arena that was unlike anything he'd ever seen before. It was a theater of untold luxury with expensive carpets, velvet draperies and curtains, Italian-made chandeliers and sconces with different-colored lights, and sumptuous moldings all around, including on the opera-like stage where the ring was installed. The number of people in the audience was far less than Joe had seen at any of his other fights. In fact, they occupied less than one-third of the plush armchairs and showed little excitement or anticipation. The New Winter Garden Theater was another cultural shrine in which boxing intruded to generate money.

Joe was scheduled for the second bout. Wearing the glittering burgundy dressing robe, he confidently approached the ring with bouncing steps. His slow shadowboxing routine attracted increasing applause. He walked through the ropes to the middle of the ring, looking like a champion, and saluted the audience that was already on his side. In his corner, Renzie watched Joe as the crowd politely applauded when the announcer introduced him: "The only Second Dempsey of bantams with twenty-four KO victories in a row, and one of the best fighters of New England and New Jersey, soon to become a full-time resident of Pittsfield, I give you Geeentleeemaaan Joeeeeeee!" Joe raised his arms in thanks while Mike whispered in his ear, "Did I do a good job, or what!"

From crossing himself before the bell sound to the first blows exchanged, Renzie proved to have what other Italians showed in the ring: determination, ambition, and pride. This was a classic confrontation between Renzie the hitter and Joe the boxer, the type of match that always pleased the crowd. The New Yorker turned out to be a solid distant aggressor. Two rounds quickly passed in favor of Renzie, who punched nonstop, ignoring how Joe tried to set himself up to carry out his own fight. At the break, Coach Nick warned Joe that he was behind in points. Mike was nervous about the outcome of the fight and ordered, "Take him home, Joe!"

Rounds three and four tilted in favor of Joe, who ripped one knockout punch after another, but Renzie proved to have a granite chin. Still, his face swelled and bled so badly that his eyelids were almost closed. Two more rounds of punishment followed with a twist no one expected: Renzie gained a miraculous second wind, and his fists still stored much of their power. Joe's response came with equally merciless rapid-fire punches, and eventually the Italian wore out and walked with a stagger to his corner.

Joe was also happy to sit on the stool. "Are you going to lose to a nobody?" hissed Mike between clenched teeth at the break while showering his tired brother with icy water.

The seventh round passed with many clinches by Renzie, who sneaked rabbit punches to the back of Joe's head. The public turned against him. The final 180 seconds belonged entirely to Joe, who ended the bloody affair with a terrific flurry to the head and body, raising the screaming audience off their chairs. Joe would have won by a knockout, but this time, the lack of training, the senseless diet, and his weaker-than-normal punches worked against him. He kept delivering one well-aimed wallop after another and nearly collapsed Renzie several times, held up against the ropes by Joe's uppercuts. Finally, the bell ended the bloody round, and mercifully, the fight ended.

After eight rounds of nonstop action, the judges decided on a split decision in favor of Renzie, who could not believe he was a winner; the decision stunned the public for a second, after which they erupted with hoots and screams. The *Berkshire Evening Eagle* reporter wrote in his column, "Renzie was given the verdict and earned it but Grimm who was clever, although not as heavy a puncher at Renzie, fought hard to the final bell." After commenting on the rest of the bouts, the reporter concluded that "the greatest applause of the evening came at the close of the semi-final bout as Grimm and Renzie proved very pleasing owing to their steady and clever fighting."

By any measure, Joe was entitled to at least a draw, but he left the ring defeated. Equally humiliating for Joe was the $50 handed over in the locker room by Tickle, who had received half of that. To his surprise, Mike had been unable to place a bet—no betting was allowed in the fancy theater.

The next evening Louis and Emma invited a few business associates to their home for dinner. Using the opportunity, Mike did his first exploratory work as a promoter, asking about boxing arenas in Pittsfield. He was told that baseball, tennis, and golf were far more popular and economically profitable in the city, with its many white-color workers who were proud of their large country club and golf course. Nearby North Adams, with more factories than Pittsfield, was the place for boxers and their gyms. The news didn't discourage Mike: the more he learned about Pittsfield, the more his imagination fired plans to make it a boxing metropolis, just like Chicago and New York City. But one step at a time. First the Hashim family needed to move to its new residence.

❖❖

Back in Fall River, the two brothers and the rest of the Hashims were invited to the Simons for dinner. The teenage daughter Eva and her mother served the food, while her younger sisters Julia and Elizabeth took the dirty dishes to the sink. It was the end of May, and through the opened windows the perfume of the blossoming lilac and lily of the valley competed with the aroma of the Lebanese food. The two families of almost twenty members talked until late; when the Hashims left, Joe received a present that he was told had to be opened at home. "It will bring lots of luck to you!" The six Simon girls giggled, hiding one behind the others.

The little package was very light, as if it contained a flag or a scarf, but to everyone's surprise, it was green boxing trunks. They were made of heavy-duty cotton with a wide elastic band sewn inside the top, and a red border on the bottom of each leg. Joe never learned who made the trunks that fit him perfectly, but he loved them. In fact, he wore them on June 5, when he was booked to fight Jimmy Wilde of Taunton. This was the same guy whom Joe two years before had battered so badly that the referee stopped the fight in the eighth round.

The fight took place again in New Bedford at the cycledrome, now packed beyond its six thousand capacity with boxing fans eager to see Joe Grimm in the ring again. It was a beautiful Friday evening with an ideal summer breeze making everything look glorious and feel great. Joe, who was down to his best fighting weight of 118 pounds, never felt better. "What do you think?" Mike nudged him before placing his bet. "A final KO in the eighth, just like the last time," answered Joe, full of confidence. "Unless you want him out in the first round!" Mike shook his head no. "The stakes are higher for the last round." With a plan in place, Joe put on his green trunks and burgundy robe, and then he lay on a bench in the dressing room. He heard the roar of the crowd from the arena and, eyes closed, realized that career-wise he was right back where he started—fighting local guys whom only relatives and neighbors had heard of. From a $300 purse in New York and New Jersey a few months ago, he was back to $50. He began to feel sorry for himself, and then he chuckled, remembering Doessereck's "no guarantees in the ring."

Only Mike, rubbing his hands, looking like a cat that ate a canary, was happy about his bets. Joe began his walk to the ring, wearing the beautiful burgundy robe. The cycledrome became like a scene in the ancient Roman arenas: spectators were cheering and waving, screaming Joe's name. He ran

200

up a few steps to enter the ring and shadowboxed in the middle of it as the pitch of the cheers rose even higher. Once again, Boy Scout Troop 41 was there, outscreaming everyone else: "Go, Joe, go!" and "KO Joe!" He bowed in their direction and threw a few jabs of salute to the faithful fans. The Irish crowd roared their approval when they saw Joe's green trunks.

As for Wilde, who usually had a solid fan base of his own, this time was quite different. He sat in his corner and shook his head in disbelief at the unending acclaim for his opponent. It got worse when the announcer presented "our homeboy, Gentlemaaan Joooeee, who victoriously battled the beee-st in New York and New Jerseeeyyy!" He then turned to Wilde. "The scraaappper from Taunnntooon!" Referee Tickle called the boys for instructions, and finally the bell rang. Unnoticed by Joe, among the spectators was the most prominent New England manager and promoter, David Lumiansky, probably the best-dressed guy in the crowd and actually the most interested in Joe.

The first few rounds offered a splendid sparring demonstration by Joe, while dutiful Wilde responded and slowly began regaining confidence. But after the sixth round, Coach Tickle warned Joe that so far the decision was a toss-up and he was risking a loss. "Remember the eighth round?" Mike hissed, emphasizing each word as he leaned over Joe.

Brought back to the grim reality of possibly losing, Joe switched gears and began to take over the fight by increasing the power of his punches. Wilde fought back with stiff jabs that shook Joe a few times. Joe knew it was a round he needed. He moved closer. He landed a few crashing shots, and the crowd roared, anticipating a knockout! But the bell sounded, and Wilde, now sporting a purple eye, made it to his stool. "This is the last round!" shouted Mike when the bell announced the last three minutes of the match.

Wilde was not the type to lose without first putting up a good fight. He charged Joe, sending him into the ropes and keeping him there with rapidly fired blows. The audience was in a frenzy! But Joe fought his way out of the tight spot, and his right cross crashed in full force into Wilde's chin! Joe saw the livid face, the glassy eyes, and the tremble of the knees, and so did the referee, who stepped between the two. Joe walked to a neutral corner and watched the crowd going wilder. It was the moment of fulfilled expectation that possessed each boxing spectator, looking to see savagery in the ring. The next second Joe hooked his left glove in Wilde's liver and his right cross smashed in Wilde's face. The heavily hit guy fell flat on his back, arms and legs apart. The fight was over. Joe, with his right arm pointed to the heavens, saluted the delirious public with a special nod and grin for deliriously cheering Troop 14. Joe was back!

In the dressing room, Coach Tickle handed him $100. As he left, he turned back to Joe and said, "Great job! See you in the gym." Moments later, Lumiansky entered the door. The fowl-smelling, dark dressing room turned into a delightful scene as, arm outstretched, the promoter said in an almost singing and velvety baritone voice, "Great fight, young man! We've met before. I'm David Lumiansky." They shook hands, Joe's still wrapped in sweaty gauze. He felt a slender-fingered, slippery hand that quickly distanced from Joe's grip. The elegantly dressed gentleman in a three-piece gray suit with an art deco tie wiped his hand with the red breast pocket handkerchief. Careful not to touch anything in the filthy room, he invited Joe to come to his office in New Bedford and "discuss business concerning national and international representation in the boxing world." Then he handed Joe an engraved business card and added, "Call my office and tell my secretary I said you could make an appointment. Good day and good luck, young man!" Joe remained open-mouthed with his right hand up in the air, since Lumiansky had no desire to touch anything dirty. He left as majestically as he had appeared, leaving a scent of French perfume trailing in his wake.

"What's going on? And what's that smell?" Mike sniffed the air as he urged Joe to hurry because the Simons and Tickles had asked the brothers to join them for ice cream cones. Joe handed Mike the money envelope and business card. "Lumiansky was here?" exclaimed Mike, shaking his head in amazement as he lit a cigarette and listened to what had happened. After a few deep inhalations, he promised to take care of business, voicing his skepticism. "I don't trust these guys. Especially this one. What do you think?" Joe's answer was very clear. "I'll go with Lumiansky. How bad can it be? At least I'll have another chance!" Mike closed his eyes and blew a cloud of smoke, saying nothing.

With no fights now lined up, Joe kept reminding Mike to call Lumiansky's office and make an appointment, but Mike refused. He wanted Lumiansky "to beg" for Joe. Setting himself up as Joe's manager and promoter, he had fancy business cards printed, attended boxing events in the area, introduced himself to everyone from trainers to matchmakers, and entertained them, spending a lot of money in expensive restaurants. Despite these efforts, he was frustrated to find no useful leads that could advance Joe's career.

Mike presented himself as a big shot and talked the talk—but to those who knew the industry, he was a typical example of someone trying to fake it until you make it. Slowly Mike began to realize that he still had a lot to learn. He was determined to do that—he would learn and learn fast, he told himself. In the meantime, he told Joe to keep training, since "big things were in the works."

Unexpectedly the news came out that the New Bedford Cycledrome was going to be demolished. It had been the prime arena for boxing and other sports for four years, but it had turned no profit in the last two seasons. The owners couldn't pay their bills and maintain the place unless they doubled the cost of tickets—which the public would not accept. The cycledrome's lumber track was to be sold in a public auction, and the vacant lot was slated to become a housing development. Only Mike didn't care. In fact, he saw opportunity in the news of the cycledrome's end—he might be the one to build a new cycledrome that would be the one and only in the state of Massachusetts! In the meantime he had arranged for a match on August 28, 1925. His brother would again fight Tony Thomas, the handsome local boxer who was determined to win against Joe this time and claim a higher status among countless nobodies from New England.

The fight took place at Capital Park in Rhode Island, on a Friday afternoon in a country fair-like setting. Joe kept looking around and could not believe he was the main attraction of this kind of circus act scheduled for ten rounds in scorching summer heat. If there was one instance when he did not want to walk in the ring, this was it. Annoyed and overheated, he kept drinking one soda bottle after another, in defiance of all advice. The entire bout was a mismatch, since Joe was a superior rival who could end the ordeal in a few seconds. But Mike insisted he carry on the fight to the last closing round, since the organizers threatened to pay only if ten rounds were completed.

As it turned out, Thomas, from Lumiansky's stable, was not a bad fighter. At times he even looked good in flashes, especially when challenged by Joe to weave in and out of too-close encounters. Round after round, Joe, who dictated the pace, bombarded Thomas with stiff blows, and Thomas recovered by switching stances. Thomas was a southpaw—something new for Joe, who found it interesting to adapt both offensively and defensively to the slightly different boxing strategy of a left-hand fighter. The fight dragged on under a merciless sun.

The highlight of the fight was when Joe faked an attack only to slide to the side, catching the other with solid long lefts and rights, ending with a right cross to the chin. The impact was so devastating that Thomas began running around the ring until he regained his balance. Mike was screaming for a kill, but Joe felt sorry for Thomas and wrapped up the fight by winning a unanimous decision. Three bills of $20 rewarded what Joe considered the lousiest victory of his career. His morale had never been lower. From headline fights in New Jersey and New York, he was now boxing an opponent far below his level in a park in front of people who couldn't care less about the sport.

An entirely different kind of excitement was to make Joe focus on something besides his boxing career. He had other work to do—help his family move to Pittsfield before winter. Only Elias the barber would remain in Fall River. The former Pittsfield grocery store was now an empty brick building, full of debris. The Hashim family would live in the eighteen-foot-wide, three-story clapboard house attached to it. Under Mike's direction, with the approval of his brother-in-law Louis, the store building was completely renovated, including its spacious cellar that would serve as a stockroom. Large, white, electric fans and a polished tongue-and-groove wood floor completed the modernization of the "one stop store," as it was advertised in the local fliers.

Rows of tall, well-supplied shelves with large spaces between them were strongly lit from above, and a few modern weigh scales of different sizes were conveniently located where needed. Above each main section were signs hanging from the ceiling, indicating "Chops & Steaks," "Fresh Fish," "Spices," "Canned Goods," and so on. A telephone was installed next to the register, with another line next to the butcher counter and a third one in the family living quarters, all with the same number. All the improvements were cutting-edge concepts copied from the first "supermarkets" of New York and New Jersey, and they gave commercial prestige to the once cavelike place.

At the same time, good progress was made with the living quarters, urgently needed for the family. The store was opened for business on Joe's birthday, February 6. Mike proudly stood at the entrance and greeted each customer, pulling some of the men aside to tell them that prices were so low because everything was paid for with cash from Joe's ring money. The business began to grow from a trickle into a full stream of steady customers. From his butcher's counter Joe looked with pride at so many people selecting canned goods, fresh vegetables, household supplies, and meat, poultry, and fish. They left with multiple bags and a smile, for they liked everything about the store.

For a while Joe was too busy working in the store to pay close attention to what was happening in the competitive world of boxing. But he did follow the intense dispute for the featherweight title when on August 27, Louis Kaplan, the world champion, kept his title after a fifteen-round draw against contender Babe Herman. What was most important to Joe was that the title was still up for grabs. Mike was interested that the contest took place in Brassco Park in Waterbury, an obscure blue-collar city in Connecticut, where 20,000 people paid $59,180, from which Kaplan received $19,685. The title was defended a second time by Louis Kaplan after fifteen grueling rounds against Babe Herman on December 18, 1925. It took place in the new Madison Square Garden that had owner Tex Rickard opened a week before. He'd hooked up again with Doessereck as the matchmaker for the new boxing establishment. But Joe was no longer with Doessereck and couldn't benefit from that huge advantage. Mike felt this was beside the point. What fascinated and excited him was the fact that if a boxing event destined for Madison Square Garden could be staged in Waterbury, then it was possible for a similar big event to be held in Pittsfield!

To Joe, it was proof that wise management was the ultimate ticket to success in the ring. Mike vowed to do the same for his brother. In the meantime Eddie "Cannonball" Martin, whom everyone believed Joe could defeat, was still the world bantam champion.

CHAPTER 22
ANOTHER BEGINNING

Once the upstairs addition work was completed, the family moved into the new apartment smelling of the welcoming paint, clean floor, and washed windows. The clapboard house was rented immediately. Business began to pick up each day, greatly aided by Mike's vision of a successful store with tasteful displays: spacious alleys between rows of shelves showing products arranged on different levels, like an expensive store, but with discount prices. The two oversize front windows with eye-catching letters on the top advertised "Sodas & Cigars" and the recent drink, "Moxie." Between the windows was a large entrance door framed by newspaper and magazine racks. Above the door was a red sign with large white letters, lit by a bulb with a round shade above it:

Hashim Bros.
Fancy
Groceries

To the left and the right of the one-step threshold, along the outside walls, were display tables and open boxes with vegetables, fruits, bottles, and other inviting goods for sale. Green- and red-striped canopies ensured the needed shade for the food set outside, as well for the cash register located near the entrance door. On the far right, a long sign listed in firm large letters: "Groceries—Delicatessen—Stationery—Magazines. Another sign advertised that Western Union telegrams and money transfers were available inside, and a poster showing a bell promoted "Pay & Talk" (a public phone). With all these extra services provided, the previous humble store had been transformed into a "one stop shop" for the neighborhood, making it unique among the approximately 145 other grocery establishments in the city. Joe turned out to be a good butcher because, accordingly to Mike, "he had enough practice in the ring."

One week after another passed uneventfully, approaching Easter of 1926. Joe was working from six o'clock in the morning to eight o'clock in the evening, sometimes later, and business was doing really well. He wore a long white apron over black pants, a black tie, and a white shirt with rolled-up sleeves filled by his voluminous biceps. One afternoon, an elderly gentleman approached the butcher counter and ordered three T-bone steaks. Joe began sharpening his long knives; the rhythmic sounds always reminded him of the speed punching bag. While he wrapped up the steaks, the customer stared at him. "You sure look like that champion Joe Grimm." Joe smiled with a nod. "I used to box. I'm Joe Grimm."

"So, this is why we don't see you in the ring anymore. You're here all the time." Leaving the counter, he was shaking his head. As he paid Joe's father at the cash register, he leaned across the counter and softly said, "What a waste. That young man would have been a great champion."

A few minutes later, David signaled his son to come and talk with him. In Arabic, he asked Joe what the man had said. Joe reassured his father that everything was just fine and the stranger said something nice about the store. But that night he looked for Lumiansky's card.

The next day, when the store was quiet and the rest of his family was upstairs for lunch, he used the pay phone to call Lumiansky. "It's Joe Grimm," he said. "I'm ready to fight again."

"Good, good, young man," Lumiansky's singing voice came through the receiver. "I've got something for you. In three weeks you can fight in Lowell. Let's talk about it. When can you get here?" Joe looked at the calendar next to the freezer and said he could be there on the sixth, the first Tuesday after Easter. "So you're not a Muslim?" Lumiansky laughed and then asked if Joe needed a place to stay. "No, thanks, I can stay with my brother, who's a barber in Fall River." There was a long silence at the other end of the wire. Then Lumiansky wished Joe a safe trip, and the conversation was over. Things couldn't be better.

Or so he was thinking until Mike came back into the store from its large basement stockroom, where he had been taking inventory. Quietly Joe told him that he had called Lumiansky and already committed himself to a fight. Mike stiffened, stepped back, and stared at his brother while he reached for a cigarette. "Say that again?" he said, his eyes boring into Joe. The brother repeated that he was going to fight again—one more fight before hanging up the gloves for good. The entire matter would have to be discussed later.

That evening, after dinner, Mike cleared his throat and said that Joe had something to tell everyone. At first there was silence at the table. Then there was an eruption, everyone talking at once, dismissing the shocking news, but Joe was unmoved and offered an argument that calmed the uproar. "I can make more money in one fight than we make in the store in a month. We can use that money." The discussion was settled in favor of Joe, but Mike couldn't go with him. He would have to take over Joe's place behind the butcher counter and spend more time in the shop. And so Joe went to see Lumiansky.

Forty years old and six feet four inches tall, the thin but towering David Lumiansky kept some distance between himself and anyone approaching him. A graduate of the University of Boston, Lumiansky was a full-time insurance broker, his office being on Palmer Street. He was also an opportunistic salesman for his family's furniture business, but he wanted to be known and remembered as an important boxing manager and promoter. There was a rumor that he attended law school because his domineering Jewish mother demanded it. It was further speculated that this explained Lumiansky's ability to brush up against the law so many times and not lose his boxing license. Whatever the accusation, Lumiansky could demonstrate he was right, and usually he prevailed.

Lumiansky's main local rivals in boxing affairs were the former matchmaker Al Cassidy who worked at the Arena Athletic Club in New Bedford, John McGrath who managed the uprising Johnny Shepherd, and manager Harold Finell who handled the undefeated "golden boy" Jimmy Mendes and the promising Johnny Lynch. Like any other promoter, Lumiansky needed a champion-caliber fighter on his roster. Because of this, he determinedly kept negotiating proposals to own featherweight Shepherd and light heavyweight Mendes. Now, out of the blue, Joe Grimm, who fought better than any of those boys, was coming agent-free into his office to discuss representation. This could be just what Lumiansky had been angling for.

Joe met the promoter inside his office located in a very large multipurpose building. The host had a deep baritone voice with a velvety tone that made everything sound pleasant but firmly nonnegotiable. "As you can see, young man, you'll be in good company in my stable." With a flick of his manicured fingernails, he theatrically pointed to the office's paneled walls, covered with framed pictures of his best boxers, most of them standing next to Lumiansky.

His good grooming and panache in legal spats could not stop his being called the "cauliflower impresario," a reference to his large, floppy ears. He was also famous for his intricate dealings and complicated contracts. Even Joe Jacobs from New York, who managed international superstar Max Schmeling, could not match the legal ability of the small-city, New Bedford-based agent. His boxers were fighting all over Europe, from Dublin and London to Copenhagen, Paris, Berlin, Milan, and Barcelona, crossing into Oran in northern Africa. Others were touring Bucharest and Budapest in Eastern Europe. With his well-written contracts, Lumiansky could control his clients in the complicated and convoluted business of international boxing. Right now, he was planning a boxing tour in the western United States, and he wanted to test Joe Grimm in some ten fights he intended to schedule. Joe had lucked out—he couldn't have shown up at a better time, aiming to prove himself to be a high-ranking fighter.

What Lumiansky saw was a youngster with a champion's glow, the mark of all great-ranking contenders, making him an ideal marketable fighter with drawing power. Indeed, Joe radiated confidence in each move he made, even now, sitting in the chair. To Lumiansky's experienced eye, these were unmistakable qualities of a star in the making, and, on top of this, he noted Joe's oversize hands that could crush any jaw in their way. However, he was concerned about Joe's plan to lodge in Fall River when he would be training at Lumiansky's gym in New Bedford. "I'll ride the electric car from Fall River," Joe assured him.

Shifting slightly in his chair and clearing his throat, Lumiansky said okay. "For the time being, we'll sit tight and evaluate the possibilities. Then I'll draw up a contract for you to sign—providing everything goes as I think it will." The meeting over, Lumiansky stood and shook hands with his new fighter and invited Joe to visit the gym. As Joe left the room, the germ-phobic promoter pulled a handkerchief out of his breast pocket and meticulously wiped his hands; then he rubbed his mouth and nose before carefully refolding the white cloth and putting it back.

The boxing gym was inside another wing of Lumiansky's furniture warehouse. Approaching it, Joe detected the familiar noise and smell of wet gloves, sweat, and bodies, and soon he stepped into a very large space with floors free of filth, spit, and blood, with no peeling paint or dirty windows that were seldom opened. Instead, everything was well aired, immaculately clean, and well polished. Between these walls, young men from ages fifteen to thirty trained, blowing sharp breaths that helped them accelerate while skipping cords or furiously crashing their fists into heavy bags suspended by squeaking chains. Because Lumiansky hated consumption of cigars and cigarettes, no trace of smoke was to be found in his gym. There were large posters—the only ones in the gym—announcing "No Smoking" and "No Guns Allowed" in bright orange letters.

What made Lumiansky's gym well-known in the boxing industry was his stable of respected fighters, like Chick Suggs and his two brothers Louis and Oscar. Just two months earlier, Suggs, the well-known New England featherweight champion, had defeated Abe Goldstein in a ten-round decision. "Panama" Al Brown, the internationally known fighter now winning big in France and all over Europe, was another of Lumiansky's clients. Training hard in the New Bedford gym was Andy Martin, also a featherweight, who kept threatening the two older fighters of the same category. Because Lumiansky knew that "real rink money" was in the heavier categories, he managed the light heavyweights Charley Manty and Martin Burke, as well as the promising heavyweight Ed Keeley. Some twenty other boxers, like Toney Thomas, whom Joe had already beaten to a pulp a half a year before, were training with Suggs's personal coach, "Manny" Arruda, while others worked with Harry Lipsky, the trusted associate of Lumiansky, who was also a ring judge for many local bouts.

Coach Harry took an immediate personal interest in Joe, struck by two attributes: Joe's incredible arm speed and his heavy punches. According to the Jewish coach, a self-entitled scholar in boxing, neither of these could be taught, and they could improve only a little, regardless of training. One had to be born with them. Both coaches teamed up Suggs with Joe, five years younger and exactly the type of fighter whom the featherweight contender feared the most—a tireless, durable inside puncher.

Sparring with ever-confident Suggs, Joe learned to "never go in dangerous territory" and "never lose a cool head in the ring." Time and time again Joe heard Coach Manny saying to the cocky novices, "Overconfidence is worse than fear in the ring; it lets your guard down." To which Coach Harry added, laughing, "It's always the punch you don't see that puts you down!" Joe was happy to be in such good company and tried to prove himself worthy of Lumiansky's trust.

When the news reached the Fall River newspapers, one report appeared under large type:

Joe Grimm Signs Up with Dave Lumiansky of N.B.

> Joe Grimm of this city has hooked up with Dave Lumiansky, manager of Chick Suggs and Charley Manty and he is now training with these two New Bedford fighters. Grimm has a wonderful opportunity to gain a lot of experience as a trainer (sparring partner) for Chick Suggs and Manty and his daily workouts with the pair have already shown results ... Grimm is living at his home in this city and is in strict training in preparation for future bouts.

Joe had spent less than two weeks with the new stable when he entered the Crescent Rink arena in Lowell, facing an entire audience hostile to him. The reason was the same as in similar instances: Nelson was their homeboy from Lowell. They were not aware that Joe had won more fights by KO than Nelson had fought in his entire career.

While waiting for the announcer to do his pitch, Joe closed his eyes and smiled, remembering the good days of cheering Troop 14 and the adoring public and his victorious days in the ring. He opened his eyes and saw the crowd fanatically cheering as usual, but this time for Nelson, their aspiring hero who happily strolled around the ring saluting his loyal audience. When Joe's name was announced, a hurricane of disappointment covered the rest of the introduction that ended with "Gentleman Boxer." After all this, the referee wished them, "Fight clean and good luck." Joe took off his burgundy robe and waited in his corner.

From the bell signal, Nelson went like a bull in full charge, encouraged by a choir of screams and whistles, while Joe promptly landed a thundering left-right-left-right jab combination that stopped him, dizzy and in denial. It happened in seconds, but it had a lasting effect on Nelson, who was dazed for the remaining rounds. He jumped in a clinch to recover and resumed a new attack with powerful blows, proving only that he was either groggy or not a good marksman. Then he tried to dance around Joe and throw punches, as he came up with a different tactic, basically wanting to confuse Joe with his chaotic fight.

The next round he did the same, until Joe realized that the closer he stepped to Nelson, the more he neutralized his punching power that so far had kept increasing. By round three, Joe figured out that Nelson was fighting just like Suggs, like a cat; so, Joe wasted no opportunity to teach him a painful lesson for each bold move or mistake he made. By round five, many sections of the audience began to reward Joe's fast combinations that looked so good and landed so well. But the Lowell boy had his fighting spirit intact and kept carrying out his faulty attacks that always ended up the same way—in an alarming retreat with Joe in pursuit, ripping to his stomach and cracking his face. The back-and-forth actions with the same predictable result began to raise the crowd to their feet, either cheering for Joe or screaming at Nelson to fight back.

Round seven was entirely dominated by Joe, who by now could outmaneuver Nelson around the ring. His solid punches began to land at will on Nelson's body and head, and large bruises were bleeding under his eyes and from his puffy lips. The eighth round found Nelson exhausted, trying to shield himself or to block the incoming gloves that Joe shot with accuracy and speed. Joe began a long sequence of combinations that could have ended up in a KO, if the bell hadn't stopped the fight. It was a mismatched bout and the public accepted that, when rewarding the victorious Joe with rounds of applause and "Way to go, Joe!" A ring reporter described the fight as "Grim [*sic*] won handily beating Benny Nelson of Lowell … the youngster showed fine form … and he is in line for plenty of work in the near future." Lumiansky saw the entire fight and led Joe to the dressing room with many congratulatory words. The unusual gesture did not escape the jealous Suggs, who actually knocked out Rick Mercer in the fourth round out of ten scheduled. Joe received $150, and Suggs double that amount. Joe also received a contract to sign "in order to protect you and I in the brutal game of chance," explained the sober and impeccably dressed Lumiansky.

"Do not sign anything!" shouted Mike on the phone. "Sunday afternoon, I'll be at Elias's and we'll talk about it!" In the meantime, Elias gave the contract to a barbershop client who was a lawyer and agreed to study it. When Mike arrived, he found Joe and the lawyer in Elias's family room, with the contract and a notebook on the table. "It is very unusually written, with many strange clauses to accept," he said. Observing the three brothers' long faces, the man flipped further through the pages until he found a particular paragraph, which, according to the lawyer, was enough reason for anybody to void the contract. First, he reread it silently for himself and then, in a dramatic voice, read to the brothers, "The boxer, in case of death or incapacity prior to the end of the present contract, all rights the manager had do not stop but pass to his heirs, executors …"

Poking the paragraph with his index finger, the lawyer looked at the puzzled brothers and explained, pointing to Joe, "If you die for any cause, your family is responsible for paying back to Lumiansky all your debt to him." Mike stood up at once, puffed his cigarette a few times, and, exhaling a heavy cloud with each word, commented, "So, what you're saying is that we could lose the grocery store, and the house, to Lumiansky?" The lawyer lifted his shoulders and his arms, saying, "If that's what it will take to pay him back, yes, that's the case."

"We go right back to Pittsfield tomorrow and we'll show all these crooks how to handle the boxing business!" furiously decreed Mike. Joe never went back to Lumiansky, nor did he return his contract. He just followed his brother Mike back home.

Mike knew little about his new hometown of Pittsfield, nestled in the Berkshire Hills of western Massachusetts; it was quite different from Fall River. The young city had been incorporated only in the last years of the nineteenth century, and its population had grown to some 40,000 by the time the Hashim family settled there. Electric Manufacturing Company was one of the vital businesses that created the first electric transformer, and the city had the glorious distinction of having the first electric stop sign in America, if not in the world, in 1925.

The influence of the Roaring Twenties came with strict limitations to Pittsfield, where everything could be achieved in an old-fashioned way, with hard work, patience, and pride. The community was proud of its architecture—the temple-like city hall; the colonnaded courthouse; the citadel building of the library; the monolithic Berkshire Museum; monumental church, bank, and school structures; and even the imposing building of the YMCA, not to mention the beautiful hotels, like the New American and Maplewood, and many mansions. A simple stroll on North Street showed one after another expensive and elegant commercial outlet, including England Bros. department store, numerous imposing banks, and many shops, all geared to the affluent clientele living in the prosperous city. Newspapers *Globe* and *Berkshire Eagle* kept all the residents informed about the latest developments in the busy daily life of the city, with many competent editorials and news features about the social, economic, political, and cultural news and events, reserving a lot of space for reports on sports events. But the coverage on boxing tended to be amateurish and done with humor or comments off the subject.

The cosmopolitan city on the Housatonic River was an important cultural center. Since the 1850s, Herman Melville had found a refuge near Pittsville to write *Moby Dick* and to cement a friendship with his neighbor Nathaniel Hawthorne, another American novelist. Pittsfield was distant from New York's Broadway theater district, but the city had its own Great White Way known for theater productions, musical and dance events, and now movie projections housed in lavish buildings.

For those noble cultural purposes, the Colonial Theater was built in 1903 with all the elements needed to inspire admiration and respect for arts, with the yellowish brick facade with three palatial entrances towered by three oversize windows, arched on the top, as if to prepare the spectators for the gilded interior. Designed for high-quality sound, the Colonial was one of the best acoustical structures in the world. The Casino, the other theater, was less richly built in 1905 on Summer Street, changing managements and names every five years to the Empire, Grand, Casino again, and finally in 1924 the New Winter Garden, as part of a national vaudeville and movie distribution chain. Because of the huge cultural demand and profitability, more theaters opened. One, the Union Square Theater, was constructed in the Belasco architectural style, with a sophisticated lighting system.

The Capitol Theater was opened in 1922 with great fanfare, because it provided the ultimate luxuries in architectural taste; lavish decor; comfortable plush seats for 1,500 facing a modern stage that included a piano, organ, and huge screen with shades of color for movies; and most glamorous of all, 3,300 electric lights inside the theater to transform it into a magical world. The Beacon and Berkshire Public Theater completed the list, all of them the cradle of vaudeville and *Ziegfeld Follies*, when for decency reasons, men and women attended separate shows.

Sports activities were encouraged by private and public associations that subsidized baseball, golf, basketball, swimming, and rowing events that attracted the young and the old. Wahconah Park, with a stadium for professional baseball games, was the legacy of one hundred years of tradition and of some great players, such as Stephen Arienti and Ulysses Frank Grant, who was black. In 1924 Lou Gehrig played in the stadium, scoring home runs after sending the balls into the Housatonic River. Pittsfield was one of a few cities with a tradition of golf, provided by the affluent country club.

All in all, Pittsfield was in a class of its own, quite distinct from neighboring rural Lenox, the farm community of Lee, the mill town of North Adams, and the vacation land of Stockbridge.

With Gene Tunney defending Jack Dempsey and 39 million people listening to the fight's transmission on the radio, and then Jack Sharkey versus Dempsey in Yankee Stadium with a $1 million gate, Mike believed he would succeed in Pittsfield with Joe Grimm as his top fighter. The city had theaters that could easily hold a ring and good-size population with a lot of money. This venture had all the makings of a money machine, and Mike was determined to make it happen.

Chapter 23
Tackling the Boxing Business

With no fights lined up, Joe stopped training and put all his energy into the grocery store. Meanwhile, Mike was certain that managers and promoters would beg him to have his brother box in their events. The recent ring success of Joe's was going to give Mike the needed negotiating leverage to make Pittsfield a "mecca of boxing." While the bankers silently stared at him, he waved his cigar as he explained how other "obscure places," namely Jersey City and Providence, had prospered when promoters like himself involved local businessmen in the financing of projects that would attract quality boxers and countless paying spectators to watch them. To his surprise, Mike received a firm "no" to all his inquiries.

Then, on a Friday afternoon he received an unexpected phone call asking if Joe Grimm was still a bantam or a featherweight and was available for a fight the next Monday. The caller was Mr. Bob from the New Winter Garden Theater, who was promoting the event. Mike was stunned. Someone had already used his idea and was setting up a boxing match in Pittsfield—with Joe! As if to prove he were Joe's manager and promoter, Mike agreed to bring his brother for the weigh-in before the fight.

Hanging up the phone, he looked for Joe and found him coming out of the meat freezer. Joe asked who the opponent was. Mike opened his mouth, and nothing but silence came out of it. "How much do we get paid?" was the next question, and Mike arched his eyebrows and lifted his shoulders. "And we blamed Doessereck!" Joe laughed but acknowledged to himself that it had been seven months and he hadn't trained at all.

✦✦

It turned out that the match on November 15, 1926, was against Johnny Melrose of Albany, with seven wins, seven losses (four by KO), and two draws. The out-of-state boxer was originally set to fight someone else who could not honor his commitment, and Mr. Bob was grateful that Joe had agreed to step in at a moment's notice. He had been able to schedule only four bouts for that evening, and if one was called off, the small audience, mostly from North Adams, would ask for their money back. The evening exhibition started late, because Mr. Bob waited for all the ticketed customers to arrive, but the place was more than half empty. As Joe prepared to duck under the ropes and step onto the canvas, Mr. Bob begged him to go the full eight rounds with no KOs, because "that was good for the business." The announcer described Joe as "the Gentleman Boxer from Pittsfield," and this attracted lively applause and cheers. In the same shouting voice, he presented Melrose as "a talented fighter."

After the first round, Joe realized that a rapid-fisted attack could finish Melrose in seconds. The Albany boy was happy to display his top form in the first three rounds and believed he was winning by points until Joe planted a darting straight at the tip of his chin, leaving him stunned and paralyzed in the middle of the ring. The referee stepped between the fighters and ordered Joe to go to the neutral corner. Joe's next punch led Melrose to the stool at the end of the round. Legs buckling, the boy collapsed in his corner.

The next four rounds were identical: Joe sparred well with Melrose, but seconds before each break, he stunned his opponent with another right cross to the face or a left hook to the liver. Melrose's knees bent out of control, and he wobbled to the safety of his corner. If a second punch had followed, Melrose would have been in dreamland for a long time. But Joe kept his promise and won by unanimous decision a fight that he would have won even easier five years before. What he did well was to entertain the audience from which he received long-standing ovations, and $30 "for a job well-done." But, to Mike, more important than anything else was that everyone present learned who Jim Grimm was: a tremendously entertaining fighter!

After the theater cleared and Joe had gone home, Mike and Mr. Bob, himself a former boxer with a pug nose and scars on his face, had a long talk. Bob was friendly and honest with Mike, talking about how hard it was to stage a fight in Pittsfield. To his annoyance, Mike also learned that

Mr. Bob had already scheduled other boxing events. He also was told that anything regarding sports activity had to go through the Pittsfield Athletic Club, which issued permits for any event.

Armed with Joe's new victory, Mike renewed his crusade and relentlessly knocked at any door that had names written in gold letters. He had polished his arguments and now showed newspaper clippings about Joe's countless victories as he described his vision that would draw a flood of thousands of boxing fans into the shops, hotels, and restaurants of Pittsfield. While the Pittsfield money people listened with one side of the brain, with the other they recalled the disaster of Tex Rickard's project in Shelby, Montana, that bankrupted banks and ended in a financial disaster that made history. Moreover, the businessmen and bankers knew for a fact that the cycledrome in New Bedford was losing so much money that it was due for demolition.

January and February were always hard in New England, with the cold and the endless snow. It was a slow time for the grocery store, and the family began to worry about money. Out of the blue, Mike received a call from Melrose's manager, who was asking for a rematch because his boxer believed he'd had a bad day when he lost. The fight would take place in Albany on March 8, 1927, and Mike asked for $100 to be paid in advance, plus another $30 for expenses. The manager agreed on the spot, and Mike felt cheated that he hadn't asked for more money. Without any further ado, Joe began training at the YMCA, where the local amateur guys met to spar and confront each other. One of them was the promising local skinny boy, Frankie Salvagio, who would soon walk in the ring under the name of Frankie Martin. Four years younger than Joe, they would become lifelong friends. A wealthy observer offered to build a gym that Joe could run, a proposal that Mike flatly rejected.

With each passing day, Joe's popularity increased and many fans turned out to be steady customers, coming to see Joe, whom they called "champ." The ever-opportunistic Mike ordered an oversize eight-by-two-foot vertical poster for the side window listing services offered by the store. At the bottom was an invitation with the words, "Come in and wait for car, or talk to Mike and Joe." Many did come to speak to Joe, and Mike rubbed his hands, repeating with joy, "Build and they will come!" The store's business went up in sales.

But, according to Mike, the fight in Albany was "the real business for

Joe," who had to do well for two good reasons: his reputation was at stake, and if he scored a KO, Mike would make a bundle in betting. "I even forgot the smell of that kind of money," he complained. Louis Massery offered to drive the brothers to a hotel near the Knickerbocker arena in Albany, and all three shared a room the night before the fight. At the weigh-in, Joe faced a changed Johnny Melrose, who for months had trained with his friend Young Testo from Troy, a local middleweight celebrity with twenty wins in a row, half of them by knockout.

There was no doubt this time that Melrose was physically and mentally ready to defeat Joe in six rounds; that determination was written all over his face when he entered the ring. The audience, which had filled the old arena to capacity, stood up for their favorite boxer, assisted by four cornermen, including the popular Testo. In the opposite corner, Joe was wrapped in his burgundy robe, with Massery acting as the spit-bucket man as both waited for Mike, who went to place his bets. Joe was introduced as Jimmy Haskins, since he had renewed his boxing license in the state of New York. Hearing that he was called the Gentleman Boxer, the public booed him with all the enmity fans can devote to the opposition. Their affection was showered on Melrose, "a promising up-and-coming fighter," who kept dancing around the ring, sending pugilistic salutes left and right. The referee delivered his instructions, and Joe went to his corner, where Mike, all in a sweat, grabbed his head and whispered in his ear, "I bet all our money that you'll put Melrose to sleep in the first round! All the bets are against you. Understood?" Joe nodded and leaped forward with the bell.

Melrose wasted no time in showing his new form and shape, coming straight for a merciless fight. He greeted Joe with rapid-fire long jabs that shook Joe, and the audience went wild with screams of joy. For a minute or so, the local boy acted like a clever fighter with a powerful punch to back it up. "Go after him! Knock him dead!" yelled Mike until his hoarse voice failed him, while Joe kept throwing punches to adjust his ideal range against taller opponent. Melrose understood his intention and threw a volley of punches at Joe. Immediately Mike recognized that determined gaze when Joe went for a killing, and instinctively Melrose froze into a turtle shell stance. It was a mistake, because Joe's left hooks to the liver and half crosses to the chin began to pour nonstop and unchallenged. Each punch was lifting Melrose off the floor, until he slowly melted on the canvas, first kneeling and then dropping facedown, ending up motionless, with both arms under his belly. The bell rang (prematurely, according to Mike), announcing the end of the fight. The spectators were in shock to see that Joe was such a superior boxer. When they recovered, they erupted in a rage of denial, while the referee raised Joe's arm.

Seconds later, the entire scene became dangerous as fans, shaking their fists, began running between the aisles toward the ring. Four policemen quickly escorted Joe, Mike, and Louis to the locker room. Mike tipped an officer three bucks to take him to the bookie, who delivered a bundle of money that hardly could fit in his inside coat pocket. Taking advantage of the audience being busy with the next fight, the three outsiders ran to their car and vanished into the night. "See why it's good to be paid up front?" Mike laughed as he patted his pocket bulging with money. He added, "We are rolling in dough, brother!"

In the beginning of April 1927, Coach Bobby Tickle called the store and let Mike know that old rival Johnny Dias was looking for another shot at setting the record straight with Joe. Mike tried to negotiate money, but there was nothing to bargain, since Dias was coming anyhow with a bunch of boxers to Pittsfield for a sports event hosted by the local Athletic Club. Unfortunately, with the store so busy, Joe had no time to go to the Y after the Melrose fight. With less than two weeks to prepare for the fight, Joe did his best to do push-ups and sit-ups behind the butcher counter when he had a few minutes for himself, and run late in the night to rebuild his stamina. The fight would take place one week before Easter.

One day prior to the fight, on April 24, the *Berkshire Evening Eagle*, tipped by Mike, paid rare attention to the fistic competition. The "Today in Sports" page had a notice headlined, "Grim [*sic*] To Fight Dias." The commentary was rather pathetic, noting that "the Pittsfield grocery man" wants "to score accounts for a defeat at the hands of Dias in Fall River some time ago." Mike immediately noticed that his brother, once held in awe and respected by all reporters, was no longer called Gentleman Joe, the Dempsey of the Bantams, the Golden Boy, or other flattering nicknames that reflected his superior boxing rank. In Pittsfield it seemed he was nothing but a man working in a grocery store, fighting to settle an old feud inside the Armory building.

But Joe was relaxed and stood in the crowd to see the preliminary bout between Al Love and Young Gates. In the second fight "Sheik" Leonard of Wallingford, Connecticut, won by decision against Walter Oliver of Fall River. Another couple from Pittsfield, "Young" Hudleston and "Kid"

Duquette, carried out a boring fight, and Joe went to his dressing room before it was over.

When Joe and Dias entered the ring as main eventers, fully charged with adrenaline, their tension was felt by the crowd. Only in boxing did such a personal feeling transmit so quickly and contagiously to the spectators. The two boys met in the middle of the ring, determined to carry out an unmistakable grudge battle, and in the first minute, they engaged in a hurricane of punches that threw each of them against the ropes, only to bounce back into the mayhem. Better trained, Dias threw powerful wallops to keep Joe at arm's length distance. Joe was slipping under the barrage of heavy shots, popping countless uppercuts and hooks to the other's midsection. Blood coming from someone was splattered around, which surprised the quiet audience. The tough exchange of gloves suddenly stopped, when, as reported in the newspaper,

> The Pittsfield grocery man fought Dias with an upper cut to the jaw and felled him … The referee counted 10. Dias happened to think he had heard that number before and furthermore he realized that the floor was no place for a successful fighter to be when a referee was pronouncing the double figure. Dias immediately declared that he was fit to fight, but Referee Dekkers informed him that the semi-final bout had been concluded and he had been knocked out. The Fall River boy claimed that somebody had made a great mistake.

The *Berkshire Eagle* reporter who covered the fight agreed that the "error was on the part of Dias, who took a long trip for less than three minutes of boxing." And he continued in another column: "Just because Johnny Dias forgot that 10 is the number after 9 and failed to get up after being hit by Joe Grim [sic] in the first round, many of the customers showered Referee Dekkers with raspberries and refused to allow Matchmaker Formel to introduce the main bout performance."

To Joe and Mike's delight, the announcer shouted the words they most loved to hear, "The winner by knockout in the first round iiiiiisssssss, Joooeeee the Gentleeeemaaan Boxeeerr …" and after a deep breath, "of Piiittsfieeeld!" As he raised Joe's gloved right arm, Joe made his biceps bulge above his head, acknowledging adoring cheers just like in the good old times. After touring the ring, he put on his burgundy robe. Unfortunately for Mike, the spectators had no concept of betting on boxing, and he made no money. But considering the ovations for his brother, he felt ready "to correct one more problem with these Plymouth Rock people," since now Joe had given him new ammunition to continue his mission.

The news about Joe's victories in a row began spreading all over Pittsfield and brought more people to the grocery store. Based on that, Mike spent the entire summer of 1927 contacting managers and promoters, aiming to convince them to join his boxing extravaganza. After five months of his "boxing crusade," he showed no results, except that many important people learned a lot about the Gentleman Boxer and liked him.

Compounding his difficulties, Mike was working against the unbeatable odds of the time. That summer, one of the most famous shrines of boxing, Boyle's Thirty Acres, built by Tex Rickard six years before, was deemed unprofitable and was scheduled to be demolished. Constructed of wood, the largest and iconic boxing arena in the world had hosted memorable battles of the century between Dempsey and Carpentier, and then Dempsey and Willard, as well as between Firpo and Wills. It was here too that other top champions—including James Braddock, Tiger Flowers, Benny Leonard, Mike McTigue, and Johnny Wilson—had thrilled almost one million spectators. But the famous structure was doomed. Its loss marked the end of a Golden Boxing Era. From that time on, titan boxing events would be hosted by the New York's Yankee Stadium and Polo Ground.

Clinging to the stubborn hope that he would build a mini-coliseum in Pittsfield, Mike learned that another boxing event was going to take place in October in Pittsfield—and nobody had bothered to let him know or to invite Joe to participate. The culprit, Mike learned from Mr. Bob, was the Pittsfield Athletic Club, whose WASP leaders chose to completely ignore the presence of two newcomers who could diminish the club's importance.

Highly upset, Mike went to the Pittsfield Athletic Club and complained about their "overlooking Joe Grimm" in spite of his amazing KO records and many fights won in the past. The meeting turned almost ugly when Mike asked for a permit to stage his own boxing events in Pittsfield. Not only did they refuse, but they also stated that they could get better boxing promoters from North Adams to run their boxing shows. Mike left, slamming the door. According to him, "Balduc was the darling of the Pittsfield Athletic Club" and therefore was booked regularly. So was "Kid" Decker, the middleweight star of North Adams. Only Joe was left out.

However, Mike was not a man to take no for an answer, and his indignation made him write a letter to the *Berkshire Evening Eagle*, directed to "The Referee's Sporting Chat" column. After a few lines of introduction, Mike made his point clear:

> I shall make my statement in the form of a challenge. I am ready to put Joe up against George Bolduc, who won his last two fights in this city, or any first rate boxer of 126 pounds, that the Pittsfield A.C. can bring here. I am not begging fight for Joe Grimm, as I can get plenty of out-of-town contracts for him. In fact, he has a business and he is in the fight game only for the love of the sport.
>
> I do wish to prove, however, to the Pittsfield A.C. authorities that we have right here in Pittsfield a top card performer, and let the local fight fans be the judges.
>
> Yours in sport,
> Mike Hashim.
> Pittsfield, November 7, 1927

To Mike's outrage, his public challenge went unanswered while another boxing event was posted at the Winter Garden Theater for November 17. Balduc was again top billed, this time against another nobody, Steve Smith, who predictably was defeated by points after ten boring rounds. It was obvious to Mike that Balduc was beefing up his record at the expense of less skilled fighters who had more losses than wins in the ring. In Mike's estimation, Joe could floor Balduc in the first minute of the first round, yet he was beginning to better understand Doessereck and many of his promotional problems.

Clearly, Mike was anything but stupid, but in desperation, he planned to borrow money from Louis Massery and finance the first independent boxing event in Pittsfield. Louis, however, gently but firmly refused. Unhappy and frustrated, Mike decided he would borrow money from the bank, using the store as collateral, but his parents were so horrified that they refused to discuss it. Soon, the name of the store and its address appeared in the *Pittsfield Directory*, showing David and Rebecca as owners and sons Michael with Nageeb (Joe's baptized name) as employees, at 139 West Housatonic Street. This made it crystal clear to whom the business belonged.

Then Mike did what he had never wanted to do—use his "reserve money" of $2,000 that he had hidden, won from betting and what was left of Joe's ring money. First he checked with Joe, who smiled and had no trouble answering, "Sure, we'll do it!" He respected and loved his brother, and if Mike thought they could do it, they could.

Mike began to look for a good location to host his first boxing event. He needed to find a theater with the right amount of seats and a stage large enough to accommodate a ring, only to receive basically the same "We're not interested!" The reason was that "barbarian boxing fans will trash the theater." Luckily, Mike didn't have to spend any of the hidden stash, because on November 28, Mr. Bob promised to provide "a good rival for Joe."

In the meantime, Joe was working behind his butcher counter and kept shaking hands with many fans who brought their relatives and friends to "meet the champ." It really felt good for Joe to have a little recognition, even though it was awkward to be repeatedly asked, "Why are you here and not working out in the gym or winning in the ring?" After a while he found a comfortable answer he believed to be right: "There's a lot to do in life besides boxing." Joe worked a double shift to prove the point. Still, he remained open-minded about returning to the ring, and if an opportunity arose, he was ready again to train and prove his gameness.

The Hashim family celebrated Thanksgiving 1927 in their new home. The oldest son, Elias the barber, came with his wife and their baby daughter to Pittsfield for the holiday. Lebanese food and turkey were continually replenished on the dining room and kitchen tables, but unlike in the past three years, no one spoke about boxing. The only memorable event was that brother-in-law Louis took everyone who was in the house to a photo studio for a family picture.

The photographer seated Rafka in the only armchair in the middle of the group. She looked saintly as ever and had the aura of motherhood. Behind her was David, her mustached husband, who looked thin and tired but content. On his right was Mike, hands in his pockets like any successful businessman, his suit jacket parted and showing the silver watch chain across the vest. He was the only one to look straight at the camera, as if he was investigating it. In front of him were seated his younger sisters Catherine and Evelyn. To David's left was Elias, standing behind his wife, Adele, who held their daughter, Florence. Next to Elias stood Joe, who had gained weight and was impeccably dressed in a double-breasted suit with a white handkerchief tucked in the breast pocket. His face showed not the slightest mark of his brutal profession in the ring. His left large hand sporting a gold ring rested on the shoulder of his youngest brother, George, age nine. Everyone was smartly dressed, showing how well adjusted they were in their new land. However, like most immigrants in front of the camera, none of them smiled.

It was a very timely photograph, because days later David Hashim fell on the steep stairs as he rushed from the apartment to work in the store. He had broken his hip. Refusing to see a medical doctor, he instead trusted a Lebanese shaman who believed that rubbing, pulling, and twisting the wounded limb would heal it. The mishandled hip, with not enough calcium to recover, deteriorated so badly that before long David was confined to his bed with excruciating pain. Since only Joe was strong enough to lift the elderly half-paralyzed man, he became the main caretaker for his frail father. He had no time to train, and Mike had to spend more time in the grocery store, which limited his time to look for money to fund his boxing project. Sister Evelyn worked more hours than ever, and the two younger siblings, Catherine and George, tried to help as much as they could.

Mike proudly announced his new motto, "Today a grocery shop; tomorrow a national chain of stores." His logic was simple: so far, each megabusiness originated in a corner street store, which the Hashims already had!

CHAPTER 24

NO GUARANTEES IN THE RING

Mike's slamming the door of the Pittsfield Athletic Club was bad manners, but it had an unexpected good impact: he was asked back for further talks. This time he was offered the opportunity to be the matchmaker for the boxing events at the New Winter Garden if he was willing to pay 10 percent of the gross to the club and all expenses that ticket selling did not cover. "Who said good guys finish last?" Mike relayed the story to anyone who was willing to listen, happy finally to have an official boxing title and a place on the fistic map.

Like any other manager, promoter, and matchmaker, Mike slaved over the telephone to call everyone he knew and convince them to send their fighters to Pittsfield. After two restless weeks of negotiations, Mike realized that ultimately any boxing decision was based on financial profit. Soon he concluded that boxers who would fight for under $50 were a good catch for now. Locals from North Adams and Pittsfield would be favored, because their transport expenses were minimal. They also brought large crowds of relatives, friends, and fans. Another smart thing was to bring boxers from the same city, because they could share a ride and a hotel room; he found many in Holyoke who were happy to do this. The same thing applied to the announcers, referees, judges, ring doctors, and so on. Most importantly, he learned from Mr. Bob to provide as many bouts as possible with lots of rounds, as the public was more likely to pay more "to see a lot of bloody action."

Joe received the next fight announcement as his brother explained that "if enough spectators don't show up, we probably won't make any money." Joe's main concern was that he had one week left to train and lose some weight. That evening he did his first two-mile run around the store streets. Late in the night he did calisthenics in the backyard, while the neighbor's dogs kept barking at the fast-moving silhouette. He shadowboxed early in the morning, and, during the day when the store was quiet, he did sets of push-ups and sit-ups and lifted weights behind the butcher counter.

Once Mike had scheduled five fights (a coup, considering there were usually up to four) for Monday evening, November 28, he ran with his good news to the *Berkshire Eagle*; now it was time to get the publicity. There, by a stroke of luck, he had made a good contact with editor Edward Karam, who was a fan of Joe. Because of that, he had published Mike's previous letter. Now, on the day of the fight, he announced, "Lively Card at Garden Tonight," with a subhead, "Pittsfield A.C. Has Booked Boxing Bouts Which Promise To Be Attractive." The news item noted that "three eight-round bouts, one six-round tilt and one four round affair are the program arranged by Mike Hashim, the match maker." A list of all ten combatants followed, with brief information about the ring participants. Mike was flattered to see his name in print.

Joe, who was now a featherweight, continued his training routine until the afternoon before the fight, when he went for the weigh-in. There he met his opponent, Leonard Cook of Bridgeport, Connecticut, who tipped the scale exactly ten pounds heavier than Joe. Even though Joe was okay with this, the officials barred Cook from that competition. Somehow, Danny Morey of North Adams, who had the positions of manager and promoter of the evening event, found a last-minute substitute in Georgie LaFay from nearby Albany, New York. He was two pounds heavier than Joe and a beginner with only fourteen fights, winning only a few. Compared with Joe, he was a nobody, but a well-trained and fit nobody, who, for $30, was willing to step into the Pittsfield ring.

Mike wanted a full house and urged Mr. Bob to reduce the ringside ticket price, and hundreds rushed to take advantage of it. Eventually they ended up standing around the theater walls, and for the first time the entrance fee covered all expenses. Mike walked away with $23 after paying everyone, excluding Joe but including Morey, who for the first time got paid for his work, namely $36. To Mike, this was the most important money he had ever made, and wrapping an arm around Joe's shoulders, he said, "You don't mind if you aren't paid, do you?"

In the first of the evening's fights, welterweight Frank McClusky of Pittsfield won by points against Young Bartini of Lee, both novices and equally unskilled fighters. Next, "Young" Duquette, Joe's only direct rival in Pittsfield, lost by decision after six badly fought rounds to Rene Shabutte of Holyoke. The third fight featured welterweight Harry Lagess of North Adams, who fought with style against "Cowboy" Danny Long of Holyoke, who was knocked out in the fourth round. Then, "Kid" Decker of Housatonic, New York, won a pitiful decision over "Cannonball" Cote of Lewiston, Maine, the worst fight of the night. Joe left in the middle of that bout to get ready for his own fight.

After Morey, now acting as referee, had done the presentation and fight instructions, the bell sounded. In a few seconds Joe and LaFay were at it, exchanging sizzling punches that raised spectators to their feet. It was unlikely that LaFay knew Joe's KO reputation, as he began to throw one haymaker after another, hoping that one would flatten his dangerous rival. Arms low, ready to swing wild, he began a stormy attack, which moments later Joe mercilessly halted when he darted his right cross to the chin. LaFay dropped to the canvas with a thump. He stayed there, reluctantly got up, and again experienced a similar devastating punch. The audience went wild—a rare thing in Pittsfield, even though the entire episode lasted only a few moments. A very unhappy Morey kneeled next to motionless LaFay and, instead of counting, whispered in his ear that if he quit, he wasn't going to get paid, not even gas money for the return trip home. The referee confessed to a reporter after the fight that he "went to LaFay's corner and said: 'Get in there and fight. Grimm has no punch tonight. He has worked himself out in the gymnasium and should be easy for you.'" The warning convinced the scared boy to get up and throw himself in a tight clinch around Joe until the end of the round. The public booed while the scrappers walked to their corners.

During the break, Morey went to Joe and Mike and begged them not to finish off LaFay immediately. Again LaFay pushed his luck, surprising the relaxed Joe with a volley of tough punches, some of which landed on his face and body. The pain instantly reminded him of Coach Manny's warning about how dangerous overconfidence could be. The crowd was screaming support—the underdog might score a KO! Joe leaped and sidestepped the punches to get out of the messy situation and kept dodging another storm of blows that delighted the public.

With his eyes glued to his opponent, Joe decided he'd had enough of giving this guy a break. Ignoring the promise he'd made, Joe stepped forward to hammer a powerful left and a right, flush to LaFay's chin. The boy melted to the floor. The referee took his time as he bent to kneel next to him and then waited for him to get up. LaFay struggled to his feet at the count of seven, only to find himself at the mercy of Joe's salvos that laid him on the canvas again. People were losing their voices from so much yelling as the bell ended the round. The referee also told the reporter that after LaFay went back to his corner, "he remarked to me: 'I thought you said Grimm could not punch.'" At the same time, Mike splashed Joe with icy water and whispered in Joe's ear, "What're you doing? Don't sabotage my event by killing the sucker before the middle of the eighth round!"

"Hey, you're not the one taking the blows!" responded Joe.

For the next two rounds, Joe dragged out the fight with a kind of sparring, while Referee Morey "urged" the fighters to be more aggressive. By the eighth round, the action was nonstop and intense. Joe put LaFay down on the canvas again and again, and while the New Yorker got up for the last time with glassy eyes and a shaking body, he met one single right cross planted on the exposed chin. Joe moved back, waiting for his adversary, now a sleepwalker, to hit the floor any moment. He did not, because the referee caught LaFay in his arms and dragged him to his corner, signaling that the fight was over.

That late night on their way back home, Joe was listening to his brother complaining that "it was a real fight to match two good boxers and not easy at all, because of money issues." Joe stopped him with a laugh and said, "How about that Doessereck?" Mike frowned, puzzled. "What about him?" Joe laughed again. "I was just wondering how he's doing!" Mike didn't respond to the irony.

The next day the *Berkshire Evening Eagle* reporter summarized the fight: "LaFay went down a couple of times in the eight round and referee Morey stopped the boat awarding decision to go." The reporter concluded, "It was unfortunate that Grimm should figure in such a bout as Mike Hashim, the matchmaker and his manager. Grimm tried to fight, but this affair did not help him in his campaign to be considered capable of performing in the main bout here." It was not a flattering comment for the Hashim brothers, but days later the paper had a more favorable story under the headline "Fight and Fighters":

> Pittsfield is back on the fighting map after the splendid show the Pittsfield A.C. put on last week. It was the best card that the club put on in a long while. Despite the rainy weather the fans turned out pretty good. It's too bad Joe

Grimm's opponent was not willing to mix with Joe. It takes two to make a fight and as Lafay didn't care to fight it out with Joe it made the local boy look bad at times but surely Grimm is a much better fighter than he showed that night.

Wonder when Hashim will give us another show? If the fans will turn out the way they did in the last show we will be in store for some good bouts this winter.

Come on Mike, give us another good show.

Mike was happy to see his name in print again. His dream of becoming a boxing promoter was rekindled. After reading the article out loud in the grocery store to his customers, Joe and sister Evelyn, he grinned and said, "Watch out, Charlie Doessereck. Here comes Mike Hashim!"

Meanwhile, in the boxing community there was chaos and confusion when the world title in the bantam division was unexpectedly awarded to Teddy Baldock, who, at age nineteen, was the youngest world champion declared by British boxing authorities. The problem was that a few months before, the undisputed world champion Charley "Phil" Rosenberg forfeited his title, because he was too overweight to fight Bushy Graham, whom he defeated in fifteen rounds, but lost the world title anyhow. The complicated saga of "who was the champion of the rooster fighters" was being played out far away from Pittsfield, where Joe was butchering large chunks of meat behind a counter instead of mauling his rivals in the ring.

Regardless of the bantam title saga, Mike was on top of the world, especially on December 16, which was the day before another boxing event he had arranged. When the local newspaper was delivered to the store, he saw in print that "Matchmaker Mike Hashim is pleased with his entire card. This is the second show put on by him. The first one drew practically a capacity house and another big gathering can be expected tonight." He sighed happily. Indeed, it was going to be a great night with five good fights scheduled. The four-round opener would be between two local boys, "Kid" Kanappe of Pittsfield and "Young" Villa of North Adams. Next would come a six-round bout matching Pancho Villa of New Bedford against Rene Shabutte of Holyoke. Then there would be the much-anticipated eight-rounders: his brother would face Mickey Roberts of Worchester, New York; then Decker of Housatonic would fight against Tracey Ferguson of

Northford, Connecticut; and the evening would wrap up with K.O. Brown of New Bedford versus Red Garren of Waterbury. Once again, Balduc's trainer and manager had denied the invitation.

For some reason, the *Berkshire Evening Eagle* announced the boxing event under the banner of "Decker and Ferguson to Meet in Feature Bout Here Tonight," with Decker's picture. The news item pointed out that he'd never been knocked out, and if he passed the test of Ferguson, a very heavy puncher, he would be "worth taking to some large city to train and present in the ring." Mike, who was smiling when he picked up the paper and stood reading it near the cash register counter, was quickly red-faced and furious. "Idiots!" he screamed as surprised customers turned and looked at him. Crunching the paper and slamming it on the counter, he continued his rage. "Joe Grimm did all that already! He's the star, not Decker the Candlelight!"

The next night the fight went on as expected. Mike, who had collected himself, now stood proudly at the entry door to the glitzy theater, greeting the ticket holders. When Joe entered the ring, the public immediately noticed that Mickey Roberts was heavier, taller, and more athletic than their homeboy. Even so, from the first sound of the bell, Roberts was totally outclassed and outboxed, as Joe dominated the fight without any challenge. Roberts was a feather dust puncher and reduced to playing the role of a sandbag. He was a typically glove-shy and arm-weary, and his head snapped back at each blow; and Joe began to throw mild punches only to please the public. It was clearly an uneven fight, and the newspaper's ring reporter severely criticized it the following day:

> Joe Grimm of this city, 125, stopped Mickey Roberts of Worcester, 129, in the fourth round of the scheduled eight-round semi final. It was the least interesting bout on the card and the close of it brought about the only raspberry chorus of the evening. The first two rounds were tame. Grimm knocked Roberts down three times in the third round. A left to the head and a right to the body felled Roberts for the count of nine. A body punch then dropped the Worcester entry for a count of five. A right to the head sent Roberts down just before the bell which saved him from a full count. Grimm knocked Roberts down twice in the fifth round and then Referee Dekkers stopped the bout, awarding the decision to the Pittsfield battler.

In contrast, Decker's fight was enthusiastically described: "He brought the big crowd out of their seats ... scoring a clear knockdown" after he had sent Ferguson "in a corner like a rubber ball." Indeed, the fight was full of suspense, as the boys put each other down to the canvas, got up, exchanged wild punches, and dominated different rounds, ending up with Decker's victory by decision. That was the fight the public expected to see, not the one where Joe punished his opponent like he was a rag doll. Joe received no money, while Decker pocketed $90 for his spectacular victory. The rest of the winners—Garren, Kanappe, and Shabutte—walked away with $50 each. For whatever it was worth, only Joe was complimented at the end of a bout with "Ladies and gentlemen, the winner by a technical knockout in the fifth round, and still undefeated, is the Deeemp-seeey of the Baaan-taaams, Gentleman Jooo-eeey Grii-immm!"

It just happened that Denny McMahon, the manager of "Kid" Kaplan, the featherweight champion of the world, was in the audience. "Smelling champions and big money" was his job, and he saw gold in Joe. But, as the night went on, he observed Mike, who was strongly in charge not only of the event but also of his brother. Deciding Mike wasn't a person he wanted to deal with, McMahon decided not to touch Joe, who would never know that in a split second, he missed a great guide and patron.

For Mike, with Joe having one more KO under his belt, it was a successful evening. The local newspaper wrote, "It was the second show staged by matchmaker Mike Hashim and both drew well." Finally, after a long and humiliating struggle, he was a name to be respected. From now on, before any fight he would say, "Joe, go the distance, give them their money's worth!" Without doubt, he and his brother were a winning combination.

After celebrating the new year of 1928 with his entire family, things were becoming clear to Joe. There comes a point when you can hold onto a dream, even though the facts show it's not going to happen, or you can let it go and look to a different future. He trained less, and then he stopped working out altogether. When Mike asked why, Joe told him he had decided to retire from the ring. Eyes bulging, his jaw dropped and his face wrinkled in disbelief. Mike whispered, "Why are you doing this to me?" Joe looked into his brother's eyes and quietly responded, "Brother, I am done with boxing. It's over." Mike took a deep breath and stepped back, shaking his head. He had to think about this. He'd figure something out. However, Joe never trained again.

The January 23 event was still on, and Mike had already found someone willing to walk into the ring with Joe. He was Al Beauregard from Waterbury, who had just defeated Eddie Madden of Fall River, who in his turn won over Pancho Villa, a New Bedford guy with a decent record (the real-world champion Pancho Villa had died three years before). Joe agreed to fight again, to save Mike's business.

The weigh-in took place Monday afternoon at three o'clock, but only Beauregard was present since Joe was waiting in his store for a meat delivery. He came running and sweaty three hours later, when he discovered he was six pounds heavier than his rival, who accepted the fight anyway. Walking back home with Mike, Joe expressed his concerns about being too tired and out of shape to be in the ring. Mike reassured him, "This punk doesn't stand a chance to win, but remember, any KOs must be in the last round; otherwise you put me in a tough spot with the public!"

Before he knew it, Joe was walking in the packed arena, facing the noisy crowd. More than two thousand pairs of eyes waited for him to climb in the ring and glide around it as usual, flashing his burgundy gown and his good-natured wide smile, shadowboxing and saluting the fans. By now, everyone in the audience knew that when "Joe was fighting, the arena was rocking" in anticipation of a knockout. But this time was different. He quietly sat on his stool, listening to his agitated brother talking about the fight being a piece of cake. He went calmly through the introduction and other prefight routines and returned to his stool, looking at Beauregard in the opposite corner, noting how his rival kept moving, probably animated by dreams of glory, like Joe did four years before. The bell rang.

Beauregard was a walk-in slugger, and his threatening attitude matched his actions, showing no inhibition in meeting Joe in the middle of the ring with a long set of wild swings. He was the type to throw ten punches in order to land one, and he instantly proved that he was totally exposed to counterpunches. But Joe was to go the distance. Smart and experienced, he knew how to handle the brutal hitter. He delighted the screaming spectators by showing his boxing superiority, executing a punishing dance with fake moves that irritated his bully opponent. Joe was so much in control that he could have delivered a KO shot in no time.

Joe was leading, and the fight was clearly in his favor when suddenly a solid blow to the chin stunned him. Even Beauregard was taken aback to see his superior rival drop his arms and stand still in the middle of the ring. Spectators held their breath and went dead silent for a moment. He leaped back, his arms up, shielding his body, and confidently continued his boxing routine. At the break Mike was worried. "You're too casual with this guy. Be more careful." Joe was so dizzy from the shock that he didn't hear anything.

The third round proved to be a nightmare for Joe, but it was the most exciting part of the fight for the audience. Beauregard was again throwing wild and ill-aimed punches. They came like a strong wind with furious speed and power. Joe did everything to avoid them, and most blows went astray. Referee Dekkers moved too close to the battling boys and took a shot in the chest from Beauregard that almost collapsed him. Both boys stopped fighting, looking at the poor man with trembling legs and confused eyes, catching his breath and dignity, all amidst laughter from the crowd. The fight resumed at the command, "Box," and reached the savage levels of a brawl despite how hard Joe tried to control it. At each break he pleaded with Mike to let him floor the troublemaker and end the circus, but the answer was "Don't spoil the fun—this is exactly what people pay good money to see! That's why they like you." Again, Joe did his best to offer a good fight to the paying customers.

To the thrill of the audience, in the sixth ground Joe hammered the other so badly that he went through the cords. Referee Dekkers had to stop the fight to let Beauregard untangle himself and get back into the ring. His face was that of a loser, covered with red patches and purple ringing his eyes. Joe was again in full control of the fight. But during another unpredictable melee, one of the sledgehammers he had just avoided landed on the back of his neck. Instantly, Joe sank on his knees and rolled on the floor. The public jumped on their feet, screaming. Dekkers, instead of disqualifying Beauregard for the illegal blow, jumped around Joe, who was back on his feet before any count. "Just a head rush!" he said to the referee.

So Joe got ready for the eighth-round grand finale, remembering not to blink at the wrong time. But there was no grand finale for the determined Joe, who during the next furious exchange hit Beauregard lethally hard. Like the gentleman he was, Joe stepped back, expecting his stunned rival's knees to fold and drop him on the canvas. Dekkers jumped between them. Joe looked over his shoulder and signaled to nervous Mike to calm down. Suddenly he heard the audience screaming. As he turned his head back to see what had happened, a lightning black glove coming from nowhere crashed into his nose. Excruciating pain shut off all Joe's senses of the surrounding reality, except his instinct to jump into a tight clinch. Only his pride kept him standing.

Joe had no idea how he found himself sitting in his corner. He believed the fight was over. He had no memory of the sudden attack, which was the kind only rookies would execute out of frustration and rage. Mike splashed the icy sponge on his face and kept wiping blood until the white towel turned red. Joe struggled to breathe through the clogs of blood that choked his throat. "You want to quit?" yelled Mike, trying to be heard over the hubbub of the audience. "After I finish him!" Joe spit out some blood and refused to have cotton balls stuck into his nose.

At the bell he jumped toward the astonished Beauregard, who showed increasing confusion, as he was battered over and over with blows that in normal fight would KO anyone. But with blood obstructing his windpipe and still being punch-drunk with his legs buckling, Joe felt like he was floating on clouds and was only able to deliver weakened and slower punches. In the last round, the fight had already shifted dramatically from Beauregard to Joe, but it was too late.

When the referee raised the arm of victorious Beauregard, who had one eye badly swollen and closed, there was a furious chorus of boos sounding the crowd's disapproval of the wrong decision. Joe hardly heard them. His head felt heavy because of lack of oxygen, and he was still throbbing with pain after the devastating blow to his nose. As he looked at the floor while his brother gently rubbed his back with the towel, he remembered Lumiansky's trainers often warned, "It's always the punch you don't see that puts you down!"

Joe realized he'd been carelessly overconfident, and that was why he was caught off guard at the precise moment he'd believed he won the fight. When the blood stopped, he walked home alone, mad at himself for having allowed himself to be hurt so badly.

His mother first collapsed onto a kitchen sofa when she saw the mutilated face, and then she rushed to have him sit down as she soaked a cool cloth to gently press against his nose. He refused to eat or go to a doctor. Depressed and angry, he kept going over the fight in his mind, disbelieving how such a calculated defender like himself, an easy winner, had been caught by a punch pulled from halfway across the ring to land so bluntly in his face. Mike gave him space; he quietly told the family about the fight only when Joe had gone to his room.

The next day, in the *Eagle's* "Today in Sports" column, he read the brief and colorless description of the fight to refresh his foggy memory:

Al [Beauregard] is one of those boys who keeps coming all the time, hitting well and often with rights and lefts. Joe outsmarted Al at times but Grimm did not seem to possess the punch to enable himself to take advantage of opportunities. The first round was not especially sensational but in the second frame Al brought the customers to their toes. He landed a solid left to the jaw and Grimm's hands dropped to the floor. Joe, however, was soon in the fighting posture again. Beauregard was swinging so often and so carelessly in the third round that he caught Referee Dekkers on the chest with a left.

In the sixth round one of Beauregard's wild and hard swings caught Grimm on the back of the head and felled him. Joe got up before any count was under way. Beauregard tried hard to produce a knockout but Grimm was able to go the distance.

To Joe's relief, the reporter didn't mention his broken nose. When anybody asked about his wound, he joked, "I thought the guy was a cream puff, until he proved otherwise with a right flash to my nose." And to prove that he was a winner in the ring, he told Mike to book him for the next fight, which he hoped was going to coincide with his twenty-third birthday on February 6. Mike rubbed his hands, and a grin stretched his pencil mustache from ear to ear. He simply said, "You just saved my reputation." He had already found a brave guy from Bridgeport, Julius Sambotti, who accepted the challenge to fight on February 27 at the New Winter Garden Theater.

Joe was determined to score one more knockout before he closed the boxing chapter of his life. He wanted to end this career in the same way he began it—with his head held high.

CHAPTER 25
THE LAST FIGHT

Mike's next pugilistic card was held for the benefit of the Elks Lodge, which one year before had become a national foundation involved with charity relief work for World War I veterans, orphans of organization members, and the granting of scholarships. The noble cause attracted everyone who was somebody in western Massachusetts for a fund-raising gala. Mike felt extremely honored to be in charge of entertainment, which would be a boxing event in the New Winter Garden Theater. It seemed to Joe that Mike's matchmaking activity was going astray; it had become a kind of circus to please donors who neither knew nor cared about boxing. Mike had even booked two "colored" boys from New York and included a wrestling match in addition to the four boxing bouts. It was a bad version of the ballyhoo that was so much in fashion.

At first, Joe refused to fight. He was having trouble breathing through his healing nose, and furthermore, he didn't like the entire exhibition set up. He couldn't let his brother down.

When Joe walked in the ring for the semifinal bout, he could not care less about the cheers addressed to him. He just sat on his stool and waited for the bell, planning how to pace himself for a long fight and protect his nose from another direct hit. His opponent, Julius Sambotti, was a novice but a decent fighter who could also land fast and effective punches. After two rounds it was a seesaw battle, and Mike begged Joe to win but not with an immediate KO. Joe's only concern was to keep the flying gloves away from his face.

When Joe realized that it was anyone's fight, he took firm command and demonstrated how well he could shoot from all angles, making Sambotti run for cover. In the last two rounds, Joe threw plenty of tough punches with well-aimed leather to make sure he would win by points. "Come on, Joe, drop him!" were the cries from the audience, but the bout ended with both boys standing up. Joe, with no training and a damaged nose, had fought all the scheduled rounds unable to breathe properly and overtired. He simply ran out of punching power, and so did Sambotti.

Not surprisingly, the *Berkshire Evening Eagle* reported in its title, "Preliminary Boxers Provide Best Battle of the Evening," and described how "the colored" boxers lost while Mike Carlo scored an exciting TKO in the third round against Huddy Hendelson. Both welterweights were from Pittsfield, and Joe, who watched the fight, believed that it should have been illegal to throw such little-trained boys in the ring. But the public loved the fight, as did the press, which had this to say about his victory:

> Joe was down to better weight than in some of his other fights and did pretty well although the customers as a whole were not wildly enthusiastic over his showing. The best round of the bout was the fifth and Grimm had the better of it. Neither Joe or Julius [Sambotti] showed much in the line of a damaging punch.

Again Joe received no payment for his victory, and Mike didn't make much either, as most of his money went to the foundation for its charity. He couldn't stop thinking that everything he had done in New Jersey and New York was amounting to nothing, except his first real injury. He went on with his grocery business that was doing better than ever and didn't bother with any training. In the meantime, Mike continued with his boxing shows, despite the fact that he wasn't making money from them.

It looked like April 7 might be the big day Mike had been waiting for. Best of all, he had asked Joe to fight a star bout against Johnny Mack from Hartford, Connecticut, who was said to be a tough and smart fighter on his way up. Climbing through the ropes can tell a lot about a fighter, and certainly Mack clearly knew his way around the canvas enclosure. With him came three corner aides. The announcer introduced the fighters as "Mighty Mack" and "Gentleman Joe" who "were ready to battle a ten-round war."

Back in his corner, Mike was worried about his untrained brother and asked him to "take it easy," advice he had never before used in the ring.

Mack was the type who needed to get mad in order to fight well. Being taller, Mack used the advantage of fighting at a distance, so his strong series of long lefts and rights cut short the menacing attacks. His main problem was that he needed space to punch well, and Joe was not willing to facilitate that. Bobbing and weaving under the darting gloves, Joe rammed Mack with an arsenal of punches that drove him from one side of the ring to another. His three cornermen screamed something, and Mack covered himself with both arms while running backward. Joe found himself chasing his speedy opponent and then stopped in the middle of the ring, his arms down as he looked at the "turtle" boy. The bell rang, and the crowd chanted, "Do it, Joe!" while both combatants dropped on their stools. "Take it easy, will you? You have nine more rounds to go!" Mike was concerned about his untrained brother. "Don't count on that!" was Joe's answer.

Round two was dramatic because Mack was not willing to step back and used his dominant left jabs to distance himself from Joe, who kept banging and belting him with body shots, looking for an opening upstairs, pursuing like a dog chasing a cat; soon enough, a smashing left cross to the chin sent Mack facedown on the floor. The public jumped as one, but their cheers were cut short when Mack leaped back on his feet and continued milling. His guts and determination translated into a battery of punches that forced Joe into a retreat. Joe was okay with this—he was happy to realize that his undeterred punching power was still intact. The round closed with wild cheers for both boys. Mike splashed Joe with icy water and could not muffle a "Son of a gun!" admiring exclamation.

Round three clearly showed that it was a fight that would end with only one boy standing. Mack was putting out everything he had. The round went quickly, and at its end Mike asked Joe how he felt. "Wait and see!" was the answer as he got up with the next bell.

The two warriors went toe-to-toe for a little while, and the public was delirious with anticipation. Joe realized he was beginning to tire when he felt an unexpected second wind. With the same willpower that he had in the first round, he charged forward, head cocked and that unmistakable look on his face that Mike knew too well. In a flash, eyes afire, he found an opening to Mack's chin. A thundering left mercilessly followed. Mack was no longer in control of his body; knees buckled, jaws chattering, he dropped his guard. For the first time in his fighting career, Joe doubled his KO punch, and the ever-effective left hook was merciless again and again.

In a few seconds Mack was off his feet and melted like a candle against the ropes, ending up motionless on the floor.

While Joe toured the ring to the cheers of the public, Referee Dekkers's pumping arm stopped at ten. He could have continued to two hundred, because Mack remained flat on the canvas. The ring reporter for the Fall River *Evening Herald* wrote, "Joe Grimm of Pittsfield, formerly of this city, won his bout at Pittsfield last night by knocking out Johnny Mack of Hartford in the fourth round of the scheduled 10 round encounter. Grimm is a big favorite with the Pittsfield fans and his cleverness and punch proved too much for the boy from Connecticut." It would be the last punch Joe ever threw in a ring.

Realizing he hadn't taken a single punch in the nose, Joe was jubilant. He'd won, and with no new injury or even a hit to his still-healing nose. The announcer found only Joe in the middle of the ring. "The winner by knockout in the first minute of the fourth round, ladieees and gentleeemennnn, I give youuu, the Dempsey of the Bantams, Gennntlemaaan Joeee!" Arms up in the air, looking to the sky, Joe knew this was the last time he would hear the words that had made him dream of becoming a champion. He silently made his last prayer in the ring: *God, please take care of my future!* Joe stood with his arms raised, a large smile on his face, turning slowly in a circle as he acknowledged more than a thousand people chanting, "Joe did it again!" and "Joe Joe Joe!" The sound bounced off the walls of the beautiful art deco theater, now transformed into a gladiatorial coliseum. Joe slipped into his shiny burgundy robe and paraded again around the ring, wanting to embed in his memory the adulation roar of the crowd and the taste of victory. Winning always felt good, but this time was special and different; he would treasure these generous and prolonged ovations for the rest of his life.

In his corner Mike, with an ear-to-ear grin, teased Joe. "And you said you'll never fight again!" For the first time in the ring, he kissed his brother. Joe took his gloves off and handed them to Mike. "I came to the ring with a bang, and I'm leaving it with a bang!" Both brothers walked back to the dressing room, waving to the fans. Once in the quiet room, Mike showed his puzzlement. "You're not seriously thinking about quitting fighting now that you're doing better than ever, are you?" Joe nodded yes and said, "It's time for me to go on with a normal life." Mike's cigarette dangled from his open lips, but he remained mute.

Mike never asked Joe to fight again. He knew, as Joe did, that in the ring, as in life, there was always someone younger, stronger, and better. So much for guarantees in boxing or in life.

✦⧨✦

It turned out that 1928 was not a good year for the economy in Massachusetts. Unmistakable signs of distress became more visible as greater numbers of workers in mills and factories lost their jobs. To stay in business most companies cut salaries by 10 percent, and millworkers protested with the largest labor strike in New England. The collective action backfired in a damaging way when many factories moved out of the northern cities to the South, where labor was cheaper and cotton supplies closer. Practically overnight, more than half of the regular sports spectators could not afford to buy entrance tickets to events.

Mike was beginning to lose money with each boxing event he scheduled, because he couldn't afford to bring in top prizefighters. For sure, he wasn't Tex Rickard, slipping $20 gold coins in the pockets of reporters to get them to write inflated stories about an up-and-coming Dempsey. He'd done his best, but Pittsfield, nestled in the picturesque Berkshire Hills, had neither a boxing tradition, which would have helped him attract important boxers, nor dedicated fans who would pay to watch them fight. And the depressing situation wasn't likely to change, Mike realized.

It felt great being a matchmaker and mixing with the others in the game, but the dream of a booming boxing venture was doomed. He was better off using his energy to build the grocery business while he kept his eye out for other opportunities. With his father bedridden and his mother speaking limited English, plus three younger siblings still in school, there was no question the family could use all the help they could get.

While Mike joined Joe in full-time work at the store, both brothers monitored the news about the messy bantam championship that had been dragging on since February 1927, when the title holder Charley "Phil" Rosenberg couldn't make the weight. Anyhow, he had KOed and mauled challenger Bushy Graham in fifteen rounds, because the Madison Square Garden tickets that were already purchased had to be honored. In the same event, the new champion was officially defeated, and the New York State Athletic Commission disqualified both fighters and their managers for deceiving the public. Once again, the title was up for grabs, and one by one, "Bud" Taylor, Teddy Baldock, Willie Smith, and Bushy Graham seized the $4,000 diamond-studded belt, only to give it up for different reasons, mainly moving to the next weight category or being defeated in unwanted fights. From the middle of 1927 to May 1928, the title was vacant and under bitter dispute, but Joe was neither near that controversy nor close enough to the ring to challenge it. It was the end of the Golden Era of Bantams.

As the ticket selling for boxing events throughout the country went into a steep decline, American managers and promoters hit harder and harder times in their profession, with no indications that things would get better in the near future. The lowest point was reached when the best boxing promoter, Tex Rickard, died of a ruptured appendicitis, and the entire young boxing structure collapsed with him. Only a handful of managers and promoters could still fill the boxing arenas, including Mike Jacobs (Rickard's "money man"), who eventually would promote all the Joe Louis fights; Joe Jacobs, who managed Max Schmeling (Hitler's propaganda champion); and Joe Gould, who shaped James Braddock into the Cinderella Man.

Fortunately, Joe had a successful business and made good money, so he was not forced to continue fighting like many broken boxers he knew who ended up poor or homeless.

A short time after Joe retired from the ring, his father died of pneumonia. Ever since he had fractured the head of his femur bone, he had been confined in bed, lying only on his back. Because of all the heat and perspiration beneath him, his lungs became congested. What was believed to be a nasty cough and temporary fever turned out to be a terminal case of pneumonia. The tragedy affected the entire family, and Mike took over the role of patriarch. He and Joe continued running the grocery business.

The Depression had come with staggering unemployment, bankruptcies, and personal tragedies, but regardless of all the disasters, people still needed to eat. Sometimes Mike would lament about the "rotten business of boxing," often quoting Doessereck. Joe would nod and smile. He still had fans who begged Joe to return to the ring, and sometimes he wondered what he would do if Doessereck or Lumiansky came around and asked him to return. Smiling to himself, he would hear the ring announcer shouting over the noisy crowd, "Ladieeees and Gentlemeeen, tonight we are proud to introduce to you in this corner, Joeee Griiimm the undefeeeated Gentlemeeen Boxeeer!" Still smiling, he'd go back to making sausages or dusting the canned goods so the colorful labels would attract the customers' attention.

Early one winter morning, a lady in a lavish fur coat stood at the butcher counter, her light floral perfume gently surrounding her.

"May I have four nice rib eye steaks?" she softly asked.

"Yes, ma'am, I'll cut them fresh for you." Joe began to trim the steaks with a long shining knife. The woman studied Joe. She couldn't help but notice his short sleeves showed bulging biceps and triceps, and the fitted white apron did nothing to hide his muscular chest and torso.

"Excuse me, are you Joe Grimm?"

"Yes, I was, but not any longer," Joe answered as he kept working.

"I know you from the church. You were a great fighter. My husband and his friends talk about you all the time. Why aren't you fighting? Don't you miss the ring?"

"No, ma'am. Those days are over for me."

"But you are still young—you could go back. My husband says so."

"I had my days in the ring. Now I'm doing this." Joe gave her a polite smile as he wrapped the steaks and then put them on the scale. He wrote the price on the wrapping paper.

"You have a point," the woman responded. "Besides, who needs the boxing business with those mobsters hovering around the gyms and the rings? That's what my husband says. You're a good young man, and you seem very happy with your life."

"Yes, ma'am, that's for sure," Joe said as he gave her the package.

Mike, restocking a shelf in a nearby aisle, overheard the exchange. It was clear his brother was still a powerhouse regardless of what he was doing. His inborn qualities had made him a first-class KO fighter, and then he turned into a better-than-okay grocery man. "It just goes to show," Mike said to himself, "things work out, even though they don't go where you originally wanted." He finished emptying the carton, carried it to the back door of the store, and rushed to take the lady's money. He was dressed in his usual three-piece suit, looking like a successful banker instead of a grocery store co-owner. He stopped at the butcher counter, where Joe looked like he was daydreaming. The brothers smiled at each other and nodded in approval.

"I've been thinking," Mike said. "We've got enough money saved to invest in something, and it's a good time right now to buy real estate. This bad economy is going to recover at some point, and people will want to buy houses again and set up new businesses. In the meantime, we can rent the space and fix it up slowly. We can't lose! We can't get hurt. Every great business starts with a street corner store, and we've already got one!" Joe laughed with his brother, and both shook their heads. Yes, they'd do it. They'd go after another big dream together.

Epilogue

There are no guarantees in life, regardless of what one does. Certainly this is the case with professional boxing, where success in the ring can change in an instant; in fact, it is almost inevitable that one day a fighter will cross gloves with someone who potentially can reduce him to an invalid or even kill him. When Joe Grimm faced the brutal fact that it would take years, at best, and even then he might never have a chance to battle for a title, while meanwhile his family urgently needed him, it became clear to him that it was time to make a change. As for where to go, his brother Mike had the answer: home, to take care of the grocery business bought with the ring money. It turned out that his fortitude in the ring was easily transferable to other work and another kind of life.

Joe retired in 1928, when he was in the best shape of his fighting career, and he never fought again. He bore no scars of any kind and had no regrets. For the rest of his life, he considered himself to be a winner with nothing more to prove. In brief, Joe knew when to let go. This turned out to be a wise and timely decision: one year later, Wall Street crashed and the Depression bankrupted millions. For the boxing industry, the economic disaster meant fewer and fewer spectators trickled into the arenas. As businesses in Fall River, New Bedford, Bayonne, and Pittsfield, as well as throughout the country, locked their doors, so did many boxing arenas. The big era of boxing was over.

Fortunately, the brothers had gotten out of a volatile environment just in time and now had a lucrative and durable new career. Since even impoverished people needed to purchase basic necessities, their new business was safe and the Hashim family never had to fear the financial unpredictability of the next day.

⊰⊱

Joe's record of twenty-four KOs in a row at age eighteen is an impressive accomplishment, even if one argues that his opponents were largely unknown fighters. The records of many renowned boxers show that they began winning against opponents similar to Joe's, but they did not score such a remarkable string of uninterrupted knockout victories. Jimmy Wilde, the "Mighty Atom" of England, won his first 103 victories in a row, scoring one hundred KOs, 16 of them consecutive. Because of that record, he was considered the third-greatest puncher of all time. The British Ted "Kid" Lewis won 170 matches, 70 of them by KO, but 9 in a row. Jack Britton won twenty-one fights by KO, ten of them in the first round. Glorious Dempsey dropped fifty of his rivals during his sixty-one victories in the ring, but in small strings of eight KOs or less in a row. Primo Carnera, the giant Italian, was world champion with an impressive seventy-two KO victories, mostly rigged by his mafia handlers, and still the longest string of consecutive knockouts was only seventeen. The black champion Henry Armstrong was the first prizefighter to hold three world titles (featherweight, welterweight, and light weight) at the same time, when only eight divisions existed. By 1937 he won by knockout twenty-one out of twenty-two bouts. Eventually he scored twenty-seven knockouts in a row, ranking him as the second-best professional boxer of all the time. Disputable is Stanley Ketchel's record of knocking unconscious thirty-five of his first forty opponents.

Between 1940 and 1985, some thirteen boxers, mostly unknown, scored more than twenty-four KO victories in a row. Max Foster, George Foster and Earl Hargrove scored twney-four consecutive KOs. The record holder is the heavyweight Lamar Clark, scoring forty-four KO victories in a row until he was stopped for good by Muhammad Ali, who managed only nine repetitive knockdowns out of his own thirty-seven. Formidable Iron Mike Tyson mastered nineteen KOs in a row, mostly against unknown boxers. In recent years, the Ukrainian Vitali Klitschko, three-time heavyweight world champion, scored twenty-six consecutive victories via knockout. Roberto Duran, rightly called Manos de Piedra (Hands of Stone), the world title holder in four different categories, won more than one hundred fights, scoring twenty-four knockouts in a row (out of seventy), just like Joe did.

In view of these statistics, I would argue that Joe Grimm belongs in the legendary boxers' category and should be mentioned in the history of the sport, at least in a footnote, for his remarkable knockout scoring.

꧁꧂

Many professional boxers relied on their managers and "advisers" to handle their money, and in most cases, all of them except the fighter did well financially. As the Depression escalated, numerous champions who had trusted their savings with professional investors lost everything. Mike's continuous presence prevented Joe from investing his prizefighting money with a speculator and, like some desperate others, having to become a muscleman for a mafia boss. A lucky one was Albert Wright, the world featherweight champion who was employed by Mae West as her chauffeur and bodyguard. Perhaps Joe would have had a brilliant career under the management of Doessereck or Lumiansky, or even with McMahon, who was fascinated by the talented and hard-hitting "Dempsey of the Bantams." Because of his personality and public appeal, Joe might have been one of the most applauded challengers, and he could possibly have made millions of dollars for himself and his entourage.

But when the glory days were over and the money vanished from the banks during the Depression, how much better off could Joe be than as the co-owner of a prosperous grocery store? His former gym buddy Jimmy Braddock lost almost $20,000 that he had deposited in a bank that went under a few months before the Depression struck. Because of that, the future Cinderella Man had to beg each day for a job in the shipyard to feed his family. Only a miracle turned around his doomed boxing career and his life into an unlikely boxing and financial success.

The arbitrary title of champion was no guarantee of a secure retirement. Most ex-champions opened a bar, a restaurant, or a saloon—businesses with which they were familiar, as they had been high-tipping clients. But they proved to be reckless owners. Their idea was to bring fans together and keep legends alive with stories backed up by framed pictures all over the walls and drinks on the house. It took Mickey Walker no time to lose his business and become a painter instead. Tommy Burns, the heavyweight champion of the world, retired from the ring as a rich man and ran a profitable restaurant until 1929, when the Depression ended his prosperity. He became a minister and was buried in an unmarked pauper's grave. Pete Herman, the former bantamweight world champion, lost his eyesight; he returned to his New Orleans hometown to run a restaurant. The ever-popular Jack Delaney, the light heavyweight world champion who once praised Joe, was addicted to alcohol; he retired as a tavern owner and died at forty-eight of cancer. The great Jack Dempsey earned millions of dollars and lost almost all of it during the Depression. After retiring, he was forced him to engage in countless boxing exhibitions that eventually helped him succeed in the restaurant business.

Many boxers with stellar records who made millions of dollars and were famous for being easy spenders eventually hit hard times and died homeless and in poverty. The greatest of all pre–World War I heavyweights, Jack Johnson, lived the life of an international jet-setter, recklessly spending the $1 million he had earned in his career, only to end up penniless. A pauper, he worked as a saloon porter, bartender, and cabaret entertainer, while still training in Chicago as late as 1938 for a hoped-for comeback. He even tried to use his spiritual talent "to fight the evil" and became Reverend Johnson, looking (to no avail) to serve in a black parish in Ohio. Broke at all levels, he died in an automobile crash, still with a mouthful of gold teeth, the only possession he had left. Equally famous, the flyweight world champion Jimmy Wilde made a fortune in his twelve-year professional career but got involved in too many schemes and died as a pauper at age seventy-six. Henry Armstrong made more than $1 million in his fifteen-year career but ended up broke because of his gambling sprees and his manager Eddie Mead's "investments." The legendary Jack Britton lost all of the wealth he accumulated in a twenty-six–-year boxing career, investing in Florida real-estate speculations.

Others succumbed to their vices, like Benny Lynch, the flyweight champion of the world who became an alcoholic and died at age thirty-three. Teddy Baldock, the world bantamweight champion at age nineteen who shook hands with tycoons and celebrities, retired as a badly beaten-up fighter, addicted to alcohol and gambling; he lost everything and finished as a wreck, defeated in the ring and life, dying penniless and dressed in borrowed pajamas at age sixty-four in an infirmary. Maxie Rosenbloom, the colorful light heavyweight world champion, did very well money-wise in his career of three hundred fights, so he could afford to gamble over $250,000. He turned out to be a successful movie actor and television personality, but he never saved a cent, as he indulged in hanging out in the best nightclubs and taking trips around the world. He died penniless at age seventy-one, but with a smile on his face. The original Joe Grim died in an insane asylum in Pennsylvania.

It seems incredible and unfair, but men who proved invincible in the ring ended up losers in life. The icon of bravery, Mickey Walker, who victoriously fought from welterweight to heavyweight, made $4 million in his glorious twenty-year career and lost it all. As he explained, "My managers got a lot of money; so did all my wives. They all got a lot of it except me." Indeed, he made three managers and seven ex-wives rich, while he lived on a social security check and charity from his fans. Walker was found by police in 1974, lying on a street in Freehold, New Jersey. He was admitted in a hospital, where doctors initially took him for a homeless drunken man. He died of anemia, arteriosclerosis, and Parkinson's disease. Johnny Dundee, who was knocked out only twice in his career with 194 wins, died blind in a nursing home in 1977. The great idol of France, Eugene Criqui, with an eighteen-year career in the ring, won ninety-nine fights, fifty-three of them by KO in small groups interrupted by other decisions; he was blind when he died at age seventy-three in a nursing home.

The bantam champion who once belonged to the same stable with Joe, Panama Al Brown, the world title holder for six years, conquered Paris with his flamboyant lifestyle, dancing with Josephine Baker and being the lover of Jean Cocteau. He met a tragic end; the colorful boxer, who was never knocked out in the ring in twenty-three years and recklessly spent $350,000, ended up sparring in a Harlem gym for one dollar a round. A cocaine addict in trouble with the law, he died of tuberculosis, without one cent to his name. Panama Al Brown remained famous for the quickest knockout in history, fifteen seconds, including the ten seconds of the referee's count.

The greatest lightweight ever, Benny Leonard, who lost his first two professional fights and then won ninety-one fights with seventy KOs (spread in small groups), retired at his mother's request; he was undefeated and a millionaire. Losing his fortune in Wall Street speculations, the "Ghetto Wizard" was forced to reenter the ring in 1931. He won twenty-three fights against second-rate rivals but suffered a last and crushing defeat by a TKO from a superior opponent. He was still active in the ring as a referee, where he suddenly died of a massive heart attack while refereeing a fight when he was fifty-one years old. It was a true hurrah exit for a true boxer.

Other world champions had even more gruesome fates. Al Abraham Singer, the former lightweight champion of the world, nicknamed "Battling Bronco of the Bronx," died in a bar fight. At age thirty, Bill "KO" Brennan, famous for fighting Dempsey twice, was found shot to death by the mobsters on the streets of New York.

The walking legend, Kid McCoy, who made a fortune and lost everything, shot to death a married woman who lived with him and spent seven years in jail. Three years after his pardon, he committed suicide at age sixty-six, after having had nine wives. His last written message was "… sorry I could not endure this world's madness …" He was carrying all his wealth in his pocket, $17.75. He was once the groom who remarried an ex-wife and, as a gesture of trust, gave her a $1,800 diamond pin and a check for $10,000—and these gifts took place when a skilled worker made one dollar a day. In 1936, the great middleweight world champion Billy Papke, known as the "Illinois Thunderbolt," killed his ex-wife in a bout of jealousy and then turned the gun on himself. Seventy-five years later, the former two-weight champion Edwin Valero killed his wife and then killed himself in a jail cell. He began his boxing career with twenty-seven straight KOs (nineteen of them in the first round), according to the Venezuelan boxing records. More than sixty well-known ex-boxers committed suicide.

Some champions who were once considered indestructible died prematurely. Legendary middleweight world champion Harry Greb died on the surgical table at age twenty-nine while his doctor tried to reconstruct his damaged nose. His famous black adversary, Theo "Tiger" Flowers, with 56 KOs out of 136 wins, died in similar circumstances one year later during eye surgery. He was thirty-two. Tony Marino, the bantamweight world title holder, went into a coma after he was knocked out four times by Carlos Quintana in New York and died two days later. He was twenty-five. Abe Friedman of Boston, the tireless Jewish bantam and featherweight for twelve years with over 120 fights, was forced in 1925 to retire from the ring because of blindness. One year later, at age thirty-two, he was killed by a truck. Pancho Villa, the world flyweight champion, died in a hospital at age twenty-four because of an infected tooth. His wife believed he was killed by the doctor, who injected an overdose of the anesthetic, on orders from the mob, which had lost too much money gambling on Villa.

The ferocious world middleweight champion Stanley Ketchel, one of the best prizefighters the world has ever seen, was shot to death by a jealous girl's lover. He was twenty-four. In his short but illustrious career of sixty-one official fights, he scored forty-six knockouts in streaks of eleven and twenty-one in a row, a credit to his nickname, "The Michigan Assassin." Dying with a bullet in his chest, he cried to his manager, who ran for rescue. "Take me home to Mom, Pete ..." Joe Grimm came home in one piece, healthy and industrious, to the great relief of his mother, whom he cared for in his home, the apartment above the grocery store, until she died at age eighty-five.

Only a handful of others were successful after their boxing careers. The world heavyweight champion Gene Tunney retired from the ring not only as a glorious fighter but also as a smart investor and capable business owner. His famous challenger, Tommy Gibbons, retired after a nearly perfect winning career with enough money to be a member of the $100,000 club. He owned a boxing gym, did very well in selling insurance, and was elected six times the sheriff of his county in Minnesota. He was knighted twice by the Catholic Church for his good deeds in the community. Jack Sharkey, also a heavyweight title holder, successfully retired with enough savings to own a bar; he supplemented this with earnings from personal appearances and lived a good life with plenty of money. Highly respected, he died at the age of ninety-one. Jimmy McLarnin, the double world welterweight champion, retired when he reached the top of his career. He cleverly invested his prize money and became a wealthy man who lived to be ninety-six, just like Joe.

Meanwhile, the archenemy of the American heavyweights, Max Schmeling—nicknamed "Nazi's Puppet" and greeted with garbage thrown in the ring when he boxed in the United States, especially after he defeated Joe Louis—survived all the prizefighting and political ordeals and became a very rich man after the war. He proved to be a true friend to Joe Louis, who had become an impoverished and sick ex-champion, who made $4.6 million in his distinguished boxing career but personally received only $800,000 and still owed $500,000 to the IRS. The former Aryan hero helped the retired "Brown Bomber," now also a drug addict, to live a decent life, even paying for his burial with full military honors; the former world and European heavyweight champion was one of the pallbearers. Schmeling died a wealthy man at age ninety-nine. Postmortem, Joe Louis was the first American boxer to be honored with a postage stamp.

At age twenty-four, when he was at a peak in his professional boxing career, Joe Grimm quit prizefighting and settled down to work long hours with Mike in their grocery store. Joe never stepped over his older brother, now the family leader, and never disrespected him, regardless of his wrong decisions or mistakes. Mike and Joe married sisters. After having had four children, Mike's wife would die in childbirth; he married again and had two more children. Joe and his wife were married for fifty-nine years; she passed away on their anniversary. He considered her and their four children to be the best things in his life. Mike, who once was turned down by each bank in Pittsfield and in the neighboring towns, became a successful entrepreneur and real estate investor, who was courted by all the banks that once had rejected him. Throughout his life, Mike would remain the one person the family looked to for advice, until he died at age seventy-three.

❧❧

Joe remained a living boxing legend for everyone in eastern and western Massachusetts who knew boxing and was awed by his record of twenty-four KOs in a row. Humble Joe realized that if one could not be a star in the sky, he could be a candle in his home and hometown. He channeled his relentless energy and determination into being a good husband, loving father, and solid businessman. The saying he grew up hearing—"an empty hand is a dirty hand"—meant to him that he should share and give back his many blessings. He was involved in youth associations to which he donated his time and money, especially the Boy Scouts of America. He was generous to everyone. If customers were short of money, that was okay; if a stranger came to the store, hungry, he was invited upstairs for a meal.

Virginia, his oldest child, recalls that her father "loved to have relatives, friends, and even strangers over, especially for a big Sunday dinner. He was very kind, soft-spoken, and gentle person, but stern when he stood up for his rights." Joe remained a conscientious worker and a family man with a positive attitude toward life. "He was an eternal optimist," says his daughter Mae. "He would say a cup was half full, never half empty." When I asked Joe's children if their father used his boxing skills to discipline them, they said there was no need for that—his quiet but firm voice was enough to enforce any rule. Joe Jr. explained, "You should have seen the look on his face when he meant something. Who could challenge that?" Daughter Marion agrees that her father "was strict, but never in a bad mood." She adds, "He was the best role model we could hope for!" Joe liked to write poetry for any occasion, giving his wife, children, and grandchildren handwritten poems for birthdays, holidays, anniversaries, and any special occasion. A gentle man, he was a homebody who also enjoyed hunting and fishing with his younger brother George, who became a much-respected dentist and successful investor.

For the rest of his life, Joe's training discipline was with him: each day he did his morning workout with push-ups, squats, sit-ups, and other calisthenics. He always left the table just a little hungry to maintain his fighting weight. If his boxing years came up in a conversation, his eyes would glow with excitement, and he was happy to entertain his listeners with ring and knockout stories. He remained a boxing enthusiast, dropping everything to see a good match, and he was heavily involved in amateur competitions as a local referee and a judge. Competitive boxing was still in his blood, and he enjoyed it at all levels. He loved to watch Muhammad

Ali fight and greatly admired him, proud that Ali also wrote poetry. Joe remained friends for life with ex-boxers from Pittsfield, Frankie Martin, Pat Chioffi, and Dave Skade, all successful restaurant owners.

Could Joe have had a long career in the ring if he had been guided by a professional manager and promoter, without Mike being omnipresent and making decisions for him? Probably, yes, he could have been a high-ranking boxer and even a champion. But would he then have had the life that gave him such joy? Would he have lived to a healthy age of ninety-six with no scars and no regrets? Joe's children and grandchildren are a testament to the good life he lived.

Joe Hashim, an immigrant, had a shot at the American dream and lived it. He had a run at glory that most could not even dare to think about. He retired from the ring in good times and would always remember the announcers trying to be heard over the roaring crowd, shouting, "The winner and still undefeated, here is Gentlemaaannn Jooooeeee!" Those words would resound in his ears, and he lived by them for the rest of his life. Wisely, he didn't wait for the cheers to change into tears. After Joe traded the ring for the butcher block, he never looked back with a chip on his shoulder and was never sorry about his decisions. He was happy with himself. It was that healthy pride and unscratched dignity that made him a dashing octogenarian and a youthful-looking nonagenarian.

Certainly, there were no standing ovations after carving a T-bone or selling a pound of olives. But Joe had had a taste of real glory—enough to last a lifetime. The entire Hashim family continues to this day to thrive and honor ambitious Joe and Mike, who so generously provided for them by making the best of the Golden Age of Boxing and the Roaring Twenties.

Behind the Story

The boxers, trainers, and managers described in this book are all real. There is little information on the Internet about some of them, especially the non-champion bantam fighters, but the details of their fights can be found in archived local newspaper clippings. And while we cannot know the words that were spoken nearly one hundred years ago, the characters of Joe and his brother Mike, Charlie Doessereck, Dave Lumiansky, Bobby Tickle, and other coaches remain vivid in the memories of their children, associates, and even members of the public who briefly intercepted their lives at that time. The dialogue in *The Gentleman Boxer* is based on those recollections.

Gina and her brother William are fictional characters. At the time Joe Grimm was fighting, flappers liked to be seen in the company of "tough guys." Certainly the Gentleman Boxer would have been attractive to the women who flocked to the ring, and Gina represents one of them. Typically women were accompanied to the ring by a male companion—thus, William, her brother.

Mario, the barber, is also a fictional character, but we know that Mike worked in a barbershop in Bayonne. Mario's shop is representative of the elegant establishments of the era that specialized in the bob cuts that were so popular with flappers like Gina and boxing fans.

To the best of my knowledge, based on my extensive research and time spent in the libraries of Fall River, New Bedford, Pittsfield, Bayonne, and Jersey City, this book describes the time and places in which Joe and Mike lived. The other boxers, managers, and trainers were key figures in the Golden Age of Boxing, also known as the Golden Age of Bantams.

Acknowledgments

While there is little information on the Web about Joe Grimm, BoxRec (boxrec.com) and Cyber Boxing Zone (HobbyPlow.com) were rich in content regarding many other prizefighters, boxing events, and other information pertaining to the early years of the Golden Age of Boxing. The ever-resourceful Wikipedia helped with my writing about many biographies and events from the boxing world.

In Joe's scrapbook I found newspaper clippings with descriptions of his fights, but neither the name of the newspaper nor the reporter were included. I was able to trace many, but not all, of the clips, finding commentary about his fights in the 1920s archives of *The Fall River Herald*, *The Evening Herald*, and *Daily Globe* of Fall River, Massachusetts; the *Evening* and *Morning Standard* of New Bedford, Massachusetts; the *Bayonne Times* and *Bayonne Evening News* of Bayonne, New Jersey; and *The Berkshire Evening Eagle* and *The Berkshire Eagle* of Pittsfield, Massachusetts. My thanks to the newspapers that gave me permission to quote from their articles. *The New York Times* also featured helpful trivia about the boxing events of the era. To all of these newspapers, their staff writers, and ring reporters, I am most thankful and impressed with the quality of their insightful reports.

The following books were particularly helpful with background material:

The Encyclopedia of World Boxing Champions by John D. McCallum (Chilton Book Company, Randor, Pennsylvania, 1975); *Heroes & Ballyhoo* by Michael K. Bohn (Potomac Books, Washington, DC, 2009); *The Lawless Decade* by Paul Sann (Crown Publishers, New York, 1957); and *PITTSFIELD ... Where Legends Begin* by Phyllis E. Kerle (Berkshire Visitors Bureau).

The vital content of my book was inspired by the living children of Joe and Mike and their relatives, who gave generously of their time to help me write this book. Since I didn't have the opportunity to talk to Joe and Mike, I have done my best to recreate their personalities and actions as young men in the adventurous 1920s. Thankfully, Joseph Hashim Jr. provided me with the boxing record notebook handwritten by his father, the scrapbook stuffed with newspaper clippings, family pictures, and countless stories about family, as well as showing me items belonging to Joe Grimm, like his green boxing trunks. Marion Muhlfeld, the sister of Joe Jr., was a constant support throughout the writing of this book. She put me in touch with her two sisters, an aunt, and an uncle, and she helped in tracing other relatives who had stories about the Hashim family in the 1920s, as well as sharing photographs. It was Marion who mentioned that her father was flat-footed—a key factor in his boxing style. Joe and Marion's sisters Virginia Tobia and Mae Atter had recollections that helped give me further insight into Joe Grimm's character, and Virginia, who created the scrapbook of newspaper clips and pictures when she was just twelve years old, provided additional photos. She also had samples of the poetry her father wrote.

Mike's family was equally helpful. His daughters Dolores and Elinor, along with Dolores's husband, Dan Gerardi, made a special trip to meet with me, give me family photos, and share stories about their father and uncle. Michael Hashim Jr. showed me family picture albums and 8-mm films, while also sharing stories about his father and uncle. His brother Robert contacted relatives on the West Coast to answer questions about the family's early days in the United States.

Dolores and Marion put me in touch with their aunt Catherine Simon, who, now in her nineties, spent her life in Fall River; her two older sisters, Alice and Elizabeth, married the Hashim brothers, Mike and Joe. Catherine, who for many years worked for the Fall River Public Library, was always glad to answer any question about the history of the city, the Lebanese community, and Joe's young years. Marion told me about George Haddad of Salt Lake City; George, the grandson of Rafka's Orthodox priest brother, supplied information about the Hashim and Haddad family lives in the area of Aley, Lebanon, at the beginning of the twentieth century and their early lives in America, as well as specific traditions and aspects of Lebanese culture. George Hashim was always close to his older brothers, Joe and Mike; he used to love hunting and fishing with Joe. George's sons, George Jr., James, and John, remembered many details about their sturdy uncle with his crushing handshake, and they encouraged me in my quest.

Philip Massery, Emma's grandson, and Louis Bidar, Edma's grandson, were also supportive and helpful with information about their grandmothers.

Outside of the family, there were many others who generously offered their time, support, and efforts. Jeffrey Whitehouse, a close friend of James Hashim, engaged the customers of Patrick's Pub in Pittsfield, Massachusetts, in a most informative discussion about the boxing past of the city, resulting in many helpful names and events. He also supplied information about former local boxers who were lifelong friends of Joe Grimm. Jim Tickle, the grandson of Bobby Tickle, who was Joe's first coach, manager, and mentor, described his grandfather's family, his business, his boxing activity, and showed the picture of Bobby Tickle with his three sons, all Joe's friends.

People from neighborhoods were an unexpected resource. John Sousa, of Sousa's Mini Mart on Morgan Street in Fall River, took time to show me around the bygone Casino and former Capitol Theater, now under renovation. Donna Viveiros e-mailed me vintage photos of the theater in its glory days. Chuck, the maintenance engineer of the Fall River YMCA building, provided details on the history of the building's structural changes. Jay Avila, from Spinner Publications, came up with the only picture of the cycledrome that I could find, and provided other information about New Bedford in the 1920s. Roger Fristoe of Louisville, Kentucky, coached me on how to restore the old pictures that were otherwise unprintable.

I made trips to Massachusetts, Rhode Island, and New Jersey, where Gentleman Joe lived and fought. There, I researched in local library archives for pertinent documents and reviewed rolls of microfilm with newspapers articles written about Joe's boxing career. Michael Holtzman at the Fall River *Herald News* thoughtfully referred me to local boxing and history buffs. Lee Blake from the New Bedford Historical Society and Paul Cyr from the New Bedford Library history archives were helpful with specific information about the history of the city and other interesting facts about the Fall River area. I was impressed by the Pittsfield Athenaeum's records and files, and the expertise of Anne-Marie Harris in the Local History Department, who responded to my specific questions and gave me many helpful leads.

At the Bayonne Library in New Jersey, a temple full of valuable references, librarians Jeanette Torres and Lisa Attanasio were greatly helpful with my intricate investigative mission. Joe Grimm's spirit seemed to be hovering over me as I approached the man sitting next to me, also searching newspaper clippings on the microfilms. It turned out that Mr. Willard (Bill) Miller was well informed about the local history of the 1920s and took pride in being able to recall facts about people and places in those years. He was, in fact, an amateur "genealogy researcher," and from the moment I introduced myself, he was ready and willing to help me. He made most of the findings about Charles Doessereck's life and boxing activities, and diligently searched for any information I was seeking after I had returned home. Regina Adriolo, a former boxing manager from Brooklyn, made exhaustive efforts to trace Doessereck's photo, but she ran into constant dead ends.

My final thanks and gratitude go to my wife, Diane, George's daughter and Joe Grimm's niece. She introduced me to the Hashim family and implicitly to the subject of this book, with which she helped me in innumerable ways. I dedicate the book to her and the entire Hashim family and to all readers whose relative walked in the ring and dared to dream big. Because of these anonymous fighters, boxing became the king sport in America, and the American champions took over the world of professional boxers. To all who did not have a glorious career but gallantly fought and entertained countless millions, I bid with this book a long overdue homage.

Bibliography

Books

Bohn, Michael K. *Heroes and Ballyhoo: How the Golden Age of the 1920s Transformed American Sports.* Washington, DC: Potomac Books, 2009.

Evensen, Bruce J. *When Dempsey Fought Tunney: Heroes, Hokum, and Storytelling in the Jazz Age.* Knoxville: University of Tennessee Press, 1996.

Goldman, Herbert G., ed. *1986-1987 Record Book and Boxing Encyclopedia.* New York: Ring Publishing, 1987.

Gorn, Elliott J., and Warren Goldstein. *A Brief History of American Sports.* Urbana: University of Illinois Press, 2004.

Kerle, Phyllis E. *PITTSFIELD ... Where Legends Begin.* Berkshire Visitors Bureau.

Kimball, George, and John Schulian, eds. *At the Fights: American Writers on Boxing.* New York: Library of America, 2011.

McCallum, John D. *The Encyclopedia of World Boxing Champions.* Radnor, PA: Chilton Book Company, 1975.

Mowry, George F., ed. *The Twenties: Fords, Flappers & Fanatics.* Englewood Cliffs, NJ: Prentice-Hall, 1963.

Perrett, Geoffrey. *American in the Twenties: A History.* New York: Simon & Schuster, 1982.

Roberts, Randy. *Jack Dempsey: The Manassa Mauler.* Urbana: University of Illinois Press, 2003.

Sann, Paul. *The Lawless Decade: A Pictorial History of a Great American Transition from the World War I Armistice and Prohibition to Repeal and the New Deal.* New York: Crown, 1962.

Other

Nahmias, Leah, *"Providence's Lost Stadium: The Providence Cycledrome and the City's Sporting Past," prepared for an Historic Preservation class, December 12, 2007.*

Schonauer David, *"Spokes and Splinters," Smithsonian, April 2011.*

About the Author

Ion Grumeza is the author of the international best seller about sports hero Nadia Comaneci, *Nadia: The Success Secrets of the Amazing Romanian Gymnast*, and of several nonfiction history books, including *Dacia: Land of Transylvania, Ancient Cornerstone of Eastern Europe, 500 B.C.–A.D. 500*; *The Roots of Balkanization: Eastern Europe, C.E. 500–1500*; and *Admiring the Goose-steps: How Hitler Succeeded in Intimidating the World Powers*. Grumeza had formal boxing training in his native Romania, and he created and managed a boxing program for a YMCA in Connecticut. He is retired in Louisville, KY, where he presents courses for the Veritas Society at Bellarmine University.